PARADISE
FEVER

PARADISE FEVER

GROWING UP IN THE SHADOW OF THE NEW AGE

Ptolemy Tompkins

A LIVING PLANET BOOK

AVON BOOKS ◆ NEW YORK

The author would like to thank the following parties for permission to quote from copyrighted material:

Garber Communications for passages from Edouard Schuré's *From Sphinx to Christ* and Rudolf Steiner's *Cosmic Memory: Prehistory of Earth and Man* © 1987 by Foundation for Advancement of Arts and Letters, in memory of Rudolf Steiner.

Jeremy P. Tarcher Inc. for passages from *Memories and Visions of Paradise* by Richard Heinberg © 1989 by Richard Heinberg.

The Theosophical Publishing House for passages from *Legends of Atlantis and the Lost Lumeria* by W. Scott-Elliot.

"Sunset" and excerpts from "22" and "Archaic Torso of" from *Selected Poems of Rainer Maria Rilke*, edited and translated by Robert Bly. Copyright © 1981 by Robert Bly. Reprinted by permission of HarperCollins Publishers, Inc.

A portion of this work, entitled "Lost Atlantis," appeared in the January 1997 issue of *Harper's*.

AVON BOOKS
A division of
The Hearst Corporation
1350 Avenue of the Americas
New York, New York 10019

Copyright © 1997 by Ptolemy Tompkins
Interior design by Rhea Braunstein
Visit our website at **http://AvonBooks.com**
ISBN: 0-380-97438-X

Library of Congress Cataloging in Publication Data:
Tompkins, Ptolemy.
    Paradise fever : growing up in the shadow of the New Age / Ptolemy Tompkins.
        p.   cm.
    1. Tompkins, Ptolemy.   2. New Age persons—United States—Biography.
3. Authors, American—Biography.   4. Tompkins, Peter—Family.   I. Title.
BP605.N48T56   1997   97-23607
299'.93—dc21   CIP

First Avon Books Printing: November 1997

For my mother, Jerree
my sister, Robin
and my wife, Rebecca

For my mother, Jerree
my sister, Robin
and my wife, Rebecca

Acknowledgments

I'm very happy to have the opportunity to express my gratitude to my agent Gail Ross, to Josh Horwitz at Living Planet Press (without whose many hours of energy and guidance this would not be a book at all but a bunch of manuscript pages languishing painfully somewhere in my apartment), and to my very able editor Rachel Klayman at Avon Books for her skill and enthusiasm all along the way. Thanks for kindnesses small, large, and extra-large, to: Robin and Stuart Ray, Greg Mirhej, Karl Greenfeld, Jerry Smith, T. C. Tompkins, Jerree Tompkins, Max Gimblett, Nicky and Alexander Vreeland, Damon Berryman, Elise Wiarda, Sarah Golden, Elliott Goldkind, Phil Dawdy, Lew Grimes, Charis Conn, Molly O'Neill, and Arthur Samuelson. To my wife Rebecca, a special thank-you for her patience and confidence, both throughout the course of writing and long before. Last but not least, thanks to my father for suffering without protest the discomfort of being dragged, unasked, into these turbulent pages.

Note from the Author

From the eating of calculators to the nude maintenance of bees, the following pages describe real events and real people. However, the identities of a number of these people have been disguised to protect their privacy, and the sequence of some events has been changed. I hope everyone involved will forgive me any errors of memory or judgment.

Contents

PARADISE
FEVER

"Then listen, Socrates, to a strange tale, which is, however, certainly true. . . ."
—Critias, introducing the story of Atlantis, in Plato's <u>Critias</u>

Beginnings

I n the spring of 1975, on my thirteenth birthday, my father presented me with a scuba tank and regulator. It was his hope that by practicing at the bottom of our pool I could be of use during an underwater expedition he was mounting to locate the lost continent of Atlantis on the floor of the Caribbean Ocean. For a few weeks, I practiced basic maneuvers like removing and replacing my mask underwater, sucking in air straight out of the tank, and breathing with deep regular breaths to get maximum use of my air supply. Once I had mastered these skills there was little else to do at the bottom of the pool, but by that time I had come to like it quite a bit down there. Sitting in the calm and quiet, breathing the dry, rasping air from my tank, and staring through my face mask at the bright patterns of water-distorted light that moved back and forth across the pool's floor, I felt miles away from the world up above, with all its tensions and uncertainties.

One day while passing time down on the bottom, I looked up to see the silver ceiling of water broken by the naked body of a young woman. Floating above me with her long brown hair trailing after her, she stared down with wide open eyes, unblinking in spite of the chlorine. She seemed to see me as clearly as I could see her through my mask.

Unnerved, I roused myself from my spot and clanked reluctantly over to the pool's shallow end. When I poked my head above the surface, the girl swam in my direction and crouched in the water next to me. Staring at her through my face mask and still breathing through my regulator, I assessed the situation. A pair of large, white, water-dappled breasts stared back at me. Above them was the equally daunting gaze of their owner, pretty but with a bug-eyed intensity that suggested a novice hypnotist working on her first subject.

I pulled the rubber regulator from my mouth. "Who are you?" I said.

"I am Cheryl," she replied in a toneless, mechanical voice. "I am a changeling. You are a changeling too, and the hour of the changelings will arrive soon. Don't be frightened, for the changelings can withstand the fires that the mortals cannot."

Deeply uncomfortable and not wanting to look directly at either her face or her breasts, I opted at last for a freckle on her left shoulder and fixed my gaze resolutely on that while she continued.

"In the great time that is to come, there will be no more confusion about the secret questions. The secret questions will be answered by the invisible ones—the ones who watch us now. I can feel their eyes burning down on us from heaven."

With that, she gave me a knowing, crooked smile that hovered somewhere between deep, confident wisdom and dementia. Then she slowly made her way to the other end of the pool, where she floated on her back, gazing up at the blue afternoon sky.

I put the regulator back in my mouth and returned to the bottom of the pool. Once down there, I tried to get back into the relaxed, contemplative mood I had been in before Cheryl arrived, but it was no good. The sight of her bobbing about above me was too unsettling. I squirmed free from the straps of my tank, leaving it at the bottom of the pool, and climbed out into the air. From the safety of my room overlooking the pool, I watched Cheryl's naked form drift across the surface and wondered to myself where she had come from and how long she would be staying.

As I suspected, Cheryl turned out to be the latest in a series of young seekers anxious to spend time in my father's company. Like many before her, she showed up without much in the way of warning but was welcomed in all the same, for my father was disinclined to turn away anyone who went to the trouble of searching him out. In Cheryl's case, however, he ultimately made an exception. After a few weeks her cryptic pronouncements started to get on my father's nerves, and he sent her packing— but not before she impressed upon me the wondrous possibilities of the great time to come.

"All is mystery now," she would stop and assure me at odd moments around the house, "but in the future, all will be answers."

I didn't know what she was talking about, but when I returned to my pool-sitting, I mulled over her words as I breathed the metallic air from my tank and stared at the trembling silver ceiling. Yes, I thought to myself, a time of answers sounded like a very good idea indeed.

My father, Peter Tompkins, was a spy in World War II. Having spent much of his childhood in Italy, he spoke such fluent Italian that he was able to pass himself off as a Roman fascist. From his hiding quarters in Rome, which featured a secret room accessible only by a small trapdoor, he led the intelligence group largely responsible for securing the Allied victory at Anzio. Hunted by the Nazis with whom he consorted under his assumed Roman identity, my father watched helplessly as many of the Italian partisans working under him vanished into Nazi torture chambers when their true identities were uncovered. The Nazis never caught my father, but it was no doubt in part from them, and the months he spent living under the fragile shield of his assumed identity, that he learned his lifelong love of secrets.

In 1941, when he was twenty-two and working as a radio correspondent for NBC, my father stopped over in Kenya for a few days while researching a story. There he had occasion to meet the American consul, who offered this impressively serious-minded young man a place to stay. My father took the consul up on his offer, and soon thereafter met his daughter Jerree, a sheltered but free-spirited twenty-three-year-old who was slated to marry one Eric Heinrich, a local aristocrat who raised polo ponies on an estate outside Nairobi. She fell in love with my father on sight, and the two eloped down the east coast of Africa soon thereafter—with the consul, his wife, and the heartbroken Eric in close pursuit.

Thanks to the consul's influence, a great deal of effort went into finding and detaining the fugitive couple. Roadblocks were set up, hotels were searched, and finally, in a port town called Lorenço Marques, far down on the coast, the two of them were apprehended. My father was sent away on the next available steamer, and my mother entreated by her parents and Eric to return to the life that had been laid out for her. But all to no avail. A few weeks later, Jerree boarded a ship that carried her to America, out of the consul's sphere of influence and into my father's, and never again would anyone succeed in drawing her back out of it.

America entered World War II, and my parents-to-be embarked on their romantic wartime adventures. While my father spied, my mother—like him the product of an almost exclusively European upbringing—translated German documents for the Allies in London. Moving from one country to another, raised primarily by governesses from a bewildering variety of backgrounds, my mother had been a deeply solitary child and was now turning into a deeply solitary adult as well. During the months she spent amidst the daily bombings of the London blitz, she distinguished herself not only as a capable worker but also as something of an oddball: an attractive, charming one, but an oddball nonetheless. When the air raid sirens sounded, she refused to take shelter. The smell, the claustrophobia, and the forced intimacy that came from being cooped up with a bunch of people one didn't know all struck her as a worse bargain than the possibility of being blown to bits out in the open air. And so my mother would sit—in an empty bus if the raid came on her way to or home from work, or high up in an empty office building if it came when she had already got there—and wait, by herself, for the planes and the bombs to leave and her fellow humans to come back up out of the ground. And, like my father, over in Italy, she was lucky. The bombs fell all around but they never fell on her.

After the war my mother and father came together again, and my father resumed the writing career he had begun in the '30s. Working first as a newspaper correspondent, then as a screenwriter and editor, he gradually evolved into a writer of books. After Robin and Timothy—the daughter and son born to them in the years immediately following the war—had passed through infancy, my mother worked at a series of office jobs to earn the food money. My father kept typing, and with the help of my father's parents, Robin and Timothy passed through their haphazard bohemian childhoods and were sent off to boarding schools. In the early '60s, when I was born, the first fruits of my father's labors were published. Book followed book from then on out, often with only a year or two between them.

From the very beginning, my father's books dealt with secrets of one sort or another—with things hidden, ignored, unspoken, or outright denied by the world at large. He published an account of his adventures as a spy in Rome, along with two other titles focusing on the hidden side of the war—or, as my father liked to say, "what really went on." In 1962 he wrote *The Eunuch and the Virgin*—a history of "castration as a political tool"—with the intent of shedding light on an area that until then had been shrouded in darkness and denial. My father also produced two books detailing the relationship between his mother and George Bernard Shaw—a relationship that had its share of secrecy as well, for it had long been hinted that the Great Man was not only a close friend of my grandmother's but her lover.

For most of my childhood my parents lived in or just outside Washington, D.C., so that my father could make use of the Library of Congress for his relentless research. Underneath the high, light-shot spaciousness of the Library's main reading room there lies a maze of dim, cramped, and seemingly endless book stacks connected by an intricate series of passageways. My father had complete access to this hidden world—off-limits to the general public—thanks to a special arrangement he cooked up with a high-ranking member of the Library he knew through his days in the OSS. While ordinary patrons had to make do with ordering up books through the central desk in the reading room, my father could enter into the stacks himself, hunting for the books he wanted with his own two hands, and even taking them home with him once he had found them.

These sunken walkways and the countless rooms of books to which they led were for years the closest thing my father had to an office. As a child, and later as a young man, I would often go with him on his voyages there. What duck hunting or trout fishing is for some fathers and sons, visiting the Library became for my father and me. Watching him in action—head bowed, a handful of books under his arm, his corduroy trousers blending in with the tans and ambers of the walls—I understood that hunting for strange books full of neglected information down in the depths of the earth was what he was born to do. There, as in no other place, I got the sensation, as I walked along behind him, that we were engaged in a common and achievable adventure in a common and understandable universe. A universe full, from top to bottom, with secrets waiting to be discovered.

Year followed year and secret followed secret. In 1971, after several years of especially intensive hunting down in the depths of the Library, my father finished work on *Secrets of the Great Pyramid,* a book which argued that the ancient Egyptians possessed a body of wisdom about the universe and the role of human beings within it that far surpassed anything the modern world had knowledge of. Two years later, he and his friend Christopher Bird wrote *The Secret Life of Plants,* which made the claim that plants were conscious beings capable of communicating and communing with humans. Plants were such spiritually evolved organisms, my father argued, that if we listened to them attentively they could teach us how to live more happily and harmoniously on earth—so harmoniously that our frayed and tired planet could be transformed, in my father's words, into a new Eden.

These two books—especially *The Secret Life of Plants*—swiftly and irrevocably changed my father's life, transforming him, then in his early fifties, from an obscure writer of eclectic nonfiction into a best-selling author and household name. A potted daisy with its head bent over a copy of my father's book showed up in the pages of *The New Yorker*. *Doonesbury*'s Zonker Harris started talking to his houseplants, while on TV characters on *Bob Newhart* and *The Mary Tyler Moore Show* did the same. Sunk deep in my favorite beanbag chair, I watched in amazement as *To Tell the Truth*'s Bill Cullen asked the astonishing question "Will the real Peter Tompkins please stand up?"

Nor was my father's influence on the national imagination confined to jokes in magazines and television sitcoms. Along with a battery of other books—Richard Bach's *Jonathan Livingston Seagull*, Jane Roberts's *Seth Speaks*, Robert Pirsig's *Zen and the Art of Motorcycle Maintenance*, and Carlos Castaneda's Don Juan series—his quirky, impassioned exploration of plant consciousness became a talisman for an emerging body of ideas about the expanded limits of human knowledge and experience. A well-thumbed copy of *The Secret Life of Plants* on your bookshelf signaled that you were open to hearing new and surprising information about the universe— and that you expected and invited such revelations on a regular basis.

By the mid-'70s, my father had become a walking, talking concatenation of the sort of ideas that these days are grouped under the general umbrella of "New Age." Bearded, bald, and with a perpetually intense and preoccupied expression on his face (as a young child I suspected that he must have lost his hair from thinking too much), my father was in appearance and character perfectly suited for this role of New Age avatar. Merely by being himself, he became the definitive model of the Fringe Investigator: the mysteriously authoritative figure with the whitening beard, khaki bush jacket, and unfazably open mind who was forever lurking on the outer edges of accepted science and conventional thinking in general. From Peter Tompkins you could always count on learning that the impossible wasn't really impossible at all, and that your not having been alerted to this fact before was due purely to the untiring efforts of the self-serving charlatans in the academic community who were working overtime to keep you in the dark. He was the one to suggest that ancient astronauts had visited the earth, that psychic surgeons could cure your inoperable cancer, that the ancient Egyptians possessed magical techniques for levitating twenty-thousand-pound rocks, and that you yourself might even have been one of those Egyptian magicians in a previous incarnation.

The romance with things occult and miraculous that gripped America in the '70s—a romance which was eventually to evolve into the New Age phenomenon as it exists today—created a great gulf between the believers and the nonbelievers, between those who became heavily invested in these new ways of seeing the world and those who thought them nothing more than an exercise in self-indulgence and willful credulity. Emotions ran very high on both sides of this divide, and no one was more adept than my father at stirring up indignant opposition in the tents of scientific orthodoxy. When he told the news media that apples experienced the equivalent of an orgasm when eaten with a loving and respectful attitude, or that invisible, humanlike nature spirits swarmed within the greenery of a well-tended garden—and worse, when these pronouncements were greeted with enthusiasm by journalists and readers alike—botany professors around the world felt their throats constrict and their scalps grow hot with rage. With his blustery demeanor and his love of sweeping prophetic generalizations, my father was an inviting target for attack, and for a time the debunkers were falling all over themselves to get in a shot at him.

This war between the believers and the unbelievers in which my father loomed so large was an eminently televisable event. From Mike Douglas to Dick Cavett to Johnny Carson, my father made the rounds of virtually every talk show of the day, usually in the company of a representative of the scientific community with whom he was expected to fall into passionate and vitriolic debate. The standard menu of events on these shows would be for Mike or Dick or Johnny to introduce my father and then stand back while he flared his eyebrows menacingly and described whatever improbable phenomena he had been investigating that week. In the appearances following the publication of the plant book, a table full of plants would be wheeled on-stage attached to a galvanometer—a lie-detecting device that my father's friend Cleve Backster had found could register what appeared to be the emotional reactions of plants as well as humans. The plants would then be threatened with uprooting, burning, and other such abuse, and the TV cameras would zoom in on the galvanometer's wildly fluctuating dials. Finally, a suitably dour scientist would emerge, and he and my father would square off like a pair of fighting cocks in a Mexican bar, trading accusations for however much air time remained to be filled.

My father brought a trademark intensity to the subjects he explored. When he argued that the ancients had lived in an expanded state of harmony and cosmic integration that the modern world had fallen tragically away from, and when he insisted that the door back to this expanded state was open to anyone who would simply listen to the whisperings of the plants they ate and walked upon, his fierce conviction was as persuasive as his ideas themselves.

At the center of all of the intensity and charisma my father managed to generate in those years stood a single, burning conviction: Escape into a more fulfilling world of experience was truly possible. For my father, it was not enough to spin seductive descriptions of the Eden that life on the planet could become if only we would throw off our repressive neuroses and awaken to the larger life that lay in hiding all around us. One needed to act on this knowledge.

And act he did.

In the late '60s my mother and father moved across the river from Washington to McLean, Virginia—that definitively dull suburb where the CIA nestles all but invisibly and the more family-minded of the nation's bureaucrats come looking for housing when administrations change over. At the time, McLean's affluent reputation lay in the future. Land was cheap, buildings scarce, and my father was able, with a little borrowing, to buy an enormous cow barn on a side road about a mile from a lonely highway junction called Tysons Corner.

"The Barn," as it came to be called, was built originally for cows, not people, and its white cinder-block walls and bulging green roof enclosed a space absurdly large for the three-person family that moved into it that summer. Even later, after years of renovation and reconstruction, it still looked like a place built for something larger and rougher than humans. Over time, as McLean became increasingly populated and affluent, the Barn served as a kind of massive, white-and-green ballast rock for the neighborhood. Pompous in its sheer enormity yet humble in its rambling, pigeon-speckled unkemptness, the Barn was the house my father had always dreamed of owning: the place where he would have the room to do the work he wanted to do in the way he wanted to do it.

In resolving to live a fuller, more realized life than he had before, my father was acting in the service of the spirit of the time—and the spirit of that particular time was very much a communal one. From about 1972 onwards, the Barn became a way station for an extraordinary array of self-styled seekers, finders, and aspiring awakeners of the slumbering modern world. Yeti hunters, psychics, free-form visionaries, and reincarnated Atlantean alchemists—one after another they showed up at our door, sometimes with advance warning and often without. And if they liked what they saw they stayed . . . in some cases for years.

So it was that at the same time America and the rest of the world were beginning to fall in love with my father's ideas about the rebirth of a lost and magical condition of planetary integration and cosmic harmony, the rambling cow barn in which I had formerly gone about my solitary child's business became a testing ground where the systematic search for this lost paradise was conducted on a daily basis. From the couple who drilled holes in each other's foreheads to awaken their kundalini energy to the modern-day alchemist with a recipe for at last turning lead into gold, my childhood and adolescence unfolded amidst a cluttered, absurd, yet oddly heroic attempt to remake the world into the garden that my father was so convinced it could once again become. While those around me were trying to recover their lost cosmic moorings and become again as little children, I tried as best I could to go about the business of growing up. I went to school in the mornings and returned home in the afternoons. I read *Mad* magazine, puzzled over the contents of Cheech and Chong records, collected Wacky Packs, and stood in a block-long line to see *Jaws* the day it opened. But by virtue of my membership in the perplexing parallel universe of my father's creation, I also witnessed dramas that had no corollary in the lives of my schoolmates.

One of the stranger things about this childhood on the edge of paradise was the combination of solitude and intense human interaction that went on during it. Crowded with people and goings-on one week and all but empty the next, the Barn was a place where feelings of isolation and participation met and mingled—a place that could seem like the center of the world at one moment and the largest, loneliest of wastelands at another. It was also predominantly a place of adults—of adult-style dramas and adult-style diversions, where other children showed up infrequently and didn't know what to make of things when they did. As a result of this combination of elements, I became at once the most innocent and the most cosmopolitan of children—one who consistently saw both more and less of the world than other children my age, and whose tools for living were at once overrich and oddly anemic.

The single event that most defined this more-yet-less, better-yet-worse childhood of mine came in the fall of 1970, when I was eight years old. It was then, at the very beginning of the decade of limitless possibilities that the '70s were to be for my father, that he brought Betty Vreeland, a Manhattan socialite and the then-daughter-in-law of Diana Vreeland, home to meet my mother and me. That night after dinner, my father announced to my mother that Betty would be leaving her husband and two children and coming to live with the three of us. Shortly after Betty's arrival that night, the pyramid book appeared to much acclaim and outrage and my father became a celebrity. From then on, nothing was ever to be the same again.

In the course of remembering the things that happened to me as a child, I have often felt as if I were stuck on a narrow path amidst a tremendous wilderness—a wilderness that calls to me from all directions but which I cannot enter. My memory of the past is like a film of a fascinating countryside made by a photographer who traveled there without getting proper directions on what to record. He lingers inexplicably in one place while spending a maddeningly brief amount of time on some other that, had somebody been there to direct him, he could have captured properly.

According to occult literature there is a way out of this problem. This way involves gaining access to something called the Akashic record—a vast, intangible storehouse of every event, both subjective and objective, that ever occurred throughout the history of creation. The Akashic record is a supremely comforting notion for people like me who are prone to brooding imperfectly on the past, for it tells us what, secretly or openly, we have always wanted to hear: that nothing is ever really lost, that no event goes unrecorded, that no action of any sort ever really passes out of being once it has occurred. Good, bad and indifferent, each and every event and interaction that ever took place is suspended in perfect clarity and peace, waiting for us to find our way back to it.

I first learned about Akasha when I was seven or eight years old. My father and I were eating lunch down in the basement cafeteria of the Library of Congress, and I was looking at an illustration of a dinosaur in a book we had just found together in the stacks.

"How come," I asked my father, "the guy who painted this picture knew what that dinosaur looked like?"

"He had a skeleton to work from, I suppose," said my father. "But mostly it would have been just guesswork."

"Yeah. But it's weird how real it looks, isn't it? I wish I could see what a dinosaur really looked like instead of just somebody's guess about it."

My father leveled his sandwich and looked over it at me. "You could, you know."

"What do you mean?"

"I mean you could do just that. Name two dinosaurs."

"What kind? Any at all?"

"Just two different species who had contact with one another."

"Tyrannosaurus and brontosaurus."

"Good. Now, the tyrannosaurus ate the brontosaurus, isn't that right?"

"Right. When they came up out of the swamps the tyrannosaurus would jump on them."

"Okay. Imagine one specific brontosaurus coming up out of a swamp one afternoon, and another specific tyrannosaurus waiting for him and going in pursuit. Imagine all the little details, like the wind and the twigs stuck in the brontosaurus's toes, and the fear it felt as it heard the tyrannosaurus approaching through the trees. Imagine all this going on, then imagine that all of it still exists, as if a movie crew had been there to record the whole event. Wouldn't you be interested in seeing that?"

"You bet."

"Well, some people can. People who can see into the Akashic record discover all sorts of things like that."

"What's the Akashic record?"

"It's a place a bit like this library, only it exists on another level—a higher, more spiritual one—than we do. Everything that ever happened, down to the smallest detail, exists there. It's like a giant *living* library."

"Wow. What do you have to do to get to see into it?"

"You have to be clairvoyant."

"Are you clairvoyant?"

"No," my father said. "But I could be, I suppose, and so could you. Anyone can be if they try hard enough."

It was around the same time as our conversation about Akasha that my father took to reading *Pinocchio* to me in the evening, before I went to sleep. On the night when we finished its last pages—in which Pinocchio awakes to find that he is no longer the wooden doll of Giepetto's handiwork but a round-cheeked, flesh-and-blood child—I asked my father about something in the story that bothered me.

"So it's kind of like Pinocchio was a real boy all the time?"

"Yes, exactly," said my father, apparently pleased that I had come up with this idea. "In essence, he was a real boy all along. He just needed someone to tell him so."

"And he was happy he got changed into a person?"

"Of course! Wouldn't you be?"

"I guess," I said tentatively. "But how come he had to wait so

long? Why didn't Jiminy Cricket or the fairy godmother or someone just do it right away?"

"He needed to *wait*, because he needed to *learn* that he was a
boy, just the way we all do." My father closed the overlarge book
across his lap. "You see, we're all a bit like Pinocchio really. I
don't suppose you know what an allegory is, do you?"

"No."

"An allegory is a story that pretends to be about one thing,
when in fact it's about another. Pinocchio isn't really about a
wooden puppet at all."

"What's it about, then?"

"It's about people, and what they really are. Do you know what
people really are?"

"No," I said, extremely interested.

"They're *spirits*. That's what Pinocchio found out, and that's
what everybody finds out someday, sooner or later, when they
wake up—like Pinocchio does at the end of the story—to their
spiritual nature. All of us are like Pinocchio to one degree or
another, because all of us suffer from not knowing who, or what,
we really are. If we knew what we were from the start, the world
wouldn't have all the problems it does."

"Okay, so the story isn't really about Pinocchio turning into a
boy at all. It's about how people are really spirits."

"Yes."

I explored this notion a little further. "If I go to sleep tonight
thinking I'm a spirit, will I wake up one, like Pinocchio did?"

"No," my father said. "I'm afraid not. You'll still wake up in
your body. But you just might wake up with the *knowledge* that
you are a spirit. And that's all you really need."

Is the business of living really, as my father always maintained,
about waking up to one's true nature after undergoing the long
dream of a life that is only half realized? The following pages tell
the story of my childhood within the odd yet sometimes brilliant

world my father built around me, and of a brief period in adulthood when I experienced an awakening of my own from a set of
limitations that I, much like Pinocchio, had never really noticed
before. Like most people, I am forced to live and write beyond
the gates of Akasha, and the tale I have told, while true, is so in
the dim, distorted, and diminished way that the truths of human
memory always are. Mark Twain, himself probably not a believer
in Akasha, once wrote that the autobiography is "the truest of all
books, for while it inevitably consists mainly of extinctions of the
truth, shirkings of the truth, partial revealments of the truth, with
hardly an instance of plain straight truth, the remorseless truth *is*
there, between the lines." Between the lines of the following, I
hope, at least a few such straight and remorseless fragments may
be found.

ONE

Get Back to Where You Once Belonged

"From the earliest times, human beings have believed that there is a quality in themselves that sets them apart from the animals—a quality that manifests itself as a sense of alienation and insufficiency and as an abnormal capacity for destructiveness and cruelty."
—Richard Heinberg, Memories and Visions of Paradise

IN the summer of 1969 my father traveled to Europe to conduct some research for a book he was planning to write on L. Ron Hubbard and scientology—topics that had interested him deeply since the 1950s, when he had actually met L. Ron himself. Though his involvement with the scientologists was always peripheral, the language and trappings of scientology often made their way into my father's thinking and his conversation. "Old Hubbard really was onto something there," he would say in reference to thetans, clears, engrams, E-meters, past life recalls, or some other such scientological tidbit. Like many of his projects, the scientology book never got written, but it did serve the purpose of getting my father to Europe that summer, and my mother and me along with him.

We spent the first part of the summer in the south of England, where my father did research at an institute devoted to Hubbard's ideas. For the second part we traveled to a spot in Italy on the

Tuscan coast where a few well-heeled Italian families my father knew from his war years had summer houses. One of these families had offered to put the three of us up for all of August, but this plan changed abruptly one afternoon when our hosts had the poor sense to show my father an abandoned mill that was one of the more rustic local landmarks.

This mill was basically a Mediterranean counterpart of the Barn—only older, bigger, and even more impractical. Huddled in upon itself like a small city, the mill was made up of a seemingly endless succession of stone rooms, most of them empty save for the occasional prop left over from busier days—like the long and deeply sinister iron hook that dangled like a question mark from the ceiling in one of the larger rooms. The mill had sat idle for so long that much of it lay open to the elements. Here and there a wall or ceiling had dropped away entirely, letting in summer light that coaxed weeds and flowers up from the cracks in the floors.

As luck would have it, the owner was one of my father's friends. Having no use for the mill himself, he would have been happy to let my father buy it—were it not for a centuries-old prohibition against letting the property pass to someone outside the family. Undaunted by this technicality, my father devised a contract that named him as the renting tenant for the next ninety-nine years—or until 2068. With this impressive lease supplying the warm, proprietary feeling he so loved, he moved us into a group of rooms at the front of the mill that had resisted the wear of the centuries more successfully than the others, installing a few amenities like a stove, a phone, and a refrigerator while he was at it.

Swept up by the ruined mill's mighty proportions and ancient atmosphere, my father was ready to forgive its many inconveniences and outright dangers. Early on in our days there, I woke my parents up to tell them that there was a lobster on the ceiling of the giant stone cell that served as my room, and from then on my mother had to make a scorpion check before sending me to bed. On another occasion, I took a wrong turn while exploring the maze of ruined rooms and walkways that branched out from our living quarters, and got lost for a half hour or so before the sound of my mother's voice guided me back. The mill was a challenging and labor-intensive place to live by anyone's standards, but it didn't matter, because the place was generously endowed with the single quality that, for my father, counted above all else: potential. Where others saw only ruin and disarray, he saw the chance to exercise his creative abilities, and like a bird that abandons its own egg when presented with the opportunity to sit atop a larger one, he found his transformative instincts hopelessly inflamed by the vast and long-neglected mill.

Having signed on years earlier for what my father had assured her would be an uncompromisingly bohemian life, my mother was ready to take the mill's inconveniences in stride. More difficult to accept was the social life that came along with it. Vigorous disdainer of the haute bourgeois that he was, my father nevertheless had a soft spot for certain substrata of high society. Though he himself was untroubled by this apparent contradiction, my mother was. What made hanging out on one person's yacht a sign of acquiescence to the Establishment and tagging along on another one a countercultural statement?

"Money's got nothing to do with it—real people are real people, and phonies are phonies." So said my father, but my mother continued to have her doubts about all the endless picnics, boat trips, and lunch parties that life with the "real people" entailed. Watching my father heat up and boil over with sunny Mediterranean enthusiasm among this crowd of titled landowners and captains of industry day after day, she found herself growing increasingly distant—both from the so-called real people who were co-opting so much of my father's attentions and from my father himself. After twenty-some years of marriage with the person she would always describe as "the only man I ever loved," my mother was watching as the world began to pull that man away from her. The fancy Italians and all the picnics they dragged us off on were the symptom of the moment, but the problem was much bigger than that and my mother knew it.

One of the most noticeable signs of my mother's new sense of discomfort was her growing interest in Abbie, a shih tzu my father had purchased for her in England the month before. With Abbie's arrival my mother became, in my father's rueful words, "one of those dog people." The more involved my father got in his new social circle outside our family, the more Abbie's comfort, moods, and inclinations received top billing during our home hours at the mill.

So began what was to grow into an ever more pronounced rift between my mother and father—a rift that I sensed only in the vaguest, most impressionistic way at the time, but which soon enough would become overwhelmingly apparent even to my self-preoccupied child's eye. In the years to come, I would spend much of my time drifting back and forth from one side of this divide to the other, depending on where my sympathies lay and which side was more inclined to serve my needs at the moment. Yet drift though I did, in those early days at the mill just as later, my true and lasting alliance was with my mother.

The reasons for this were obvious enough, especially during our days at the mill. On one side was my father and the fancy Italians—people with odd and intimidating names like Vittorio and Vincenzo and Elaria who were all too thin and too tan and had an indefinite aura of cruelty about them. On the other side was my mother, the shih tzu Abbie, and me—the less flashy set perhaps, but clearly the more sympathetic one.

Every now and then my father would attempt to interest me in playing with the children of his Italian friends—themselves an equally tan and handsome bunch, and as coolly suspicious of me as I was of them. But his efforts with me enjoyed no more success than they did with my mother, and as a result the two of us were often left alone. In an attempt to instill a superficial sense of hominess at the mill, my mother played her portable radio for much of the day, carrying it from room to room and taking it along when she, Abbie, and I went out to play in the stony, sun-flooded fields surrounding the mill. The big hit on Italian radio in the summer of 1969 was the Beatles' "Get Back," which would interrupt the incomprehensible stream of Italian chatter with reassuring regularity. Like most children, I was a tireless theorist, and enjoyed nothing more than building up my understanding of the world using whatever materials my daily experience threw at me. Pop songs were a particularly useful resource for me in this regard, and during our time at the mill, "Get Back" came in very handy indeed. I didn't bother trying to figure out who Jo-Jo was, or why California grass was something he left his home in Tucson, Arizona, to find. But there was something in the repeated suggestion to "get back to where you once belonged" that made immediate sense to me.

The meaning of this hermetic directive tied in with another source of information I had at hand that August. I had brought a small collection of books with me to Italy, and one I had a special fondness for was a volume from the Time-Life Nature Series called *Early Man*. Large, slick, and seductively adult in flavor, this book was full of wonderfully violent color illustrations capable of occupying my imagination for long periods of time. Like most of the books I really liked, it was at once frightening and compelling, so that opening its covers always gave me a mild but pleasant pornographic charge, as though I were looking at something I wasn't supposed to see. In one illustration, a group of lean, long-haired proto-humans labored inside the body of an elephant they had just killed, passing the massive, shiny internal organs up out of the chest cavity to others hunched atop it. In another, a group of monkeylike women with short, spiky hair and long, socklike breasts used sticks to extract roots and grubs from a hole in the ground.

My favorite image in the entire book—the one which filled me

with more fear and unspecific desire than all the others—depicted
a fight between two kinds of cavemen: one hairy, huge, and ape-
like, the other more slender, sophisticated, and manlike. The slender, more advanced group held small, chipped stone weapons in
their hands, while the primitive group held large, unworked boul-
ders over their heads. Baring their teeth at the more advanced
group, the primitives appeared to be attacking them, but the cap-
tion explained that they were really only frightened by the more
advanced men and were trying to scare them away. The two
groups faced off amidst a field of long yellow grass much like
that which grew upon the fields and hills around the mill. Mountains rose up in the background, while pink, wonderfully familiar-
looking clouds floated across the ancient afternoon sky.

Time and again I would stare down into these scenes and wonder that so many things could have taken place upon the earth so
long ago, before any of the people I knew were even alive. Sitting
on the sun-warmed stone floors of the mill, with my mother brush-
ing and talking to her dog and the song that told me to "get back
to where you once belonged" in the air, I would be overcome
with a nameless and aching nostalgia—a sense that somewhere,
somehow, the world had been a different, and infinitely better,
place than it was now.

For as long as I can remember my mother has been a great
believer in the theory, not original to her, that dogs are better
than people. "Human beings!" I have heard her say on countless
occasions over the years, her exasperation always plainly evident
in her voice. "Give me a dog any day of the week. *They* won't let
you down." Spending as much time alone with my mother as I
did throughout my childhood, I was privy to a great deal of this
kind of pro-dog propaganda, and it was during the time in Italy
that I first remember taking this information to heart. Walking
alone on the beach or hanging around at the mill with my mother
and Abbie while my father was off with his Italian friends, I de-

voted much time to analyzing the difference between animals and people.

Early Man was very handy in this regard, for its garish pictures provided a number of important hints as to how this difference had originally come about. The first and most important fact I uncovered from these pictures was that humans had once been animals themselves. An extralarge illustration at the beginning of the book featured a long line of creatures, the first small and monkeylike, leading in a gradual progression to an upright man walking along with a stick in his hand and sporting a beard similar to that worn by my father and some of the fancy Italians.

The second fact this book drove home was that in the course of human beings' turning from animals into what they were today, something had gone wrong. As much as I identified with the cave people in the book—with their intense, open expressions and their simple menu of survival-oriented activities—it was plain that there was an evil and savage quality to these creatures. Page after page showed them poking, clubbing, and otherwise harassing the peaceful and streamlined animals who shared their primordial world. In one particularly horrific spread, a prairie dog, a baby deer, and a singularly innocent-looking piglet were menaced in various ways by these ugly, potbellied monkey-men. It seemed that in becoming human, these creatures had lost the basic decency that informed the animal world. Who, with their spears and their clubs and their arrogant and cruel actions, did they think they were?

The Wolf Man and the Girl in the Wall

"For now truly is a race of iron, and men never rest from labor and sorrow by day, and from perishing by night."
—Hesiod, <u>Works and Days</u>

MUCH to my father's frustration, at the end of the month he was forced to abandon the mill and move us back to the Barn so that I could return to school. So happy had he been in Italy for this brief interval that he considered giving up on America altogether and making a new life for us there, but my mother, appalled at the idea, convinced him that for my sake if for no other it would be far better if we all went back to America. I entered the second grade, my mother bought another shih tzu to keep Abbie company, and my father spent most of his days at the Library of Congress, working on the last stages of a book about the Great Pyramid of Cheops at Giza—a book that, I was given to understand, would be unlike any of the others he had written. In this book, my father was to reveal things that nobody had told about before—entirely new things that, had he not come along, would perhaps have remained hidden forever.

"If nobody knows about them," I remember asking my mother one day as she was working on a pencil drawing of one of the

Great Pyramid's inner chambers, for inclusion in the book, "how come Peter does?"

"Your father is very intelligent. He finds out about all sorts of things that other people don't know about. That's what he does when he goes to the library every day."

"I know, but if he finds them at the library doesn't that mean somebody else found them first? Otherwise they wouldn't be in the library at all, right?"

"Well, I suppose so," said my mother. "But they were put in the library a long, long time ago, in books that nobody reads anymore. Everybody had forgotten all about them, and now people will be excited that your father has discovered them and is telling everybody what all these secret things really mean."

"Do you know what all the secrets mean too?"

"Oh, no, I'm too dumb for that kind of thing. But I can still help out by typing and drawing and things like that. That's your mother—dumb but useful!"

Ever since I could remember, my mother had assured me that she was "not very bright" but that she was not bothered by this handicap because it seemed to her that intelligence was a mixed blessing. "Your father is a very clever man," she would say ambiguously, "and he's welcome to all those brains. I'm like the dogs—sweet, dumb, and happy—and that suits me fine."

This celebration of stupidity and the fruits of happiness that it bestowed drove my father to distraction.

"Jesus Christ, why do you have to run yourself down like that all the time with this nonsense about being stupid?"

"But I'm not running myself down," my mother would respond in a tone lying maddeningly between complete sarcasm and complete sincerity. "I like being stupid. Why shouldn't I? I'm much better off that way than wishing I were full of brains like you. Look at all you have to worry about with your great thoughts. I'm much better off with my dogs and my TV."

I never knew for sure if this dumbness to which she clung so resolutely was only a defensive ploy, but from early on it was clear to me that I had a place of my own in the smart/dumb dichotomy as well. I, so the theory ran, was smart like my father but, by virtue of being a child, was able to cross over and enjoy things in dumb territory with my mother and her dogs. At least for the duration of my childhood, before my great brains took over and carried me off into the sterile and serious lands of the intelligent, I could enjoy the best of both worlds.

One dull Saturday afternoon, slowly rotating the clunking dial on my big General Electric black-and-white TV, I came across a show that I had never heard of called *The Twilight Zone*. On it, a man and a woman were searching for their little girl, who had somehow walked into a wall in their house and gotten mysteriously lost inside it. The parents, stuck on the outside of the wall in the normal world, could dimly hear their daughter's voice from the vague, white, cottony space beyond, but they couldn't get to her. At the end of the show the girl came back out of the wall and rejoined her parents—a conclusion that I found deeply disappointing. Wouldn't it have been better, I thought, if the child had been allowed to stay off in that land beyond?

Similar thoughts occurred to me when I came across *The Wolf Man* late one Saturday night while taking advantage of the total lack of TV curfew that I, alone of any of the children I knew, enjoyed. Far from being frightened when Lon Chaney Jr. grew a bristly coat of fur and a set of shining white canines, I found myself overcome with a piercing and inexplicable sense of envy. Watching as Chaney ran about through the mists of the Transylvanian countryside ravishing solitary Gypsies, I was overcome with a feeling of convulsive homesickness for this gray-white wasteland—a feeling that was very similar to the one I had felt so often at the mill while looking at my book of early man.

Why did I like the Wolf Man, and this misty landscape he

moved about in, so much? The Wolf Man, I realized, was clearly a sort of avenging agent from the world of animals—the world that had existed far in the past, before humans had come along and ruined everything with their cruel and unfeeling ways. Knowing the evil that humans did, the Wolf Man attacked and bit them so that they might turn back into animals during the full moon. And yet, tragically, this good work was not rewarded but punished. Humans—and the Wolf Man himself when in human form—did not want the old animal side to win out, for they had been deluded into thinking that it was evil.

I, of course, knew better, and with this complicated salad of theories filling my head, I became obsessed with the Wolf Man and the dim feeling of mystery, joy, and animal freedom I associated with him. I would stare at my teeth in the mirror, looking wistfully for signs of their growth into sharp points, and wait at each full moon for my features to be transformed into those of an animal. Every week I would scan the TV listings for films featuring the Wolf Man, and I soon discovered that other old movie monsters gave me a similar feeling when I watched their exploits. In addition to movies about Frankenstein and Dracula, there were such exquisitely mysterious Hollywood concoctions as *The Creature from the Black Lagoon*, which featured a final scene in which the beleaguered and again wholly lovable monster, fatally wounded by the spearguns of his pursuers, swims off into the depths of the ocean, merging before my eyes with that gray and grainy Beyond that so stirred my imagination. If only I could be like one of these creatures: human on the surface but inside a citizen of that ancient world of animal grace and beauty.

As neatly as all the pieces fit together, I still had questions about the fate of these old movie monsters. How come, at the end of each film, the angry villagers or the scientists always won out? If the forces of mystery and animal strangeness always perished at the hands of torch- and gun-wielding normality, what was the point of it all? Throughout that winter and into the spring, as my father labored away in the stacks of the library and my mother looked after things at home, I watched my General Electric television and pondered.

Back in the '50s, my father, always on the lookout for land to be had at a bargain price, had purchased some six hundred acres in southern New Hampshire near the town of Claremont. The centerpiece of this spread was a pair of old farmhouses, one half-way up and the other at the top of a thickly wooded hill. A grimly atmospheric yet somehow likable ruin, the top house sat at the end of a rain-softened dirt road that wound patiently up the hill for about a mile before coming to a resigned halt at its front door. Though in better shape, the bottom house lacked the impressive view of the one at the top, and it was the latter that my father set aside for himself, keeping the bottom one filled with an endless procession of local people who functioned as caretakers. My father had been returning to the hill in fits and spurts since purchasing it, but it had been some years since he had spent a significant amount of time there. When my second grade school year came to a close, we packed up and headed for the house at the very top of the hill to spend the summer of 1970.

Utopians always make bad landlords. This is primarily because their faith in the potential harmony that could drive the world also makes them sloppy about details, chief among those details the complexities of human psychology. Because my father never charged the occupants of his assorted houses rent, he assumed that they would be only too happy to look out for those houses while he was away. Why shouldn't they? He was giving them a break, so it seemed only reasonable that they would want to return the favor. Yet somehow it never worked out that way.

In New Hampshire, my father had grown used to returning to find his house at the top of the hill a shambles of broken doors and shattered glass. Local hunters, it seemed, made the place a sort of informal sportsman's lounge over the course of the winter months. Somehow sneaking past the caretakers in the house half-way up the hill on their battery of noisy snowmobiles, these people not only made themselves at home in my father's house but left aggressive evidence of their disdain for him scattered everywhere throughout it. The broken plates and rotten food took long enough to clean up, but it didn't stop there. "My God," my mother would say, emptying the feces from the cereal bowls in the kitchen cabinet where the hunters had left it, "how these people must hate you."

Whoever was staying in the house down the hill always claimed ignorance of these winter offenses, but I would sometimes wonder if they really were so innocent. Especially when I was older, I began to notice that there was something about my father's sweeping manner, showing up out of the blue, building and tearing down and making a grand ruckus, and then taking off again, that the locals just couldn't tolerate. As for my father, the whole business just puzzled and disappointed him. All he wanted to do was be a positive force in the area, and for that his cereal bowls filled up, each year, with shit. It didn't make sense.

Because TV reception was bad at the top of the hill I was forced to look elsewhere for outside material to feed my imagination, and I found this by chance one day with my mother while in Rand's News Depot in downtown Claremont. In the late '60s and early '70s a great number of horror comics were available, and Rand's seemed to carry them all. Among these titles two in particular—Creepy and Eerie, published by the same company and for all intents and purposes identical—stood out. They had more violent and convincing covers, better stories, and a wry wit that was noticeably absent from their competitors. Not only that, but the stories often had an au courant feel that made them wonderfully specific to my own life situation. On the cover of the first issue of Eerie I ever purchased, in June of that summer, an enormous

mummy staggered toward a couple dressed in conspicuously con-
temporary, early-'70s-style garb. At the mummy's foot, a boy of
nine or ten with the kind of absurd Brian Jones pageboy cut that
was popular among preadolescent boys in the '70s, and which I
happened to sport as well, yanked at a trailing bandage, sending
a powdery blast of mummy-dust into the air.

The idea was that the mummy was attacking this '70s-style
nuclear family and the boy was coming to the rescue. But something in the picture, or in my life, made me look at it in a different
light. As I saw it, the mummy was not a threat to the family
but a necessity. Like the Wolf Man with his predations upon the
Transylvanian Gypsy community, the mummy was doing work
that needed to be done. Sure it was huge and frightening, but
where would the family have been without it? The picture appeared to have both an apparent and a hidden meaning, and a
quick check with my father only firmed up what I already knew.

"Peter, what are mummies?"

"Mummies?"

"Yeah, like inside pyramids. Are they monsters like the Wolf
Man is?"

My father's answer was a little long and convoluted, but I managed to find, somewhere within it, the information I was hoping
for. Mummies, said my father, were made from dead people using
mysterious and magical processes that existed long ago and which
nobody really understood anymore. Were mummies really alive?
I asked my father. Yes, in a manner of speaking they were, for
when the mummy was properly prepared, it meant the spirit of
the dead person would not perish but continued to survive, perhaps forever. Being half dead and half alive, like being half animal
and half human, struck my child's imagination as about as mysterious and exciting a condition as one could ask for. Like Frankenstein's monster, who was alive but made out of pieces of dead
people, the mummy on the cover of my magazine was clearly yet
another representative of that lost, wild place that I felt such keen

nostalgia for. On the surface, like other monsters, he seemed evil and threatening, but underneath it was a different story. Lurching out of the darkness toward the terrified couple, his eyes red and full of power behind the ancient bandages, the mummy was an agent from the land of mystery, sent to change the humdrum world of humans into something larger, stranger, and better.

The Lost World

"Polygamous customs were prevalent at different times among all the
sub-races, but in the Toltec days while two wives were allowed by
the law, great numbers of men had only one wife. Nor were the women—
as in countries now-a-days where polygamy prevails—regarded as
inferiors, or in the least oppressed. Their position was quite equal to
that of men, while the aptitude many of them displayed in acquiring the
vril-power made them fully the equals if not the superiors of the other sex. . . .
It was the rule, too, and not the exception, for complete harmony to
prevail in the dual households, and the mothers taught their children
to look equally to their father's wives for love and protection."
—W. Scott-Elliot, Legends of Atlantis and Lost Lumeria

ONE night in early fall after all of us had returned from the
hill to the Barn and I was a few weeks into the third grade, my
father stuck his head in my room as I sat watching my General
Electric television and told me he had someone he wanted me
to meet.

"This is Betty," my father said, gesturing toward a blondish
woman a little younger than my parents, dressed all in black and
looking inexplicably interested in making my acquaintance. "She's
come all the way from New York to help you with your poetry."

My third grade class had been reading and writing poems recently, and I had started sharing my day's efforts with my parents in the evening while they were having their dinner. Keen

as I was about this new pursuit, there was something distinctly
fishy about the idea that my father would go to the trouble of
traveling to New York just to secure me a writing coach. As it
turned out, Betty was my father's new love, and he had brought
her home that night to meet my mother and to be on hand at
our dinner table when my father made a very important
announcement—an announcement of which Betty herself had
no previous knowledge.

"From now on," my father revealed to us that evening, "Betty
is to be an integral part of this family. We are about to embark
on a unique and potentially very important adventure—one that
will change all of us in radical and hopefully very beneficial
ways."

My father's "Great Plan," as he outlined it to my astonished
mother, involved leaving behind the suffocating blanket of prohi-
bitions and inhibitions that characterized life in twentieth-century
America and entering into a way of being in which absolute freedom of mind, body, and spirit was the first and greatest goal. "We
must become free," he explained, "and in order to become free
we must learn to listen to our true desires and to follow those
desires to their end. None of us knows how to do that anymore
because we've been trained to think and act like corpses—dead
bodies moving about in a world of shit. From here on out, I've
decided to start acting like someone who is alive, not dead, and
part of doing that means loving both you and Betty equally, without jealousy and without reservation."

I reconstruct these words of my father's now, twenty-some
years later, without benefit of access to the real ones, floating beyond my reach in Akasha. How much of what was said at the
dinner table that night really penetrated? Did I pay close attention,
or was the camera of my attention trained elsewhere? That my
father said something very much like this I know because my
mother told me about it years later, just as I know from her that

throughout the dinner the strange new woman looked at once pleased and embarrassed to be there, and that my father's statement that she would be living with us at the Barn from then on had shocked her almost as much as my mother.

The moments from that night that I do remember clearly began later, in the small hours, when I awoke to go to the bathroom. Looking across my room, I noticed in the half darkness that the stuffed animals that usually sat in a long line on a little daybed were all down on the floor and my mother and the two shih tzus were asleep on the bed. When my alarm went off the next morning, the stuffed animals were back up where they belonged and my mother was sitting on the edge of my bed, my breakfast on a standing tray beside her.

"Good morning," she said.

"Hi," I said back, wondering whether I was supposed to know she had slept on the daybed or not.

My mother held out her hand. "I've got something for you to keep for me," she said, picking up my hand and pressing the object into it. It was a broad, gold band—the biggest and most impressive of several rings she normally wore.

"What's this for?" I asked.

"I'm going away for a little while," my mother said in a weird, whispery kind of voice—the kind she had after she had been crying. "It's for you to look after while I'm away. Peter and Betty— the woman you met last night—are going to look after you now. But don't forget that I'll always love you and I'll always be there if you need me. You're going to be very happy."

It had been my experience up to this point that when anybody talked too much about being happy, it meant that something not so happy was going on, and this was very much the sense I got now.

"Where are you going?"

"I'm going to Robin's. She's looking forward to having me, and she's looking forward to seeing more of you too, when you come to visit."

Sixteen years older than me, Robin lived in the Boston area with her husband, Stuart, a "square" banker—as my father sometimes disapprovingly called him. Though an important figure in my life, Robin, like my brother, Timothy, was not a part of the regular routine at the Barn, and it was strange to hear about a visit to her so early in the morning, without any advance warning at all. It was also very strange to hear that I would not be coming along on this adventure. My mother had visited Robin and Stuart without my father in the past, but she had always taken me with her.

"But what about school? Who's going to take me there and pick me up and stuff?"

"Well, I'm sure Betty will be happy to do that. Your father is right about her. She's going to be very good for you, and you'll end up being very close."

"She's not going to stop at the 7-Eleven on the way home like you do."

My mother leaned down and gave me a hug, and I could see that she had started to cry again. She got up and went quickly out of the room, leaving me to contemplate, for the first time ever, how remarkably unequipped for life I was without her. Suddenly, I could no longer remember the first thing about my morning routine. What did I need to do to be ready for school? Was there something to think or worry about that I was unaware of? If so, who was going to tell me about it now? This mysterious Betty? Not likely, I thought. How on earth was she going to know anything about my life, with all its small complexities, having never even met me before the night just past? She probably didn't even know how to get to my school, much less how to help me prepare for it.

This stream of thoughts slowed as I lowered my eyes to contemplate the ring my mother had just given me. It was, in fact, her wedding ring, but I don't remember making this distinction at the time. As far as I knew, it was just one of the three or four rings she always wore—the nicest one—and the fact that it was now in my possession filled me with a little bit of courage. I wondered, though, about my mother's phrasing. Had she intended to really give the ring to me, or was I merely in charge of its safekeeping for a while? Surely she wouldn't just hand over an object so precious to her, so much a part of her adult life, without realizing that I might lose or damage it. After all, I was only eight years old. This last thought led me to the conclusion that the ring was not a loan but was really and truly mine.

Secure in this knowledge, I slid it down my index finger, hoping for a good fit. I thought of a boy who lived just up the road from us for whom I had a keen dislike. This child was physically stronger than me, and given to pinning me on the ground, which I found infuriating. This boy wore a thick silver ring on his right hand, which in my illogical way I had come to associate with his physical superiority. Perhaps, I thought, with this new gold ring, I would now be the superior one. In my imagination, I saw the two of us clashing in furious combat, the gold of my ring clinking against the inferior silver of his, and me, thanks to the power generated by my new magical charm, sending him to the ground with a victorious crash.

To my great disappointment, the ring was too big to stay snugly on my finger. Suddenly, a wave of fear and depression swept over me. If I didn't keep the ring on my finger I would surely lose it, as sooner or later I ended up misplacing just about everything that was smaller than a tennis ball. Along with the fear and depression, guilt now made its way into the mix. I would lose the ring, and my mother would know that it was my fault—all my fault. She had placed her trust and her confidence in me, and I had let her down!

No. I had not lost the ring. It was right there in my hand. As quickly as all these emotions had flown in and settled down upon me, they now blew away. How foolish I was to be worrying about making a mistake I hadn't even made yet. In my bathroom, in the medicine cabinet, there was a box of dental floss which I ignored except when working on projects that demanded string. I rose from bed now, went to the bathroom, and got the floss down from the cabinet, pulling off a foot or two of it. I would wear the ring around my neck! That would be as powerful and impressive as having it on my finger—maybe even more so. And I would be careful—very, very careful—not to lose it. At some point later on, my mother would return, and she would see that I had kept the ring safe and I would tell her all the good luck it had brought me, and she would tell me how glad—how very glad—she was that she had thought to give it to me in the first place.

As it happened, I didn't have a chance to lose the golden ring, for my mother returned in about ten days and asked me, politely and perhaps a little embarrassedly, if I might let her wear it again. I was happy to do so, for ten days was time enough for most of its charge of mystery and novelty to wear off. Far better to lose the ring and gain my mother back—my mother, who knew the way to school and the things I liked to do when school was over and the things I liked to eat, who understood what was good in life and what was to be avoided, and who had my interests in mind in a way that no one else could.

As for the other woman, she had not succeeded much in impressing me with how necessary to the house she was. Indeed, the longer she stayed, the more I wondered at how my father could have possibly got the idea that we needed her around. There was something peculiar in everything she did—something untrustworthy. With her too-dressy clothes and her suspicious perfumy scent, she walked about in the Barn as if she had lived there for years, making suggestions to my father about things she didn't know anything about, and even going so far as to tell me what to do.

"Ptolly, do you have any regular chores to do?"

"Chores?"

"You know, little things you do regularly around the house to help out."

"No," I replied decisively, and not at all sure where she could be going with this line of questioning.

"Well, don't you think it might be fun if we gave you a few? Just simple things, like perhaps taking the trash out."

"My mother does that."

"That's just the point, Ptolly. Your mother's not here right now, and . . . it's an awfully big house you and your father live in, isn't it?"

Betty gave me a broad, winning smile. "Well? What do you say?"

"You really want me to take out the trash? I'm a *kid*."

"But that's just the thing, Ptolly. Kids can help out too! Both of my boys do. And when they do, they get a very special feeling inside—a good feeling that comes from knowing they're doing something useful!"

Thus began what was to become a protracted campaign on Betty's part to enlist my services as a responsible member of the household—a campaign that, though I vigorously and successfully resisted it, scandalized me all the same. Where did this woman get off requesting such things of me? Watching her mouth go up and down as she ate, or her hands as she searched the kitchen cabinets for the right plates or utensils, I knew full well that she wasn't really comfortable in our house but was just pretending to be. Why didn't she come clean about it?

One day, shortly before my mother returned, Betty came into my room with two presents for me. It seemed to be my week for receiving adult gifts, for the first of the objects was plainly not for children.

"These," Betty said, handing me a long, heavy pair of bright, orange-handled scissors, "are for you. They're new, and they're wonderful! I almost cut my son's tie with them the other week, because they make cutting such fun!"

Betty mentioned her own family a lot, sometimes to me but mostly in conversations with my father. It seemed that Betty's family was sad she had gone and wanted her back, but she preferred to stay at the Barn, even though anyone with a brain could see she didn't really belong there. I tried the scissors out on a piece of my drawing paper, and it was true. They had a sort of magical sharpness to them, and cut so cleanly through materials ranging from paper to fabric to bath sponges to shoelaces that cutting with them became irresistible. In the next few days I applied them to an extensive number of items in my room, until the sensation of cutting clean, straight, unexpected chunks out of everything around me began to grow stale. The other item Betty had presented to me was a small wooden cross with fuzzy, colorful thread woven around and around through the sticks. Betty said it was called a God's eye, and that it was meant to suggest the eye of God looking at me all the time. It was a pretty object, but the taut, fuzzy thread was simply too much of a temptation, and it succumbed within the first day of my cutting binge.

Whatever else happened while my mother was away has vanished into Akasha. Someone drove me to school, someone picked me up, and someone fed me my breakfast and my dinner and even did my laundry, but all of it had a provisional and sloppy quality to it, so that when my mother finally walked back through the door of the kitchen one afternoon, it seemed not so much a relief as an inevitability that she was once again in charge.

On the way to school the morning after her return, and in the days that followed, she and I discussed Betty and the "new situation," as she and my father called it.

"How much longer is Betty going to be here?"

"I don't know, Ptolly. She may be here forever, so we had better start getting used to having her around."

"I hate her."

"No you don't, Ptolly! You don't even know her yet. Nor do I. We both have to be patient and *get* to know her. She's very good for your father. He *needs* her, because she knows about all sorts of things—things I don't know about that are useful to him in his work. And if she's good for your father then she's good for all of us. We have to try not to be selfish."

"I hate the way she tries to tell me what to do. And the way she grins at me, like she's my friend or something."

"Oh!" said my mother with relief and enthusiasm. "So do I! That phony, Cheshire cat, electric grin. But we can't let details like that bother us. You know what my German governess used to say when I was little—'Every beginning is difficult.' "

And difficult it was. If my father's plan had been to introduce Betty into our life so abruptly that we could not help but accept her presence, the plan did not go as he had wished. Selfish or not, neither my mother nor I could seem to go through a day without in one way or another calling into question the idea that this woman, with her suspiciously broad smile and her habit of following my father as he moved through the house, really belonged among us. What on earth was there about her that my father needed so desperately?

On the way to and back from school, my mother and I would discuss the issue again and again. Though she pretended to side with my father as best she could, it was plain enough that she agreed that Betty had some kind of nerve trying to be so friendly with us. My father had been quite visibly undone by my mother's departure, and when she at last consented to return he was over-joyed, assuring her that the "new adventure" was one from which she too would end up benefiting. But the new adventure turned out to be a lumpier business than my father had bargained for— a fact which was apparent to me from the endless slamming of doors, trips to the airport to see Betty off or pick her up again, and the frequent three-way arguments during which my father and his two tearful women would trade accusations and recriminations.

From early on, Betty was billed as a sort of intellectual assistant—someone to help my father wrestle with the gargantuan ideas that it was his job to bring to the attention of the unknowing outside world. "It's not just a sex thing," I would hear my father explain mysteriously to my mother. "It's about work! Betty understands my ideas and wants to help me get them down on paper and out into the world. You know my ideas don't always interest you. I had hoped you would be happy that I'd found someone who can fill that need in my life."

"I *am* happy," my mother would reply. "I know I'm very simple really, just a peasant at heart, and I can understand if you've decided you need to have someone smarter in your life. I'm the *first* to admit how dumb I am, but why then do you need me too in that case?"

"I'm not *saying* you're dumb, you idiot!" my father would return. "I'm saying—I'm *showing* you—that just because a person comes across something good in life—a treasure he realizes he doesn't want to do without—it doesn't mean he has to turn around and say good-bye to everything else in his life that's good as well. Betty and I get along, we understand one another. That doesn't mean that I suddenly don't understand you, and love you, as I have for all these years. For me to say that would be to give in to what the world out there—the world of Mr. Nixon and Mr. Agnew and the whole lot of creepy, hypocritical bastards who run this country—wants me to say. *Screw* growth, *screw* possibility. Don't do as you like or be as you like, but be *as we tell you to be. Or else.* Can't you see why it is I don't want any part of that— why it is I want to rescue you from that sort of poisonous self-denial, even if it means turning this household upside down?"

As my Christmas vacation approached, my mother came into my room and told me that we were going on a trip.

"You remember how much you like Florida, don't you, Ptolly?"

"Sure," I said. "I love Florida."

"We're going on a visit there. For your vacation—just you and me and the dogs. Doesn't that sound fun?"

"What are Peter and Betty doing?"

"They're going to stay around here. Betty is going to help your father with his work, then they're going up to New York, I think, to see Betty's two sons. They still miss her a lot, and she needs to spend some time with them. This whole business has been just as difficult for them as it has for us."

"What are we going to do there? Who are we going to visit?"

"Well, we're not going to visit anybody, really. We're just going to drive around, stay in some nice motels, and do what we like."

I didn't know why my mother decided on Florida, nor did I really understand why my father would not be coming along too, for up until then, with the exception of occasional visits to my sister, trips had always centered on something he was doing, be it a work project or some friends he wanted us to see. But I didn't question the plan. Certainly I was not about to complain about a trip that involved driving from motel to motel with no one calling the shots but my mother and myself. If Betty's appearance had rearranged the normal adult rules so much that trips like this were now to be a regular occurrence, perhaps she was not such a bad thing after all.

Indeed, if anything positive could be said so far for Betty, it was that she had transformed my mother from someone who worried about my well-being eighty percent of the time into someone who worried about it ninety-five percent of the time. By now I had overheard enough conversations with the words "for Ptolly's sake" to understand that my mother didn't really want to accept the "new situation" but was sticking around largely on my account. Later on, she would not disguise this from me at all, telling me time and again that she would not have lingered had she not suspected that had she gone away I would be "plonked in a boarding school"—a fate that lay just short of the firing squad in my imagination. To the question of why she had not just taken me with her, or made my father leave the Barn, my mother replied that a boy should not be separated from his father if at all possible. Not only that, but such a radical action would have amounted to "rocking the boat"—a favorite expression of both my parents— and though angry, my mother did not want to counter a bad action with another bad one.

The day after school let out my mother and the two dogs and I piled into one of the cars and left Betty, my father, the Barn, and all the new dramas it contained behind. Three years previously, when I was five, my father had taken us all down to live on the Gulf Coast for a time near the town of Fort Myers. As the days of driving slipped by and we moved ever farther south, it felt like my mother and I were moving back into that calmer and more understandable period of our lives. For several weeks during that original stay in Florida, my father had suffered from the mumps— an illness he had managed to avoid contracting as a child but which I ended up giving to him via a neighborhood friend. The case was a severe one, and left me with weird memories of my father lying flat on his back in a darkened room, robbed of all of his usual energy. Florida, as a result, lived in my memory as a place where my mother was in charge, and so she was again. Or rather, we were, for all the decisions about where to stay for the night and what to eat were passed by me for final consideration.

Florida was also the place where I had developed my initial interest in dinosaurs, cavemen, and things ancient in general, and as we moved down into the South, where the swamplands crowded up to the side of the road and the overhanging trees dripped with gray, primordial moss, my old passion for these subjects was reawakened. As we drove, I remembered that years before I had been excited by a series of highway billboards for a tourist attraction called the Lost World. According to the signs, the Lost World was a dinosaur park full of life-sized models, and on that previous trip I had indulged in a great deal of theatrics in the backseat when I learned that our route would not intersect it. Perhaps on this trip, where my mother and I were in charge and I sat up in the front and took part in all decisions, the Lost World would be mine to visit at last.

Down, down, down we drove, stopping early every day, walking the dogs around the grounds of each new motel. At seven my mother sat with her drink and her cigarette and watched Walter Cronkite, followed by a chain of sitcoms at eight. It was all "dumb stuff," as my mother said—the kind of simpleminded fare that clever people like Betty and my father wouldn't have time for. Once we got down to the Gulf, we continued on in the same rambling manner, stopping wherever we liked and feeling my father's absence at every turn as both a pleasure and a lack.

"Peter would never eat in this restaurant."

"I know what your father would have to say about this show."

"Peter wouldn't like this view."

"Your father would hate that man's shoes."

Without my father to tell us what to do and why we needed to do it, there was the prospect of more fun, but also a certain amount of insecurity. Freedom from him, it seemed, carried a price—the price of making and living with our own decisions. But on this peculiar trip, my mother and I managed to make out well enough in spite of the occasional doubts we would have about whether we knew what we were doing.

One day I decided it would be fun to try fishing from the side of a bridge, the way all the old retired men did, sitting for minute after minute without moving, like the pelicans out on the wharf poles.

"I don't know how to fish," my mother said. "But maybe if we go and buy a fishing pole somewhere, we can learn."

At a gift shop we bought a pole complete with line and hooks, then drove to a bridge with neither too many nor too few people on it. My mother parked the car on one side and she, the dogs, and I walked out past all the old men with their big, broad-brimmed hats and pastel shirts. We sat down and with difficulty I disengaged the hook from the reel, baited it with my mother's help, and let it down into the water.

My mother stared down after it. "Now I suppose we just sit and wait, right?"

"I guess so," I said.

"Well, let's see what happens," she said, trying to sound enthusiastic.

After some minutes, one of the old men sitting nearby got up and made his way over to us.

"You two are new at this," he said.

"Yes," my mother said gratefully. "I wish his father were here to help, but he's not."

"You'll do okay," said the man. "You just need a little coaching, that's all. First off, the line has to be further down, son. There's nothing on the surface that's going to bite your hook. It's got to be more towards the bottom. What are you using for bait?"

"A piece of Swiss cheese," my mother said.

"Oh, no, that won't do. Reel the line up, son. I'll be back in a minute."

The man, brown and lean like a piece of sea wood beneath his canvas hat, walked back to his spot on the bridge and fished about in a big white cooler.

"He's a nice man," I said to my mother.

"Yes, he certainly is. We're lucky we ran into him."

The man came back with something small and wet and slippery-looking in his fingers.

"There," he said, sliding it along my hook. "That's a clam. Best bait around. Now, let that sink down to the bottom, and just wait patient. You might get something."

I let the line down, and my mother and I sat on the bridge, half uncomfortable and half happy, watching the surface of the water. And amazingly, I caught a fish—a curious flat one with a dark back and a white belly and both its eyes on one side of its head. The man came back over when he saw my pole dipping down and coached me as I reeled the fish out of the water and up, up, to where we sat on the bridge.

"That's a flounder," the man said to my mother, genuinely surprised. "It's good eating. You should be proud of that boy. He's quite a fisherman."

The old man gave us an extra plastic bucket that he had on hand and explained to my mother, who listened dubiously, how to clean the fish once we were back at our motel. We thanked him and headed back down to the car, less than an hour after we had arrived. The whole adventure had all gone remarkably smoothly, and neither my mother nor myself could quite believe that we had ended up with an actual fish. I got in the car with the bucket on my lap, and we headed back toward the motel. Halfway there, I turned to my mother.

"Do we have to eat it?"

"Well, to be honest, I wish we could just let it go."

"Me too. Why don't we try? Maybe it's not too late for it to be okay."

It was the sort of half-baked thing that I could suggest to my mother, and know that she would listen. We pulled over to the side of the road at the next stretch of water we passed, and I walked down with the bucket and upended it. The flounder sank down into the darkness, and though I suspect I knew better, I told myself that the water would soon bring it back to its senses and it would swim off, unaffected by its contact with us—two more humans doing pointless, destructive, selfish things the way humans always did.

A day or so later we started on the long trip home, taking the route that led past the Lost World, even though it was a good deal out of our way. For miles and miles, signs rose up by the side of the highway, announcing the Lost World's imminent arrival—just as they did in my memory of years before. But when we arrived at the exit that led to it, we were greeted with a sign saying that the Lost World had closed down for good.

"*Now* they tell us," said my mother as I launched into a brief fit of outraged sniffling. "How inconsiderate to leave all those signs up."

To make up for missing the Lost World, we stopped at another attraction farther along: a park set on a waterway where people skied back and forth, standing on one another's shoulders and waving to the tourists on shore. The place didn't do much for me, with the exception of the mermaid show, which featured a number of women dressed in elaborate bathing suits with long fish tails. The women swam about in a big indoor tank and waved out at us through a thick glass pane. Every now and then, the mermaids would discreetly suck a little bit of air from a rubber hose that each of them held off to the side, as if it were a cigarette they were casually puffing. I knew the women needed the air in those hoses badly—that without them they would drown down there in their little turquoise room. But the women pretended not to need it, only taking a little bit now and then, as if it hardly even occurred to them to do so.

The women had their eyes wide open too, staring out at us as if we were clear and distinct to them through the water and the thick sheet of glass. But I knew we weren't—I had opened my own eyes underwater enough times to know that it stung and everything stayed blurry no matter how hard you tried to focus. Staring in at their smiling faces, I admired the women for trying so hard to look comfortable when I knew perfectly well they weren't. It seemed to be a kind of sacrifice they had to make, for the sake of the people who came to look and wanted to believe in them.

After a while we left the polite mermaid women behind and got back in the car and headed home, away from the Lost World, and back to the Barn.

The Water of Life

"He, being a god, easily effected special arrangements for the center island, bringing two streams of water under the earth, which he caused to ascend as springs, one of warm water and the other of cold and making every variety of food to spring up abundantly in the earth."
—Critias, describing the god Poseidon's creation of the central city on the isle of Atlantis, in Plato's Critias

SPRING came, and before long another summer rose up before me. Once again, it was time to pack up for the hill in New Hampshire, to fix the windows and empty the cereal bowls, and to visit Rand's News Depot for a fresh supply of horror comics. Only this time, things were very different than they had been the year before, for Betty was now with us. As we packed to leave the Barn the novelty of the new situation sank in further.

"Betty's coming to New Hampshire with us too?" I asked my mother, taken aback. "But there's no room for her up there."

"Well, we'll have to make room for her," my mother replied. "She and your father will get the upstairs, and I'm going to stay downstairs with you."

"But there's no place to sleep upstairs."

"No, but there will be now. Your father is going to rebuild it. He's always wanted to make the hill into a really nice place for us, and now he has the chance because of the pyramid book."

Over the winter, the "pyramid book" had been transformed from the mysterious project my father always had to go and work on into an actual object, heavy in the hands and full of pictures, as none of my father's other books had been. With its arrival, something strange happened to my father. Or, perhaps more accurately, something happened to the world around him, for my father himself never really changed. Suddenly, everyone everywhere seemed keenly interested in him and the things he had to say, just as my mother had promised they would be. His first invasions of my little black-and-white TV screen began, and every bookstore my mother took me to seemed to feature the book in its front window.

Like most writers, my father rarely sat and toiled at his craft all day. Mornings had always been for writing, and afternoons were typically given over to carpentry. Certain structures were particular favorites with my father. He loved installing dormer windows, for example, and bathrooms, and could slap one of the latter up and have the water running in it in an incredibly short time. Inevitably these were rough and provisional affairs, with plasterboard walls hammered up unevenly and hastily painted, so that the nail heads and pencil measurement markings were still visible years after their completion. Process, not precision, was the important thing. Nevertheless, one never needed to wait for a bathroom in any of his houses, and there was always plenty of light—at least in the top rooms.

The less finished a property was, the more my father liked it. If a house, and the land around it, could not be changed radically and perpetually, he had little use for it, while if it was a ramshackle mess of rotten wood and old machinery, his vision was given soft clay to work upon, and he was happy. Due to the rural setting and the dilapidated nature of the houses which sat upon it, the New Hampshire property was particularly vulnerable to my father's will-to-transform, and now that the success of *Secrets of the Great Pyramid* gave him the finances to do so, he brought that will to life there with bold and broad strokes.

The center of his activity was the house on the top of the hill. Soon after we arrived, a troop of young men my father had hired previously for help around the Barn showed up and began tearing the top of the house apart. One after another, great holes were cut into the roof so that dormer windows could look out upon the sweeping field that took up most of the hilltop. My father came and went from town, bringing up truckfuls of objects, all of them intended to serve—at least theoretically—as part of the house's general improvement. One morning at Sunday auction, along with a great deal of other items, he purchased eleven toilets. All of them, in varying states of condition and cleanliness, were trucked up and deposited in the field near the front of the house. After the wind and rain and sunshine of a few summer weeks had played across them and the grass had grown up around their edges, they started to look bizarrely appropriate out there, somewhat like an avant-garde artist's installation or a community of mammoth white mushrooms.

"What this place needs," my father pronounced one day when the construction in the house was starting to die down, "is water. A landscape without water is a dead landscape, and there's not much point in spending time in a landscape that's dead."

In the service of bringing the landscape to life, my father invited a group of dowsers up to the hill. After walking back and forth across the ground for some time with small, silly-looking forked sticks held out in front of them, these men gave my father good news. Invisible energy, my father told me, flowed up out of the earth and pulled these sticks down when the men were over water. Because the sticks had dipped down here, on our property, it meant that water lay somewhere beneath us.

Shortly thereafter, a well-digging outfit was summoned to drill for an artesian water source. The arrival of the well crew added a further dash of excitement to the lazy summer days, and I remember the pleasure of watching for hours as the noisy, machine-driven probe sank deeper and deeper, pushing out great black heaps of earth and shining, fist-sized chunks of quartz. The process stretched on for day upon day, and finally the morning came when the head of the crew told my father they would have to give up.

"I'm sorry, Mr. Tompkins, but it just doesn't look like there's anything down there."

"But I had it dowsed," my father protested. "I've been assured that there is a limitless supply of water if we just drill down far enough."

The man shook his head. "I'd love to believe this dowsing stuff, sir. It would certainly make my job easier. But there's just nothing there. You've paid for the day, so we'll keep the drill running until quitting time this afternoon. But I've got to tell you, it doesn't look at all good anymore."

Late that afternoon, about an hour before the drill was to be retracted from the earth and taken away for good, water gushed forth. Clean, freezing cold, and blasting up out of the darkness, it brought the landscape to life just as my father had promised. Under the force of the water the heaps of black earth and shining quartz collapsed and spread out onto the surrounding grass like paint on an artist's palette, and soon everything everywhere was thoroughly, triumphantly wet.

An artesian well, my father had explained to me, was a well that never ran out. Water came from it forever, from the very heart of the earth. Too young to fully appreciate the novelty of the success my father's big picture book of pyramids was enjoying, I found this more mundane feat profoundly impressive. Suddenly all the crazy adulation seemed to make sense. No wonder everyone thought he was so great.

The task of bringing the water of life to the dusty New Hampshire hilltop took a second form as well that summer. A short time after the well-diggers had departed, a fleet of bright yellow tractors and bulldozers made their way up to the top of the hill and set to carving up the field in front of the house some way down from where the little forest of toilets stood. Over the next few weeks they produced a great cavity in the earth, with a carefully modeled hump of land at its center and a delicate assortment of trees planted atop it. Slowly, the newly carved-out mass of mud around this little mound of earth filled with water, and when it had gotten deep enough a crescent of white beach sand was trucked in and dumped along its edge.

Betty took a number of snapshots during this project. Most of them show my father in high rubber fisherman's boots, standing amidst heaps and furrows of exposed red earth, his mouth open and his hands gesticulating intensely the way they did during his more passionate dinner table pronouncements. I suspect that these photos show him explaining how the whole thing would look upon completion, but to me they have the atmosphere of shots taken somewhere during the first week of Creation, with the God of Genesis busily conjuring up some new aspect of the world through a mighty act of speech.

By mid-July the pond, with its pleasant little strip of beach and tree-dotted island, was finished, and my father pronounced it good. But he had little time to take advantage of its happy atmosphere himself, for this was the initial summer of the Great Plan, when the world was erupting all around with the water of acclaim, and he had his work cut out just responding to it. In addition to keeping up with the world outside—with the phone calls from his publisher and the various newspapers, magazines, and TV and radio programs anxious to hear his thoughts and opinions—he had to contend with things on the home front. For despite his professed desire to set my mother and Betty free by creating our new, four-person household, resistance was cropping up at every turn.

"I cannot proceed," my father would announce during the quarrels that erupted almost daily on the hill that summer, "with my work and with the project of building a life for all of us in the face of these persistent petty jealousies. If the two of you cannot learn to let go and love one another as I do you, equally and without prejudice and selfishness; if you cannot learn that love when freely given and freely taken liberates rather than enslaves, then I will be forced to leave you both, and Ptolly as well, and spend my life off alone somewhere with only my work for company."

The petty jealousies my father spoke of were felt most acutely by my mother, who despite her hesitant but earnest gameness to give the Great Plan a try, couldn't help but notice that my father inevitably chose Betty to accompany him on his perpetual trips. Both on the hill and before that at the Barn, my mother had often been left alone to look after me while Betty and my father came and went, stopping only to catch their breath before going off to some other city, some other party, some other television show.

"Freedom," my father would respond when my mother came to him with her complaints, "like any other project really worth pursuing, is a matter of give and take. You look after Ptolly now, and Betty's presence will free us up in the future for adventures of our own. The shackles of sexual jealousy aren't the only ones that need to be broken—the whole bloody bourgeois business of slavery to the family needs to be upset. Once you relax and get used to it, you'll find that having Betty around makes your life much more productive and joyous than it ever was before. Look at all the couples with children we know! Whatever they might say, in reality they are held down, stifled, by the needs of those children just as their sexual desires are held down by their blind adherence to an antiquated morality. To hell with all of it! That's what I say, and that's what I mean to accomplish."

And yet, in spite of the grand sweep of my father's theories and the confidence with which he extolled them, the fights continued—sometimes generated by my mother, sometimes by me, sometimes by Betty or my father, and sometimes by all of us at once.

"How in blazes," my father would scream to the skies during these collisions, "can I be expected to keep this ship afloat and fulfill my responsibilities when I am perpetually dragged into domestic imbroglios brought on by small minds unwilling to move into the larger life that I keep struggling to get you to understand is out there, waiting to be lived?"

One bright July day soon after the tractors had retreated and the pond lay sparkling, with the red earth healing into green around it, my father assembled all of us and presented a new solution to our domestic dilemma.

"I've been giving all of this a lot of thought, and it occurs to me that Jerree's resistance to growing into the new life I have devised is not necessarily her fault. The inability to grow and change is something we bring down onto the physical plane with us when we reincarnate. It's obviously a past life that's causing her to resist the new plan, and until the specifics of that past life are recovered, identified, and addressed, we can't hope to make any progress. Therefore I've arranged that she go to New York and get treated by a new scientologist friend of mine. He's had great success with a number of people I've talked to, and I'm confident he'll be able to rout out Jerree's problem as well."

"But what about Ptolly?" said my mother. "I may be unhappy with things, but he's having a wonderful time here on the hill. What's he going to do in an apartment in New York all day while I'm getting this treatment?"

"As I've told you both time and again, freedom means sacrifice. Betty will stay on here to look after Ptolly, while I come and go, seeing all of you as my schedule permits."

Apparently my father had not tried this plan out on Betty before presenting it to all of us together. I looked over to check her reaction, and found it easy enough to read.

"Listen, Peter, it's all well and good that you've come up with this idea, and it's very nice of Jerree to say she'll give it a try, but I've got plans for the next few weeks—people I want to see. I can't just stop everything and stay put on this hill. Why don't we"—and here she turned to me and flashed one of those grins my mother and I were so suspicious of—"send Ptolly to a camp of some sort? After all, he's nine years old. He should be with children his own age instead of stuck in the middle of a highly confused threesome of adults who seem to be spending most of their time arguing with one another. What do you say, Ptolly? I think I know a place on Long Island that could take you now, even though it's late in the summer. I know the owner."

"No way!" I responded, with the unchecked vehemence of a child consistently used to getting his way. "I don't want to go to some dumb camp with a lot of dumb kids I've never seen before. I want to stay here. I like it here, and I don't want to leave just because my mom did something wrong in her past life! Besides, you just want me out of the way so you can travel around and be fancy and famous."

"That's not true!" said Betty.

"Oh yeah, right, Miss Priss," I said, my own half-understood and semiformulated resentments toward Betty now fully roused. "You're just a spoiled princess."

My father turned and glared at my mother. "Just where do you suppose he's been getting ideas like that?"

"Oh, I'm sure I don't know," said my mother with poisonous nonchalance. "Some past life situation no doubt. Perhaps as a child in ancient Egypt he had an overbearing father with a spoiled mistress who insisted on getting her way all the time. No doubt your brilliant scientologist friend could put him in a trance and coax the dirty details out of him—after he's finished brainwashing me."

This was uncharacteristically direct for my mother, and it had its intended effect. "You're crucifying me!" my father shouted, his face turning a dark and dangerous-looking shade of red. "Each and every one of you is dead set against this entire adventure, and I can see that none of you is going to be satisfied until I'm lying in a bloody, emasculated heap at your feet! Well, go ahead, then, hack away, I give up! You can't set someone free when they're so in love with the chains binding them that they bite and scratch even as you approach them with the key. Rot to your hearts' content in your happy little dungeon. I bid you good luck and good-bye!''

With that he blasted out the screen door, and in a moment we could hear one of the cars start up and race away down the hill.

My mother finally did end up going to New York to have her past life entanglements clarified, and Betty gave up her various engagements to baby-sit me on the hilltop when my father could not be there himself. I even managed, on my better days, to be somewhat nice to her and appreciative of her efforts on my behalf. Yet whatever past lives my father's scientologist friend succeeded in leading my mother back into, the things discovered there were not enough to free her from her human failings. Or at least not to the degree that she was able to pursue the cosmically open, jealousy-free relationship that my father had set as her goal. The Great Plan, whether from a flaw in its construction or the all-too-human foibles of the three who had enlisted to bring it to fruition, was simply not playing out as my father had hoped.

Meanwhile, Rand's News Depot continued to serve as Mission Control for my attempts to put the goings-on around me into satisfactory order. By now I had read enough issues of *Creepy* and *Eerie* to have come up with some substantial modifications to my picture of the human condition, and most of these modifications took the Great Plan, with all its talk of harmony and happiness and all its contradictory evidence of bickering and general misery, as their starting point.

One of the strongest messages I got from the stories in these comics came from the twist endings they often featured. Patiently and inevitably, the plot built up the reader's expectations over the course of several pages, only to dash those expectations in the final few panels. In one story I was especially partial to, a group of children pursued a vampire, only to reveal, once they had driven a stake through its heart, that they themselves were ghouls and had intended all along to eat it. In another story, a henpecked husband made a deal with a werewolf to get rid of his nagging wife, only to discover, in the final panels of the story, that his wife was herself the werewolf. In another, an escaped convict in a Southern swamp was attacked by a group of vampires in a decrepit mansion, only to kill them and escape back into the surrounding swamp, only to be caught by the posse chasing him, only to shoot the posse, only to discover that the members of the posse had themselves turned into vampires. "Eeeeeeeeek!!" "Aaaaaaaagh!!!!" The final screams of the unfortunate protagonists, written in large, wavery letters that often bled across the final two or three panels, became as soothingly reassuring to me as Walter Cronkite's nightly news reports were to my mother. Actually getting surprised was not the point. The fun, I discovered, lay in learning that the world was never the kind of place you expected it to be, no matter how well you thought you knew it.

These stories also firmed up my convictions, now fed every day by the activities of the adults around me, that there was something fundamentally wrong with human beings. One story I remember being especially interested in, from one of the lower-rent magazines that copied the style of *Creepy* and *Eerie*, concerned an evil doctor who, in the course of his fiendish experiments, locked a husband and wife away together in a cage without food, coming back in a few days with a piece of meat which he hung from the cage's ceiling. The man and woman, formerly devoted to each other's well-being, scrambled viciously for the dangling piece of meat, thus proving the doctor's grim point that people are at bottom instinct-driven savages who have built up a phony veneer of civility and decency, only to have it broken by the least disturbance.

The base motivations lurking beneath all the complicated and high-sounding activities that adults engaged in was a theme that ran through most of these tales. The lesson here was basically the same one learned during my days of caveman study back at the mill. Human society! What was it really, after all was said and done, but a hypocritical sham? My mother, in her own way, had assured me of this countless times, and these stories provided a festival of confirmation. The stuff that adults said and did was all a big crock, and the more swiftly and messily this was proved, the better.

Though my parents didn't pay too much attention to it, my increasing fascination with these comics, and with things morbid in general, was sometimes so impossible to avoid that it won comment from them. One night that summer, while Betty was away visiting her sons, I went with my mother and father to have dinner at a restaurant in town. On the way back to the hill, a policeman waved our car to a halt before a small bridge spanning a river. Then another policeman leaned down to the window and told us we would have to wait a few minutes before crossing.

"There's a girl in the river upcurrent a ways," he said. "A drowning. We've just got to get some ropes positioned, then you can move on."

"A girl?" asked my mother from the passenger seat.

"Yes, ma'am. Eleven years old. Looks like she got pulled under somehow."

"Oh, how horrible."

"Yes, ma'am. A tragedy. Just a minute or two, and you can proceed."

"Let's stay and wait till she gets dragged out," I offered hopefully from the back. Though I couldn't explain why, I found the idea of a dead girl at the bottom of a river unspeakably mysterious.

"Jesus!" my father shouted from the front seat. "This is really too much! What is going *on* with this child?"

My mother turned around in her seat so she could see me.

"This isn't make-believe, Ptolly. It's not like one of your comic books. It's very sad."

I knew she was right, and that I wasn't supposed to get excited about something bad actually happening to someone. Nevertheless, I couldn't help it. The fact that such a thing could occur— that a girl could disappear down at the bottom of a river, just like the girl in the wall had done on *The Twilight Zone*, spoke to me. Like the mummy, like the Wolf Man, like the hidden water my father had drawn up when no one had expected it, the event was a communication of sorts from a place beyond—a world-behind-the-world, the features of which I couldn't see and the intentions of which I didn't understand, but which I was becoming more and more certain did exist.

As summer turned into fall and winter, the dynamic among Betty, my mother, my father, and me continued to be one of constant and largely unfruitful ferment, with my mother and me complaining to my father about Betty, Betty complaining to him about the two of us, and my father shuttling back and forth in between, alternately lambasting and pleading with Betty and my mother to overcome their petty jealousies and open themselves to the life of harmony and splendor that he so keenly intuited was about to commence.

Around this time, as part of what was apparently a general campaign to remake herself in the wake of Betty's arrival, my mother went off to the hospital for a few days to have a face-lift. My mother had turned fifty in 1968, and from that time onward it became common to hear that she looked "good for her age." Rising at six every morning to perform an hour or so of yoga, mowing the endless lawn that surrounded the Barn with a hand-powered mower, yet at the same time remaining an enthusiast of old-fashioned amenities like cigarettes, steaks, and martinis, my mother saw herself as a woman with discipline who nevertheless knew how to have a good time. Unlike Betty, who didn't smoke, didn't exercise, and took a '70s style interest in what she ate, my mother wasn't "precious" about things. "I'm tough—tough as nails" she would say. And I wanted to believe it.

Yet the tears that came so often in her arguments with my father and Betty seemed to suggest otherwise. And there were other moments that made me doubt this supposed toughness, like the fall day when my mother went to pick up Abbie, who had been acting increasingly sluggish that summer in New Hampshire, from the vet. Returning with a large cardboard box which my father had to help her carry from the car, my mother explained to me that Abbie had cancer and that the vet had had to put him to sleep.

"All these months he's been sick, and I've been making him come on walks—making him do what he didn't want to. Oh, I feel so *guilty!*"

Standing over the box with Abbie in it, my mother had cried and cried, and listening to her from the hallway outside her room, it was difficult indeed to believe that she was really "tough as nails," as much as she or I or anybody else would have liked to.

So when my mother told me she was going to the hospital to have her face lifted, I was worried. With my child's respect for the pure physicality of words, the idea of someone's going to a hospital and having her face *lifted* struck my mind's eye vividly. In my imagination I saw the doctors, gathered around with their white robes and masks, and at their center I saw my mother— faceless now, a sort of amorphous blank—as the doctors executed their mysterious manipulations and refinements.

"It's nothing drastic," my mother told me when I voiced concern that the doctors might drop or otherwise mishandle her face. "They just pull the skin a little bit all around so the wrinkles go away. Like this." She put her hands up to her face and drew the skin back.

"See? That's all there is to it."

"Why do you need to do it, though?"

"It's just something that will make me look better. My body's in good shape because of all the yoga I do, but I'm getting too many wrinkles now, and a face-lift will make me look ten years younger."

"Why do you have to look ten years younger? So you'll look younger than Betty?"

"Oh *no*. I just want to, that's all. It will make me feel good about myself."

A few days after the procedure, I went along with my father to the hospital to pick up my mother. When I got there I received a shock. All the talk of the ease and relatively minor nature of the procedure had had its effect, and I was prepared to see a magically transformed version of my mother awaiting me. What I saw instead was an alarmingly unfamiliar figure swathed in mummylike bandages, so weak from whatever the doctors had done that she was scarcely able to talk to me or listen to my news of what had been happening at school in the few days she had been away. As I looked at her, I remembered my mother's descriptions of the procedure and imagined all the stitches around the side of her face suddenly snapping from some unexpected event—perhaps an argument with my father—and her face crumpling up into nothing.

After some days of lying in her darkened bedroom my mother went back to the hospital and the bandages came off, but beneath them she still looked distressingly worse for wear. The great change that was supposed to make the pain and punishment of the operation worthwhile was nowhere to be seen. More time passed, and at last my mother began to look herself again. The scrapes and cuts and swelling went away, and I could see that perhaps she did look younger than before. But for my purposes, the important information to be gained all lay back in the early phases of the event, when I had seen my mother in her white hospital gown, her face covered in bandages. Accustomed as I was getting to seeing my mother as someone strong on the surface but secretly frail, the operation provided me with a visual reaffirmation of what I knew anyhow: the Larger Life was having its effect on her, and that effect was destructive even as it was supposed to be good.

Along with such potent visual clues as to what was really going on with the adults around me, the endless "discussions" among Betty, my father, and my mother continued to yield a rich supply of food for thought. Images of ropes, shackles, and assorted other tools of confinement filled my father's arguments, as did a parallel set of images relating to freedom, release, and soaring flight above the land of timid bourgeois artifice. For a time, all of us lived in a world where freedom, both as an ideal and as a challenge, defined just about every aspect of day-to-day life. The general prescription of "more freedom" was, of course, a cure-all in many households other than my father's in the early '70s, but at our house it was applied with particular intensity.

Periodically, the atmosphere among this intense, freedom-obsessed trio of adults and the child who found himself among them took on a kind of giddiness, as the possibility of really breaking out of what my father called the "cage of bourgeois artificiality" seemed for a moment within reach. But it was always short-lived. One minute everyone was "lighter than air," "happy and loving," and so forth, and the next minute it all fell away into chaos and bad feelings—the result of somebody's "rocking the boat" or "poisoning the atmosphere," as my father often put it. If things were cheerful and carefree, the one thing to be sure about was that something—maybe trifling or maybe larger—would come out of nowhere to upset it all.

Thus were my suspicions about the dubious and untrustworthy nature of the human condition, born long ago in the light-filled rooms of the ancient mill, driven home. As my mother pointed out to me time and again, the human world was one of artifice and imitation, full of people pretending to do one thing but actually doing another. Wait long enough, and any pretense to harmony and happiness would blow away like so much milkweed, revealing the chaos that lay beneath. "Human beings! Give me an animal any day of the week." So my mother said, and so, I got to thinking, it must be. People let you down. Trust not in them but in nature: in trees, in animals, in the wind and the clouds, in all that lay beyond the strictly human sphere. But could even that world be trusted? Sometimes, I wasn't sure.

The Man Behind the Curtain

"Be not afraid of the universe."
—Eskimo shaman, quoting the supreme self, or soul, of the universe

"Everything means something, I guess."
—Character in The Texas Chainsaw Massacre

THE days and nights I spent alone with my mother in the years of the Great Plan were many. On these nights, when Peter and Betty were off in New York or Europe or elsewhere and no long-term visitors were on hand, my mother, her dogs, and I served as the lonely guardians of the great cold shell of the Barn, which in my father's absence seemed to become even larger and more unwieldy.

Put together by someone who quite simply didn't fear the world, the Barn was a brazenly unprotected structure. Room upon empty room, each of them outfitted with extra-large windows, looked out into the blackness. Tall, dense walls of trees rose up on either side of us, all but blotting out the lights of our neighbors. Six separate doors, all unlocked, and an Olympic-size attic that was always ready with an inexplicable noise or two in the deep hours of the night, provided rich material to meditate on as I lay, my General Electric TV finally extinguished, waiting for sleep to arrive. To my mind, there was something basically unnatural and sinister about the suburbs. From my occasional visits to the houses of school friends I knew that dysfunction—though typically of a less-flamboyant variety—was in plentiful supply beyond the Barn just as it was within it, and as I lay in bed I imagined not only the empty Barn itself but that uneasy landscape stretching endlessly beyond it.

Such was my fear of the night wrapping around us that on especially bad nights I would sleep in my mother's bed. With the inception of the Great Plan, and the ever-changing sexual politics and bed-hopping that came along with it, this habit of seeking refuge from my fears in my mother's room could create confusing situations. One night, I awoke from uneasy dreams to find that I had actually sleepwalked into my mother's room. I was further disoriented to realize that the person on the other side of the bed was not my mother but Betty. Of course! Betty and my mother had recently switched quarters, and in my dreams I had failed to take account of this. Unnerved, I got out of bed and made my way back to my room.

By the time I was in fourth grade, the concept of an invading presence—one that sweeps in and blows the ordinary world away—was something I believed in and thought about every day. And by this time I had a new source of fuel for my thoughts: the movies. Not the ones I watched on TV, but those on the big screen. For years my father and I had been going to the cinema together, for he loved films even more than I did and had the true aficionado's open-mindedness toward them, seeing whatever happened to be playing without complaint. As the Great Plan wound into its second year, I began more and more to take advantage of that open-mindedness in order to gain entrance to films that most other children my age had no idea about. *Beyond the Valley of the Dolls*, *Midnight Cowboy*, *Women in Love*—by 1972 I had seen all of these and more. Although most of the time I didn't understand what was going on in these films, I understood enough to know that in seeing them I was getting away with something—and that was usually enough to keep me awake even in the dullest and most incomprehensible parts.

By far my favorites were horror films, which in the early '70s were enjoying a lively and unprecedentedly bloody renaissance. These were not the relatively benign, old-fashioned stories offered up by the local TV stations but something different altogether. In *The House That Screamed,* I watched as the unbalanced son of a girls' school headmistress murdered one student after another so that he could assemble the woman of his dreams out of their assorted parts. In *Mark of the Devil,* I marveled as a woman's tongue was pulled from her mouth with giant iron pincers. In films like *Willard* and *Frogs,* I witnessed the deeply gratifying spectacle of rats, snakes, and alligators deciding they had had enough of human domination and turning upon people en masse.

One after another, these films drove home the now familiar idea that the adults of the world really weren't in control the way they thought they were. Beneath the crust of apparent harmony that those adults seemed so ready to believe in, chaos reigned, and it was only a matter of time before that chaos made its way to the surface. At once frightened and consoled, I watched as the safe and secure lives of the protagonists of these films were turned upside down so that the hidden dimension could at last emerge into the light. "This can't be happening," someone up on the screen would inevitably gasp at some point in the proceedings. Down in the audience, in the grips of a joy I didn't understand but couldn't get enough of nonetheless, I knew better.

There was something wonderful in all these dramas of sweeping destruction—a feeling similar to the one I would get when I stood out in the field behind the Barn watching the arrival of a thunderstorm, the trees dipping violently beneath the cold erratic blasts of air and the branches blowing silver with a sound like mounting applause. But something was definitely amiss about these films too. I was older now, and the dark forces that played across the screen were so much more sinister and dangerous than the familiar monsters of days past that my relationship to them lost its old innocence. Fascinating as I found these new, graphically gruesome movies, it was becoming apparent that the destruction of the all-too-normal world they offered was something from which I was no safer than anyone else.

"How about a film, Ptolly?" my father said one Friday night after dinner. "Go check the paper and see what's playing."

I looked over the listings, letting my instincts lead me to the most potentially unpleasant.

"Here's one. It's at the Inner Circle, at midnight. *Night of the Living Dead*. What a great name."

"Midnight. That's a bit late. It's not even nine yet."

"Yeah, but if it's on that late it probably means it's good. Can we go?"

"All right. If you're still up for it at eleven, we'll go."

Night of the Living Dead had been out for only a few years and was still considered shocking for its unprecedented violence, but neither my father nor I had heard anything about it. I had simply picked it out of the movie listings on the basis of its straightforward, no-nonsense title. It sounded like a film that would deliver.

And deliver it did. As jaded as I was, *Night of the Living Dead* managed to present me with something new—so new, in fact, that I left the theater feeling like I was not quite the same person I had been when I entered it. The street outside the theater, the cars whizzing past through the late autumn night—everything around me took on a frightening unreality, and on the drive home this sense of unreality did not decrease but instead seemed to grow. Things had unfolded on the screen that I had not previously thought possible, even in the pretend world of the movies, and as a result the world around me had become an entirely less trustworthy place than it had been a mere two hours earlier.

Upon reflection, I realized I had many reasons to gravitate to *Night of the Living Dead*. The forlorn farmhouse from which the main characters battle the encroaching army of zombies looked a good deal like the house on the top of the hill in New Hampshire. In addition, the desperate hammering of the film's hero as he nails planks of wood and bits of splintered furniture against the doors and windows was oddly reminiscent of the sloppy, rapid-fire style of carpentry my father tended to practice in his perpetual remodelings and improvements.

But these were just small and coincidental details. Above and beyond them, the movie lodged itself in my imagination because it stated in unprecedentedly direct terms what all the other horror films and comics had before it: Life was a place of deep uncertainty, ruled in secret by huge and dangerous forces. Like the lonely, pathetically vulnerable house in the film, lost in a nighttime landscape where the dead staggered and lurched about in search of human flesh, the ordinary world was a fragile and precarious island set in a sea of mystery—a sea out of which something strange and dark and truly terrible could emerge at any moment.

Night of the Living Dead gave my theories back to me in such a direct and vivid way that I was thoroughly unhinged by it. Having witnessed such an uncompromising confirmation of my darkest suspicions, it seemed perverse and ridiculous to me that the ordinary workaday world should dare to continue. Telling my school friends about the picture did little or nothing to help me make sense of it. No one else in my fourth grade class had parents permissive enough to allow them to go see it, so I was left to ponder the unspeakable events I had witnessed without the benefit of my peers' opinions. The more I tried to give my fellow nine-year-olds some idea of the uncanny and horrific truth I had uncovered at the heart of this film, the more I realized that, like a mystic returned from an encounter with the divine in the trackless wastes of a distant desert, I had no hope of truly conveying what I had witnessed.

"So the woman goes down to the basement to where the daughter is, and the daughter is *eating her father*."

"Whoa, that's cool. That's like when Godzilla grabbed that guy and just his legs were sticking out of his mouth."

But of course it wasn't like that at all. Godzilla was a plastic Japanese dinosaur, a mere entertainment. What I had seen, while "only a movie" in the technical sense, was decidedly something more. With this film, I began to realize, I had stumbled upon something genuinely adult—something which, as my mother put it, I was "not ready for." And as a result I suddenly found myself living in a world where true surprises were possible, a place where absolutely anything could happen.

Sitting on the steps outside the kitchen one day shortly after seeing the film, I overheard my mother and father talking inside. "Peter," my mother said, "I'm worried about Ptolly. He seems so preoccupied with that ghastly movie you took him to last week. He's got circles under his eyes, and he's terribly pale. He told me there's a scene in the film where a young girl eats her father and stabs her mother to death with a gardening trowel. What is on your mind that you can take a child to see something like that?"

"Pretty grisly stuff," my father remarked offhandedly. "But I didn't know anything about the film. He wanted to see it, and I'll see anything as long as I don't know what's going to happen. I like the surprise."

"Well, you certainly succeeded in surprising him! I think you ought to stop going to these pictures altogether. He has enough to cope with in his life at the moment without worrying that some zombie is going to eat him."

My father perked up at this last statement, as did I from my spot on the steps outside.

"Are you suggesting I censor what the boy sees?"

"Oh, for heaven's sake. I just think it might not be a bad idea to protect him from films he's not old enough to understand."

"Shield a child too much from the world," my father returned, "and you implant the idea that the world is a place that one needs to be shielded from. One shouldn't keep secrets from children about anything. That film may have been a little much for Ptolly, but on another level it's never too early to learn about what frightens you and to confront it. It's only by examining what we fear most that we can learn to defuse those fears and the negative energy they generate. When that happens, that negativity can be transformed into love and positive energy."

"Positive energy! I hardly see where the positive energy is to be found in a girl stabbing her mother with a gardening trowel. But in any case, I'd like you to talk to him."

I had been monitoring this conversation closely, for I understood that my future movie-going privileges were at stake. It seemed to me that if I did not want those privileges to be drastically curtailed, I had better set about giving the impression that I was not as unnerved by *Night of the Living Dead* as I obviously was. In the days since I saw the film, I had indeed been doing less sleeping than usual. Those lurching, shabbily dressed zombies appeared as soon as I closed my eyes at night, and when I opened my eyes I saw them too, crowding about in the large black windows of my bedroom, reaching out to me with their pale, rubbery fingers.

That evening, my father came into my room as I was once again steeling myself for a night of fitful sleep.

"Ptolly," he said, sitting down at the foot of the bed, "you've got to stop letting this silly movie get under your skin. We'll have to stop going to the movies—or at least some of them—if they're going to have this kind of effect on you."

"But I like seeing movies with you, and horror movies are the best kind."

"So do I, but if they're going to upset you like this . . . Listen," he said, leaning forward and talking seriously, addressing his remarks to the floor in front of him. "I'm going to let you in on a little secret. This kind of stuff only has energy to frighten you if you let it. The thing you . . . the thing most people don't realize is that they have the power to control the things that frighten them. You have the power to control your own imagination and all the images that move through it, only no one's told you so. Now, what scared you most about that film?"

"I don't know. The little girl in the basement, I guess."

"Fine. Now let's do a little experiment. Try to imagine the girl. Picture her with your mind's eye. Can you see her?"

"Sure."

"Good. Now take her out of the context of the film. Take her out of the basement and put her somewhere else."

"Like where?"

"Anywhere!"

"On a bicycle?"

"Perfect. Imagine her on a bicycle. Can you see her?"

"Yeah."

"What's she doing?"

"She's going down a hill."

"Good. Now, make her reverse direction. Make her go backwards up the hill. *You're* the boss. Just as you can decide what situation you want to see the girl in, so you have the power to control what kind of effect the images in the film have over you. It's all just pictures, pictures, pictures. They're frightening because you allow them to be frightening. All the images that move through your head every day are under your control if you want them to be. You're the one creating them in the first place, and once you come to understand that and learn to act on it, they won't have any negative power over you anymore."

"I make the images in my head?"

"Of course."

"But I didn't make the girl in the basement. I saw her."

"You saw the image because someone else made it up in their head, then got actors and cameras so you could see it as they did. You know that a film always has a director, right? The one who tells people what to do and how to do it and decides where the camera is going to be."

"Yeah."

"Well, *you* are the director of the scenes and pictures that go through your head every day. You're even the director of the dreams you have at night—the director and the audience at the same time—only you don't know it."

"Where do the pictures come from, though?"

"From you! That's the whole point. You're the boss."

"I sure don't feel like I'm the boss."

"Most people don't," said my father enthusiastically. "And if you can come to the realization that you are, you'll be better off than ninety-nine percent of the adults out there. That's really the great secret: knowing who's behind the scenes making it all happen—knowing who the man behind the curtain is."

"There's a man behind the curtain? What curtain?"

"No, no. That's just a way of talking. What I mean is there's a whole world out there that you don't know about."

"I know. That's why I'm scared."

"But it isn't the kind of world you think it is. You think it's a wasteland full of ghouls and little girls with blood on their chins and all that sort of shit we see in these movies you like so much. But it isn't that kind of place at all, really. You shouldn't be frightened of it, because it's the place where you really belong. You, me, all of us go through our lives thinking we're a tiny little person, trapped inside our own heads, and that the world out there is some big alien nightmare. And because we think it's that way, that's the way it appears to us. But it's all a big illusion. It's not real."

"So what's real?"

My father turned his gaze from the floor and stared at me, tapping his head with his finger while he did so.

"This," he said triumphantly. "This is what's real. The you that mistakenly thinks it's a frightened little nothing trapped inside your brain. It's what's real, only it isn't really so little at all, and it isn't trapped inside your brain either."

"I don't get it. If I'm not in my brain, where am I?"

"You're everywhere! You're out there in the dark beyond the window, and up in the sky, and in the past, and in the future. The real you isn't limited by time or space or the body, because the real you is everything. That asinine school we send you to tells you there's some grim-faced God up in the sky looking down at us making sure we all behave correctly. But there isn't any such God out there at all. In fact, it's really just the reverse of that, because deep down each of us, you and me, if we look hard enough, discover that we are God ourselves. We actually are the ones who have made the world and who control it. The world is really us, only we don't want to admit it because we don't want the responsibility of all that power."

"So I shouldn't be frightened about that movie because I'm God?"

"You aren't *literally* God, but you are the creator of your own reality, which is almost the same as being God."

My father straightened up now and patted my foot through the blanket.

"Listen, I've got to get back out to dinner because we have guests. But I don't want you lying awake thinking about this film anymore. Think about some of the things I've told you instead— and remember," he said, smiling and tapping his temple with his index finger, "who's really in charge."

However well intentioned, my father's insights weren't much use in helping me to fall asleep that night, or in the nights to come. The trick of picturing the zombies that crowded my imagination dressed in party hats or eating green ice cream worked for a moment or two, but the process took constant effort, and as soon as I relaxed, they went back to what they had been doing before, staggering and gaping, their tattered arms reaching out toward me with the same old grim hunger. Out beyond the dim lights and shaky walls of my nine-year-old self-consciousness, the world continued to appear a dark and deeply alien landscape, dead set on doing what it, not I, wished it to do.

Having failed to command the zombies of my imagination through force of will, I developed other anxiety-avoiding strategies—the simplest and most effective of which was to avoid going to bed for as long as possible. This was easiest when there were guests over. Around ten o'clock my mother would tell me it might be a good idea to get off to bed, but my father would always intercede on my behalf, telling her I shouldn't be discouraged from listening to the adults if I wanted to do so. There usually wasn't much to interest me in these conversations, but I stayed at the table anyhow, chin in hands and eyes half closed, letting the adult voices wash over me in a comforting and largely meaningless babble.

It was during this intensive period of dinner party attendance that I first started to notice a pattern to my father's talk, as he sat, booming away, at the head of the table. I noticed that he always seemed to be talking about secrets of one sort or another and how knowing those secrets could set you free. Sometimes, as had been the case in my bedroom that night, the "great secret" would be that you and God weren't really different, but on some mysterious inner level one and the same. But at other times it would be about something else—that love was the engine that drove the universe, or that everything possessed consciousness, or that all things good and bad that happened to a person came from actions committed in a past life.

In addition to the various "great secrets," there was any number of lesser ones. Who built Stonehenge? Who wrote the plays attributed, by the dull-witted academicians, to Shakespeare? Who ran the banks in America? What were the ancient Egyptians really up to? Gradually it became clear to me that if there was, in fact, any real "great secret" to life, it had to do not with any single, specific secret but with the nature of secrecy itself. Life was essentially a carnival of misleading appearances—a papier-mâché landscape set about with hints and inconsistencies, which, when examined closely enough, pointed the way to a realm beyond. The mass of humanity, it seemed, chose to ignore these little openings and inconsistencies with which the world was strewn, but my father, to make up for this negligence, had apparently cornered the market on them.

"That whole period has to be seen in reference to such-and-such secret society or it makes no sense at all," he would remark, or "If you want to know anything about his *true* motivations, you have to realize that so-and-so was in reality a third-degree mason," or "Of course, once you see what was *really* going on with this or that ancient civilization, it turns all of conventional history upside down." With all these innumerable hidden intrigues, secret histories, and shadowy, occult goings-on, the basic argument was the same. Nothing was ever what it seemed on the surface, but if one knew this and stared at that surface long enough, openings in the small and all-too-normal world would appear: openings that would turn into roads leading into a vast dimension where all kinds of things undreamed-of were made gloriously manifest.

Of course, I was already well aware that the world possessed a secret life. The message had been instilled in me by every comic and horror film I had ever seen, and *Night of the Living Dead* had driven it home once and for all. The problem lay in the nature of this secret world. Was it, as I had come to suspect, a place of cacophony and terror? Or was it, as my father so vociferously maintained, a place of happiness and love and communion? The paradoxical joy that even the most frightening horror movies still continued to evoke in me—the fact that a part of me couldn't help loving them even now that they had begun to destroy my nights and haunt my days—suggested that my father was correct in his optimism about the secret world and its true intentions. Perhaps all those zombies really were waiting to do my bidding once I discovered, as he so confidently put it, who was really in charge.

Perhaps in spite of all these new anxieties, there was still a chance to return to that time when the Invading Presence, the monster lurking beyond, was more of a friend than something purely alien. Yet the possibility that this wasn't so—the nagging feeling that that great unknown dimension did not hold such good intentions—continued to trouble my sleeping and my waking hours. How did my father, especially given the chaos that filled his own life so constantly, *know* it was so good out there in the dark?

Back to the Garden

"What is our body to-day, compared to what it was in former days,
when we dwelt in the garden?"
—Adam to Eve in The Forgotten Books of Eden

F ROM the very beginning Betty disliked the Barn and made
little attempt to disguise her feelings about its junk-filled, half-
painted, pencil-marked disarray. The love and fascination she had
developed for my father's visionary ideas and flamboyant person-
ality did not extend to all aspects of his life, and, as her days with
us wound on, the moments when her brave "electric" grin sput-
tered out grew. As my mother was fond of remarking to me with
undisguised satisfaction, Betty "got a little more than she bargained for" when she took up with my father, and in those inter-
vals when the bargain seemed particularly poor she took off—to
Manhattan, to visit with friends from her old life, and to Sagaponack, Long Island, where she had a house of her own. Thoughtfully and painstakingly decorated, the Sagaponack house served
as her main asylum from my father's world—the place to which
she would retreat when life at the Barn, and all that came with it,
became too much for her.

With her smart neighbors and her lunches with Gore and Tru-
man, Betty knew from the beginning that she was stepping onto
decidedly uncertain turf in taking up with my father. The Sagaponack house proved to be the place where she discovered just how

uncertain that turf really was. For before long my father became a regular in Sagaponack himself, spending weekends and then weeks there, mingling freely with friends from Betty's former life. Whatever pleasure my father may have gotten from his entrance into Betty's social world must have been dubious at best, for he did pretty much everything he could to botch his reception there.

One night early on, he and Betty were invited to a particularly swanky party in Southampton. A short time after entering, my father was approached by a gray-haired gentleman.

"Who are you?" the gentleman addressed my father.

"Who are *you*?" my father responded in good Socratic style.

"I," said the man, "am your host."

"Well, then," replied my father, "you should know who I am."

The remark had its desired effect, and he and Betty were back home within the hour, never to be invited to that particular house again.

Others closer to home received similar treatment—often for reasons less easy to understand. "And you," I remember my father thundering one evening to Peter Matthiessen, a friend from Betty's former life who had ventured over for dinner one night. "You march into the jungle with Madison Avenue dripping off your fucking shoulders!"

"I didn't think you had read any of that guy's books," I remarked to my father after this dinner.

"I haven't read a thing by him! I was just sparring about a bit, seeing if I could get him to play."

"Getting a person to play" was the phrase used by my father to describe the barrage of rapid-fire verbal abuse which he customarily showered on new visitors to the dinner table. It was a sort of initiation, as he saw it, and no small number of visitors failed to make the grade.

"Oh, Peter," I can remember Betty saying after this or that

social fiasco, "did you *have* to say that to so-and-so? He was making such an effort with you!"

"What do I care about effort? That fellow is a card-carrying member of the Establishment masquerading as an *artiste*. Why should I bend myself in two to fit into a cage like some trained literary parrot?"

Even when he made a stab at actually getting along with the literary swells, things didn't always go smoothly. One day my father handed me a paperback copy of *From Here to Eternity*. Looking inside, I saw the words "to Ptolemy with best wishes, Jim Jones."

"Met him the other day," said my father.

"Did you get into an argument with him?"

"No, no, not at all. Though"—and here my father smiled, in apparent amusement at his ability to botch social encounters even when he wasn't intending to—"I congratulated him on what I thought was a particularly powerful scene in the book. Turned out I was describing a scene from *The Naked and the Dead*."

Many of these Long Island dramas—which I would witness on the odd weekend or vacation when I left my mother alone at the Barn and came visiting myself—centered not on people but on objects—specifically, the ones my father was always trying to fill Betty's house with. In the beginning, my father and Betty seemed to have struck up an unspoken agreement that, architectural visionary though he might be, her house was off-limits. But as he spent more and more time there, Betty's hold over the house began to erode under my father's unwelcome but vociferous interest in what he saw, with characteristically unwavering certainty, as its improvement.

"Ptolly," my father said gaily one June morning, "there's a rummage sale going on at the Bridgehampton Village Center. They're having a book sale as well. Want to come along?"

"Rummage sale!" said Betty. "Oh, Peter, you're not going to go and buy a lot of crap I don't need, are you?"

"Crap is only crap until you *do* need it. Come on, Ptolly. Time's wasting. We don't want the others getting the goods before we have a chance to look them over."

When we arrived, my father gave me a few dollars and left me at the tables of dusty, swollen paperbacks on the lawn outside and headed purposefully into the building. "When you've had enough out here come and get me at the auction," he shouted over his shoulder.

"Auction?"

"Yes. Inside. That's where the good stuff's being sold."

I wandered among the books for half an hour or so, then headed inside to see how my father was doing in securing the so-called good stuff. I found him at the front of a small crowd gathered around a man standing at a podium with a gavel. He and my father, it seemed, had already established an understanding. Introducing the next item on the list, the man addressed his remarks directly to him.

"What am I bid, folks, sight unseen," said the man, gesturing toward a large, leather-strapped trunk that looked like it had been through both world wars and possibly a few conflicts before that as well. "This antique traveler's trunk has a working lock and hinges, and it's full to the top with treasures for a collector with an open mind. It's a box full of mystery, folks! Who"—and here he once again looked pointedly at my father—"will start the bidding?"

"Ten dollars," said my father.

"Fifteen," said a fellow in dungarees who looked like he might have been one of the area's remaining potato farmers.

"Twenty," said my father.

A silence followed, during which the fellow in dungarees put his hands in his pockets, so as to signal he was bowing out.

"*Sold* to the gentleman up front for twenty!" said the man, his gavel slamming the wood of the podium. "Okay"—he nodded to two young men in jeans and T-shirts—"move it over with the rest of it."

"The rest of it," I repeated to myself, watching as the two young men hoisted the crate and staggered off.

"What else did you get?" I whispered.

"Shh," my father said, staring intently at the podium. "You'll see later."

"And now," said the man with the gavel, "a set of items any home handyman would be tickled to get his hands on. Not one washer but two, and a dryer to go along with them. Don't let those little rust spots fool you, folks. These units are in complete— or in any case very close to complete—working order. An afternoon's tinkering will get you the convenience of an entire home washing system."

"Twenty-five," my father shouted, unable to wait until the auctioneer officially opened the bidding.

"Fifty," said a large man standing next to the dungareed potato farmer.

"Sixty."

"Seventy-five."

"One hundred," pronounced my father.

After another short silence, the gavel came down again, and the T-shirted youths bent and set themselves against the rust-mottled machines, moving them out through a door behind the podium to the rear of the building where "the rest of it"—the product of my father's apparent monopolization of the entire auction—had been accumulating.

Driving home an hour or so later, with the two young men following in a pickup truck piled high with the heavy and hoary fruits of the morning, I asked my father what he thought Betty might make of his purchases.

"Oh, she'll complain a bit, but she'll come around. Especially," and here it seemed as if we were experiencing one of those father-son moments in which life-wisdom is passed from one generation to the next—"when it comes in handy. You never know when that day is going to come, but . . . it always does."

"Those three toilets are really going to come in handy?"

"Those toilets," my father said in a generous and paternal tone, "are money in the bank. Do you have any idea what a new toilet costs? They're prohibitive."

"But how come you got three of them?"

"They came as a set, Ptolly! And even if I only end up using one of them, I will have laid down much less than I would for a new one at full price."

"How about the organ? It looks like it weighs about five hundred pounds."

High, heavy, and deeply battered, the organ was the morning's single largest purchase. Pressing one of its ancient yellow keys while the young men were figuring out how to hoist it onto the truck bed, I received in return not a note, out of tune or otherwise, but a kind of sick, dusty thud. Opening the lid, I saw that the majority of strings were missing, and that those still there had been serving as the infrastructure for the nests of a number of now-departed small animals.

"There's always someone," my father remarked with the assurance of a lifetime's worth of experience, "who wants to play an organ."

Foreseeing an interesting confrontation, I ran into the house ahead of my father. Finding Betty upstairs, I led her to a window that gave her a good view of the truck as it backed along the green tranquillity of the summer lawn toward the spot where my father stood, beckoning it on with great welcoming sweeps of his arms.

In a flash Betty was gone from the window, and by the time the first items in the great cargo were being set down on the grass she had reached my father. I raised the window and tried to listen.

I was a little too far away to make it all out, but I got the gist. From amid the impromptu Stonehenge of washers, trunks, and toilets accumulating on the lawn around them, the words "It goes back! It all goes back!" drifted up on the warm summer air.

"It stays!" came the booming reply. "It stays and you will thank me for all of it! Jesus bloody Christ, why am I the only one around here with the wit to think ahead!"

Long Island remained, for years after that, only a partially satisfactory place for my father because, try as he might to work against the fact, it was largely a finished product, uncongenial to massive modification. And because my father desired above all else in those years to build the world anew—to change it to meet his very definite, if somewhat unrealistic, specifications—he was forced to vent that frustration elsewhere.

One of these Elsewheres was the Barn, and with the publication of *The Secret Life of Plants* in 1973, this most quirky and enduring of his "properties" came into its own as never before. Although my father's world had dramatically expanded with the success of his book on pyramids and their magical powers, with the plant book it exploded. Entire bookstore windows filled up with copies of it, the *Washington Post* ran a review titled "I'm OK, You're Oak" that, while incomprehensible, sounded grand to my ears, and the televised arguments with the dour scientists began in earnest. The money and the attention *The Secret Life of Plants* generated, combined with the intoxicating feeling of having been on the right track all along, made it seem like the New Life was within reach after all.

One of the most vivid indicators that my father had struck a nerve was the army of visitors that now began pouring steadily into the Barn. While neither my father nor Betty were always on hand to interact with these people themselves, thanks to their endless travels, my mother and I were, and for the rest of my childhood and adolescence these bizarre fellow travelers would play a key role in my continuing education about the adult world.

The Barn being large and my father being generous, there was room for plenty of not-so-weird guests to filter in and out over the years as well. Old friends, fellow fringe scholars, and the like, these people contributed in one way or another toward making my childhood a more eventful one. But the visitors I tend to remember most clearly are the weird ones.

Most of the more visionary guests who passed through the doors of the Barn in those years showed up with empty pockets, but to compensate for this their heads were packed with extravagant schemes, and they sought my father's help in bringing these schemes to the attention of the world. "If he can do it," these people seem to have reasoned upon closing one or another of my father's books, "so can I." The great majority of the ideas they brought to my father's attention turned around the notion that ordinary, everyday life is not what it purports to be but instead exists in relation to a former time and place when incredible things occurred on a regular basis and life was a larger and ultimately more satisfactory thing than it is now. The outlines of this lost, larger dimension had for the moment been obscured, but they were destined, ultimately, to come back into focus. The tasks that these individuals had set for themselves, and which they sought my father's help in bringing to fruition, involved hurrying that process along.

A number of these individuals never actually made the physical journey to the Barn, but communicated with such frequency that it sometimes seemed as if they lived there. One of the most persistent was a maverick mathematician named Quigley, who seemed to be constantly writing or calling to request funds for another calculator. "Quigley needs calculator," I would scribble on the message pad after a brief exchange on the phone. Once, I asked my father how it was that Quigley managed to go through so many calculators—which, in the '70s, were not the five-dollar items they are now but new inventions with prices starting in the hundreds of dollars.

"He eats them," my father responded. "He tells me he absorbs the intellectual power of the calculator the same way someone who eats the balls of a bull absorbs the bull's macho quality."

Once, several months went by without a call, and I thought to ask my father about it.

"He's vanished," my father replied significantly.

"Right," I said. "So where do you think he went?"

"No, no," my father corrected. "He's *vanished*. Into thin air. He spoke about trying it, and I think he's pulled it off."

The list of the other individuals who materialized and then vanished in those years is long. Some stood out for the singularity of their vision or project—others simply for the sheer determinedness with which they attempted to get my father to listen to them. A few stood out in both categories. I remember in particular an Italian, no longer living, who showed up one day—at my father's invitation, as it turned out—with an enormous collection of stones. Soft-spoken and likable in spite of his peculiarities, this gentleman lived, like a medieval knight, within the grip of an extraordinary mission. Compared with him my father actually managed to seem the less quixotic of the two.

"Who's this guy coming tomorrow?" I remember asking one night at dinner.

"Ahh," said my father, with the usual raised eyebrow and conspiratorial smile. "Arturo Tinelli. He's an old friend of mine from Florence, and he's onto something *very very* interesting. He's got a collection of stones that tell the secret history of the world on them. There may be a book in it, so I've asked him to come and stay a while."

As it turned out, Tinelli the stone hunter was a very decent fellow. Distinguished, with deep-set, compassionate eyes, he looked a little like Chance the Gardener as played by Peter Sellers in *Being There*. Tinelli had once made a good living writing film scripts, but had given it up when these peculiar stones started coming into his path. On his first night at the Barn, it became quickly apparent that he possessed the singleness of vision that characterized so many of the fellow travelers who showed up at our doorstep in those years. Screenwriting, politics, food, his former wives—these were all well and good, but what mattered were the stones. "Peeter," he turned and said with feeling that first night toward the end of dinner: "the *stones!*" It was an exclamation I would soon grow used to hearing.

The stones. The several large suitcases Tinelli had brought with him turned out to be filled with them. Wrapped in tissue paper and tucked in boxes of every size, they shared space with boxes and boxes of slides—for the stones did not yield their secrets just like that, but needed instead to be viewed in the proper light and at the proper angle.

Whether due to my lack of the visionary eye or Tinelli's lack of sanity, I didn't see much in those stones to convince me that they held the secrets of the world's history. Where Tinelli saw a flying saucer, I saw an indentation; where he saw a man and woman having sex, I saw two indentations and a blemish. Watching the slide show felt a bit like sitting through one of those exposés of subliminal advertising. That squiggle in the ice cube might be a naked woman, but then again it might be a cat or a goat, or nothing at all.

Given Tinelli's civilized and heartfelt air, the history of the world as depicted on his stones was oddly rich in prurient fare. Male and female genitalia abounded. Sexual acts between various human and more-than-human creatures (often in flying saucers) were commonplace. The evidence, as Tinelli saw it, pointed to an alien intervention at some point in the past, in which the space creatures came down to earth and, like the unruly titans mentioned in *Genesis,* consorted with the daughters of men before disappearing back into space. The influence of the extraterrestrials continued today but was covered up by the government of the

United States as well as by the governments of other countries. Yet the evidence of that influence remained—if, like Tinelli, you knew where to look.

This combination of sex, conspiracy, and hints of huge and fabulous otherworldly goings-on was, of course, irresistible to my father. Even so, after a few weeks it became obvious that my father was not sufficiently interested in Tinelli's stones to throw himself into a full-time study of them. But that did not mean that he was about to tell the poor fellow that he had to pack up his stones and leave; for as the champion of possibility, and as a person who generally didn't like to disappoint, my father couldn't dash Tinelli's hopes of at last being able to tell the world of his discovery.

The solution my father hit upon—and I had seen him adopt it with no small number of others—was to reply with a basic "later." For weeks after Tinelli's arrival, down the dark and spacious halls of the Barn, I would hear the small, insistent voice of Tinelli saying "Peeter, the *stones*," and my father's booming reply of "Jesus, Tinelli, not now! I've got a book to write! Stop trying to paralyze me!" In time, Tinelli was forced by my father's persistent rebuffs to look elsewhere for a sympathetic ear. He even took to stopping me on occasion. Reaching into one of his pockets, he would pull out yet another stone, unwrap it from its nest of tissue, and hold it up to the light.

"Look," he would say, his dark and oddly soulful eyes trained on me to gauge my reaction. "Right there, in the light. You see? A spaceship!"

The word *paradise* comes originally from the ancient Iranian word *pairidaeza*, which means enclosed garden. The human-plant relationship, like the human-animal relationship, is often described in the world's paradisal literature as having been deeper and more direct in paradise than it is now. A Near Eastern tradition possibly predating the writing of the book of Genesis, for example, maintains that in the Garden of Eden, before the fall, Adam and Eve were able to speak to the plants that grew there, and the plants were able to speak back to them.

This mythic notion has a special resonance for me, for it calls to my mind the four-sided garden my father installed in the front yard of the Barn shortly after his book on talking to plants made him a wealthy man. I never saw too much in the way of vegetables come out of this garden, but that was because, I now realize, its real purpose was symbolic. Surrounded by a high and impractically heavy wooden fence, the garden served as a showcase for the paradisal mind-set that, for better or worse, my father was struggling to awaken in the midst of unsuspecting and resolutely unparadisal McLean, Virginia.

The little garden was created shortly after the arrival of Carrie, the first in a long series of idealistic young women who were to show up at the doors of the Barn in search of a role in my father's quest. "Just read *The Secret Life of Plants*," began the short letter that preceded Carrie's appearance. "I am willing to take whatever work is available for a chance to be involved in what you are doing." Carrie was welcomed in, given a room, and soon thereafter presented with the job of "getting the garden going." Significantly, a key aspect of getting the garden going turned around one's being naked, or at least topless, while working inside its walls. Whether this policy was laid down explicitly by my father or the new member of our household picked up on it intuitively, I don't remember. But in either case it had the effect of solidifying the Barn's reputation as a place apart.

Carrie was so comfortable laboring topless in the garden that she soon extended the practice to her work elsewhere around the Barn. My father placed her in charge of the beehives that he had purchased in order to further the sense of a self-sufficient cornucopia blossoming in the midst of the suburban wasteland, and the sight of her working at the hives, clad in little but swarming bees and a giant netted hat, was vivid and unsettling. I was eleven when Carrie showed up, and her relentless nudity received my focused and puzzled attention. Because Carrie was cheerful, straightforward, and friendly, I couldn't dislike her, but there was something about her lack of clothing that got under my eleven-year-old skin just the same. Basically, it was all right with me if she wanted to be that way, but I couldn't see why everyone wanted to pretend that it was unremarkable for her to do so. Nor, for that matter, did Betty's and my father's new habit of walking around with nothing on strike me as any more reasonable. It would have been much the same, it seemed to me, if everyone had suddenly chosen to go through the day dressed as pirates or lobster fishermen. Something unusual was going on, but for some reason those involved seemed intent on denying it.

Our neighbors had questions about Carrie too, though they tended to give voice to them in a somewhat less charitable fashion. The initial source of complaints was the Swink household, directly across the street from us. With its chilly white pillars and its immaculate, cemeterylike carpet of lawn, this house was in every way the opposite of the Barn, and life inside its walls no doubt ran according to a very different protocol as well. Peering out from my room on Sunday afternoons, I could sometimes see both Carrie, stooped over the rows of plants in the garden, and, across the street, Mr. Swink, traversing his lawn on a sit-down mower. From time to time, Mr. Swink would put his machine in neutral and stare across at us, and one day I actually saw the curtains part and Mrs. Swink stare at Mr. Swink as he in turn stared over at us.

Inevitably, a phone call came. "It's Mrs. Swink," said my mother, her hand over the receiver. "She wants to know what you think you're up to letting people run around with nothing on in broad daylight."

"You can tell her," said my father with satisfaction from his place at the long dining table where the three of us were having our lunch, "that what I'm up to is not something she's likely to have any understanding of whatsoever."

"Oh, Peter, I can't say that. Here, you come and talk to her."

"I most certainly will not. I have better things to do than listen to the Puritan ravings of some life-denying, asexual Nixonite insect with an agenda against me."

"I'm sorry about Carrie," my mother said back into the phone. "She's helping Peter around the house and with some of his manuscripts, and she's very relaxed about things. She's from California."

A silence followed, during which Mrs. Swink was apparently giving my mother the full benefit of her opinions on relaxed people from California.

"Well?" my father said when she hung up. "Is she calling in the militia? Perhaps arranging a few phone taps?"

"No," said my mother, still standing by the phone and looking out the large kitchen window at the garden and the Swink house beyond it. "She says she supposes it's just something she'll have to get used to."

My father had finished his lunch, and as my mother began clearing away the plates he sat with his elbows on the table in front of him and his head down, resting against his clasped hands.

"The amazing thing," he said after a moment, raising his head as if struck by sudden inspiration, "is that there's nothing to get used to. Absolutely nothing! Nudity is not an abnormal state but the one we're given naturally. That poor woman has been brainwashed by the Establishment into looking at the body as if it were some loathsome burden instead of the physical expression of divinity that it is."

"Well," said my mother, "I don't have anything against the human body, but I do think it's a bit much to have those bosoms waving around all the time. I think she's just trying to prove something—just the way you and Betty are, running around with nothing on at your age. At least Carrie's young. The two of you are a little old to be pretending you're water nymphs."

"Water nymphs!" said my father, bristling. "Well, I'll tell you

one thing that girl *has* proved, and that's that you haven't understood a thing of what I'm trying to bring across around here.
Nothing!"

In fact, the time of proving things—to my mother, to the neighbors, and to the world at large—was only just beginning.

At the conclusion of the first year of the Great Plan, after countless arguments and reconciliations, plane flights, sessions with scientologists, and various other urgent attempts to escape the
bourgeois world for good and all, my parents divorced. I remember the event well, as I came along for it. Deep in the winter, my
mother and father and I traveled up to Claremont, which I had
never seen under a blanket of snow, and stayed in a hotel for a
few days while the papers for a New Hampshire divorce—less
expensive than one in Washington or Virginia—were filed.

As my mother was to go on living at the Barn, the whole business struck me as fairly mysterious. Why were my parents getting
divorced if neither one of them was going to go and live somewhere else, as the divorced parents of some of my friends at school
did? And why were the two of them acting so celebratory about
the whole thing? The way I heard it from my school friends, divorces were cataclysmic affairs that changed everything overnight.
The only thing that changed at the Barn following our winter trip
to Claremont was that there was now a document—a "silly piece
of paper," as my mother called it—that said the two of them were
no longer married.

Despite all the years of office work she had logged supporting
the two of them, my mother demanded no financial compensation
from my father—a fact which made the divorce seem even more
pointless. As I understood it, fighting about money, about who
got what, was what divorces were all about. If everyone was going
to get on so fabulously from now on, why go to all this trouble to
obtain a piece of paper that all concerned knew to be meaningless?

As my mother explained it to me—both then and when I was

older—the piece of paper, though indeed only a silly formality, was to function as a sort of trophy or souvenir for the year of pain and learning she had just been through, as well as the new freedom to which my father had introduced her. By divorcing him, my mother would be at liberty to live in the same house with Betty without feeling the need to press herself upon my father as someone who *needed* love in that desperate, graspy way that normal, conventional people did. From there on out she would be, as he had so emphatically directed her to be, above and beyond such things.

The divorce took place in the winter of 1971. My mother remained very much at home at the Barn—more so, in fact, than Betty—and the wringing of hands, the daily emotional alarms and diversions, died down considerably. My father had in a way got what he wanted. Yet in another sense he had failed completely, and this was clear even to me, with my limited child's understanding. My mother had indeed remade herself along the lines of the superhuman model my father had placed before her—even going so far as to enter a hospital to have ten years magically and painfully removed from her face—but ultimately, the results were not exactly what he had expected. The difference was that, in responding to my father's urgent demand that she transcend all those "petty" human emotions he was forever bemoaning, she did it her own way, taking a step beyond where he wanted her to stop. Though still at the Barn, and as close to me as she ever had been, my mother was at the same time a thousand miles away. She was "above the heaviness," "free from the garbage of the old attachment," just as my father had wished her to be. But she was also, as she often said to me, dead: dead to the promises of freedom and possibility and bliss that my father kept throwing around, and dead to some degree even to my father himself and the old love that she had felt for him.

"Sometimes I look at your father," she would say to me, "and I don't know what I'm seeing. It's as if he's a total stranger. I just can't believe all those years we spent together. It's as though it were a different life."

Watching them talk, much in the manner of any longtime couple, about Carrie or the Swinks or some other routine topic, it was easy for me to forget that things were not as they once had been—especially when Betty wasn't around. But the reality of the brave new world my father had ushered us into always returned, and in the years to come the moments when it seemed like none of it had ever happened got fewer and fewer, until finally they stopped happening at all.

TWO

Traveling Down the White Road

"All the legends of an earthly paradise are based on distant memories of this epoch. From age to age the confused recollection of it has been transmitted and transformed into the mythologies of various races. The Egyptians called it the Reign of the Gods, which preceded the reign of the solar or initiate-kings. In the Bible it was Eden of Adam and Eve guarded by the Cherubim. Hesiod named it the Golden Age, when the Gods robed in air walked upon the earth. Humanity was to develop new faculties and make new conquests, but throughout successive races, throughout aeons, throughout cataclysms and world-changes, it still preserved the indelible memory of a time when it could communicate directly with the universal powers. This memory might change its form, but it always represented man's inextinguishable longing for the divine."
—Edouard Schuré, describing the Atlantean age

IN 1967 Dimitri Rebikoff, a French inventor and designer of underwater photography and diving equipment, looked down from the window of a small plane flying over the Great Bahama Bank and saw what looked like a man-made structure lying in the shallow water. The following year, 1968, a commercial pilot named Robert Brush spotted another, smaller structure in the same general area, near the Bahamian island of Andros. Then, in September of the same year, J. Manson Valentine, a historian and biologist,

made the most unusual and provocative discovery yet while snor-
keling in the waters off the island of Bimini, also in the Bahamas.
About a quarter of a mile off a spot known as Paradise Point, a
local guide showed Valentine a massive underwater trail made up
of square whitish blocks of limestone. A student of the classics as
well as world history, Valentine theorized that these blocks were
the first tangible evidence of the lost continent of Atlantis.

Atlantean enthusiasts tend to fall into three broad categories.
There are the levelheaded, sober types who maintain that "Atlantis" was simply one or another mundane city in the ancient world
whose identity has been concealed and distorted by the fantasies
of ancient writers. Second, there are the slightly more daring individuals who take the classical legends at their word and insist that
Atlantis was indeed located, as its name would suggest, in the
middle of the Atlantic Ocean, and that it sank in a mighty cata-
clysm as Plato says it did. This sort of Atlantean enthusiast spends
much of his or her time examining the geological record for scien-
tifically acceptable evidence of the continent's former existence and
is much concerned with things like pole shifts, ice cap meltings,
and other phenomena that might potentially account for its
disappearance.

Lastly, there are the occultists—those who base their knowledge
of things Atlantean on what is revealed about it in the halls of
Akasha. In Atlantean times, say many of them, the air was denser
than it is today, and for this reason people did not walk about
the earth but hovered and glided effortlessly above it. Like Orphic
gods, they exercised a magical command over their surroundings,
calling things into being simply by naming them and creating
immense and beautiful cities that, unlike our own, were in perfect
harmony with the earth and heavens. Houses were made from the
branches of living trees woven artfully together, and their machines—for the Atlanteans were technically accomplished in spite
of their primordial innocence—were environmentally friendly cre-

ations that harnessed the hidden energies of the surrounding world without doing any damage to it.

The Atlanteans were not mere men but rather superhuman entities only a step down from the gods themselves. Life was a charmed event for them because the gods had not yet abandoned them to a life of human freedom and loneliness, but instead provided them with direction at every turn. The inhabitants of Atlantis lived in fluid harmony with the world around them because that world, like the Atlanteans themselves, had still not fully "hardened" into the dull and intractable material dimension we find ourselves trapped within today. The gods spoke to the Atlanteans through the very objects, whether man-made or natural, that surrounded them, and for this reason they were never for a moment allowed to forget that though they lived on earth, their true home and place of origin was in a world beyond—a world of divine forces that left no desire unsatisfied.

At least, they did so for a time. As good as we are told life was on Atlantis, it ultimately proved not good enough to prevent the Atlanteans from tampering with it. Growing ever more inventive and mischievous, the Atlanteans brought about a situation in which their divine sponsorship was in part withdrawn. Atlantis sank, and the clairvoyant and magically energized world they had known hardened into the stubborn and unyielding one we know today—a world where machines run on gasoline and the air is disappointingly thin and objects do not yield easily and instantly to human desires.

My father had long held an interest in Atlantis because of the emphasis placed upon it in the work of Rudolf Steiner, the remarkable philosopher and clairvoyant who founded the Anthroposophical Movement and the Waldorf schools in Germany at the beginning of this century. Through his reading of the Akashic record, Steiner claimed to have witnessed the unfolding of Atlantean civilization over the course of thousands of years, as well as the gradual birth of our own civilization from out of its ruins.

The notion that a part of Atlantis lay in the Bahamas, however, had come not from Steiner but from another Atlantean clairvoyant named Edgar Cayce, the famous "sleeping prophet." A mild-mannered midwesterner who began his life as a stationery sales-man and Sunday school teacher, Cayce gained an enormous fol-lowing as a result of his ability to diagnose and cure illnesses while in a trance. In the course of these diagnoses, Cayce was given to lengthy asides on other topics, many of which took the waking Cayce aback when he heard about them later. A good number of these strange asides concerned Atlantis. It was the en-tranced Cayce's opinion that the lost continent would reemerge from the depths of the Atlantic—where it had lain since the cata-clysm some ten thousand years ago—in the late twentieth century. In a trance statement made in 1940, he went so far as to specify 1968 or 1969 as the year when the first fragments would begin to appear. Not only that, but he singled out the area around Bimini as the spot where these appearances were to occur.

Meanwhile, another curious phenomenon was drawing atten-tion to the Bimini area. Out in the blond enormity of the Baja Mar, as the Spaniards call the great plateau of shallow water that makes up the Bahama banks, shifting sands hid, then revealed, then hid again, a series of inexplicable markings on the ocean floor. Squares, rectangles, long straight lines that began out of nowhere and left off as suddenly as they had emerged: A whole collection of seem-ingly geometric configurations were being sighted, mainly by small planes flying over the area. Too large and indistinct to be seen from a ship, these configurations often showed up vividly from the air—though as often as not the pilots would return to the coordinates where they had originally seen them only to find that the sands had covered the shapes over once again. Stories grew up of signs and messages laid out along the ocean bottom, of stairways leading down into the depths, and even of entire temples waiting to be entered and explored.

The more cautious types argued that the formations were

merely natural curiosities in the underwater landscape, geological anomalies that, together with underwater vegetation, conspired to fool the gullible. The middle-of-the-road camp suggested that they might be the creation of the Stone Age peoples who were thought to have inhabited the Bahama banks before the end of the last ice age. But for believers like my father, such explanations were not enough. To them, these shapes and shadows were not the relics of some run-of-the-mill bunch of Paleolithic stone workers but the ruins of Atlantis itself. Temples, palaces, perhaps even the repositories of the brilliant scientific inventions that Cayce and his fellow clairvoyants maintained had powered and ultimately destroyed the Atlantean civilization. Who knew? Perhaps even the Firestone—the brilliantly advanced laserlike device that, according to Cayce, had brought Atlantean civilization to a close in the first place—was resting out among the sands, just waiting for someone to find it and bring it to scientific justice.

For my father, the temptation was too much to resist. Loaded down with income from *The Secret Life of Plants* and growing tired of looking out upon the mingled weeds and vegetables of his little four-walled garden up in McLean, he decided one day in 1974 that it was up to him to respond to the challenge of these new discoveries. Lover of film that he had always been, he was now able to afford to make one himself—one which could, if the formations proved to be man-made, establish Cayce's prophetic work to the nay-saying scientific community once and for all. If Atlantis was going to rise back up into sight as Cayce promised, cameras ought to be there to record the event. Bimini, the site of the giant limestone blocks, seemed as good a place to start filming as any. To sweeten things further, a number of people had recently claimed to have seen UFOs rising up out of the waters around Bimini. Perhaps, while he was at it, he could capture a few of these on celluloid.

My father was by no means the only person bewitched by the

mystique that the waters off Florida carried in the '70s. Thanks
first to *Edgar Cayce on Atlantis*, published in 1968, and then to
Charles Berlitz's *The Bermuda Triangle*, published in 1974, the area
became the equivalent of a giant Rorschach blot for the public
imagination. All those vanished ships, all those reports of airplanes
disappearing into a white void with a final, disoriented message
crackling in their wake, seemed to feed a long-neglected national
hunger for the mysterious and the inexplicable. Great and unknown
worlds exist, such phenomena suggested, and were as close at hand
as the waters off the coast of Florida. There was also a sense that
the strange things afoot in the waters of the Bermuda Triangle were
only the first movement in a symphony of anomalies—a symphony
that would climax with the rising of Atlantis and the return of the
magical and miraculous conditions that had reigned in the times
before it sank.

The waters of the Baja Mar were full of people looking for
things in the early and mid-'70s, and things were being found as
well—though more often than not they were not what the people
looking wanted to find. The trouble was that for centuries all sorts
of mundane items had been falling into these waters. From the
days of sail, when European ships following the Gulf Stream north
were blown off course and raked apart over the shallow reefs, to
the early years of the twentieth century, when the area had been
used by bootleggers and later for bombing exercises by the U.S.
military, objects of every description had been piling up in the
waters of the Bahama banks, and these objects were the first things
to greet the Atlantis-hunters when they went in search of temples
and magic crystals.

Flying in a chartered plane along the edge of the great trench
of the Gulf Stream one day, my father saw a dark, promising
smudge in the water below and returned by boat to dive on it.
Sixty feet down, the looming black shape of what appeared to be
a temple rose up toward him. For a moment my father thought

he had the proof that he and his fellow investigators had been hoping for, but only for as long as it took to discover that the eerie monolith was really the boiler of a ship that had gone down early in the century.

At another point in the quest, what appeared to be an entire Atlantean temple in white stone was discovered on the ocean floor. Investigation by divers, followed by a little historical research, revealed it to be a tomb ordered by an eccentric Louisiana millionaire. The tomb sank, along with the ship carrying it, en route to the Gulf Coast sometime in the 1800s.

On still another occasion my father's friend Fran Farrelly, an accomplished psychic and my personal favorite among the Atlantologists as she always had time to discuss items of interest with me, revealed the coordinates of what she believed was a sunken Phoenician vessel. When my father's team arrived on the spot indicated, the outlines of a ship were discovered almost immediately. The ship, however, turned out to be a relatively modern one. "No," Fran said, when my father came to her with this news. "That's not the one. The ship I'm talking about is *under* that one." Unfortunately, my father was never able to do the digging that would establish whether Fran had been right. In addition to these confusions, there was all of that World War II test ordnance to think about. A diver chipping away at the coral covering a strangely shaped object risked detonating an unexploded bomb dropped by the U.S. Air Force thirty years previously.

Onshore, it was a time of anomalies as well. "I can't explain it," I remember Betty saying one day, after my father had picked her up at the supermarket when she couldn't find the keys to the car she had driven there. "I put them in my bag, and when I came out with the groceries they simply weren't there anymore. I think they went somewhere."

"What do you mean, 'went somewhere.' All by themselves?" I asked from the back.

"Oh sure," said my father from the driver's seat. "Things like that happen all the time down here, on the edge of the Triangle. There's a lot of very powerful energy in the area, and it can make some pretty funny stuff happen."

It did indeed, and a lot of this funny stuff was enacted by my father.

Legends are by nature neither strictly true nor strictly false, but instead linger in the gray area between these categories. Atlantis, the mother of all legends, has been doing this kind of lingering for over two thousand years. Fact and fiction blend together in a particularly obstinate manner in much of what has been written and proclaimed on the topic, and the world of Atlantean speculation got no clearer with my father's entrance into it. Indeed, almost immediately upon the project's commencement, my father suffered a temporary but drastic decrease in his ability to distinguish truth and fantasy. With the Atlantis project, I have long suspected, my father had wandered so deep into the gravitational field of the paradise myth that he was no longer able to separate himself from it. He was living out the myth on such a grand level and in such detail that for a time it began to live *him*. I was never quite sure whether it was a documentary or a fictitious action film that my father had in mind, and the reason for this now seems to me to be that he didn't know himself.

My father's quest for Atlantis involved a more impressive amount of time, people, equipment, and money than any project he dreamt up before or after. Once again entrusting the Barn and its daily upkeep to my mother—who was to have nothing whatsoever to do with the Atlantean project from beginning to end—he purchased a house in the rich and stuffy heart of Miami Beach to serve as Mission Control. Outfitted with the swimming pool in which I was to spend so much time developing my scuba skills, the house was host to an ever-changing crew of Atlantean characters, from seaplane pilots and scuba divers to movie producers and reincarnated Atlantean princesses ever ready to slip into a trance and recount their former days on the lost continent.

Filming began in the summer of 1975, shortly after the purchase of this house, with a series of dramatic sequences in and around Miami. In one of these sequences, my father wanted to set up an appealing introduction to a short interview between himself and an affable Italian count named Pino Turolla, a key player in the recent Atlantean discoveries who lived with his wife and son on Biscayne Bay, a few miles down from my father's house.

Shallow, murky, and crowded with tour boats and intoxicated water-skiing college students, Biscayne Bay also features a few small, uninhabited islands—the sort of generic little stretches of sand decorated with a single lonely palm on which men and women are always getting stranded together in *Playboy* cartoons. My father decided that it would be a good idea to interview Pino out on one of these little islands. On the appointed day, he loaded down two boats with video and film gear and headed out to shoot the interview. The boats were brought up into the shallows and their engines cut, and the crew was about to start unloading when my father shouted for them to stop.

"Don't get any footprints on the sand. The island has to look totally uninhabited."

My father's notion was to present the viewer with a "chance" meeting between Pino and himself. The scene would open with the cameras trained on the empty island. Suddenly, bubbles appear and my father, clad in full scuba gear, clambers out of the water and sits down on the trunk of a fallen palm. Moments later, he gazes out at the water and, just coincidentally, spots another group of bubbles. Out walks his friend Pino, also engaged in a leisurely underwater tour of the bay. The two of them then sit down for a discussion of Pino's experiences with the lost continent.

"But, Peter," I remember the cameraman saying, "no one's

going to believe that you just ran into Pino in the middle of the bay here. . . ."

My father, however, was not about to engage in quibbling. He had a story to tell, and he had the viewer's attention to hold. Given the situation, this preposterous happenstantial meeting seemed as good a way of satisfying these needs as any, and it was duly filmed.

Also filmed at this time was another equally far-fetched interview, this one with Trig Addams—a Miami-based pilot who had been active in the search for underwater structures since the late '60s. Trig lived by himself just outside Miami in a house with a large garden and pool. When my father saw this house, the scenario for an interview took quick shape in his head, complete with crucial supplementary material.

"Women in the pool! We need women in the pool!"

This demand, voiced minutes before filming at Trig's house commenced, took the handful of women present by surprise. Why did he need them in the pool?

"To keep the viewer's interest!" thundered my father, momentarily unable to keep his composure in the face of such colossal ignorance. "We've got to show that Trig lives a good life so people will be interested in his story!"

Not just women but naked women were required—or, in the beleaguered director's words, "at least topless, for Christ's sake." Betty, used to these urgent demands for nudity, undressed and made her way into the pool. The other two women present, however, both of them members of the camera crew who had not been expecting involvement on the far side of the camera, needed more persuading. The viewer's interest was invoked once again, as was the threat of wasted money, of having nothing worthwhile to show for the day's filming. Eventually, the two were maneuvered out of at least some of their clothes and into the pool.

"Now," said my father, standing beside the main camera like the harried supervisor of some ancient Roman spectacle: "Frolic!"

The three women did the best they could, tossing a beach ball about and swimming here and there while my father anxiously continued to give stage directions from the side. "Okay, keep talking . . . smile . . . Okay, look up in the air. You see a plane. It's Trig! He's on his way back to the airport. Wave! Show him you're happy to see him!"

The idea, I now understood, watching with closed mouth from the sidelines, was that Trig passed over his house on the way back from some trip or other and looked down to see his pool filled, as presumably was customary, with smiling, good-natured, naked women. He waved, and, in my father's fantastically warped imagination, the women saw him and waved back.

"Okay," said my father after a few satisfactory takes, "that's good. Stop frolicking. Let's get a shot of Trig pulling up to the front of the house."

This shot was dutifully captured as well, and still lives vividly in my memory. Trig pulls up in a sports car, hops out, and swaggers up to his house. Walking through it, he throws off bits of clothing in a carefree manner, then makes his way to the pool out back. By the time he gets to the pool's edge he is wearing only a pair of briefs, which, following a directorial command from the sidelines, he flings aside before plunging in. He then swims about with his happy coterie for a few moments until my father, attired modestly in a bathing suit, approaches the side of the pool and commences asking questions about Atlantis.

Memorable as they were to me, these were only minor scenes in a larger and somewhat more reasonable drama. The focus of this larger drama was not Miami but Bimini, for it was there that the Bimini Road, as the great trail of limestone blocks was called, lay in some twenty feet of water. It was upon these rocks, and the lost civilization that had supposedly assembled them, that the whole Atlantean project hinged.

The Road stretched for almost two thousand feet along the

sandy ocean bottom, roughly paralleling the shore of Bimini. At their northern end, the stones curved around to form the shape of a reverse J, then appeared to stop as abruptly as they had begun. Leading nowhere, and made up of stones seemingly far too big and widely spaced for any vehicle ancient or modern to make use of, the Bimini Road wasn't really a road at all. Nor, according to most of the geologists who had examined it, was it a wall, a sunken boat harbor, an ancient temple to some forgotten god, or any other such romantic item. It was simply a length of soft, porous stone that time and chance had eroded in such a way as to give the illusion of having been shaped by human hands.

Many things to many people, the Road was to me one thing above all: boring. Try as I might, I could not conjure up, nor could I understand, the kind of anguish and enthusiasm that my father and his friends seemed to suffer over it, nor could I help but think that our time in the Bahamas would be better spent doing something—anything—else. Yet day after day for much of the summer of 1975 such possibilities went uninvestigated as we languished, anchored over the Road in a sixty-foot chartered sailboat, while my father and the rest of his friends tinkered endlessly about its edges with their cameras and instruments.

"When," my father asked gruffly one morning up on the bow of this sailboat as we floated at anchor over the Road site, "are we going to get you out of those abominable trunks?"

On that day, as on most days, I was clothed in a T-shirt and a pair of cutoff corduroy trousers—something which separated me from most of the others on the boat, who, like my father and Betty, wore nothing beyond the occasional pair of sneakers or sun hat. In front of the cameras, behind them, or somewhere in between, if you were involved in the Atlantis project and wearing clothing, my father would eventually have something to say about it. Nudity, I had come to realize, was not so much an option in my father's mind as a badge of honor: a sign that you were on the Atlantis team.

Since the appearance of Carrie in the garden at the Barn a year or so previously, the ever-growing amount of naked human bodies moving around me—young and old, male and female, toned and worn—was beginning to have a wearing effect. As time wore on, I found myself in the odd position of feeling envious of my friends back at school, for whom female bodies were items of supreme mystery rather than everyday scenery. Deprived of this romantic distance, the human form—more specifically, the female human form—was taking on a distressingly mundane aura for me—at the same time retaining its intense adolescent desirability. All the variously shaped breasts and distressingly concrete genitalia I was forced to maneuver among on the boat each day were turning into false idols: objects I was at once drawn helplessly towards yet at the same time distrustful of. All of which inspired in me a mood of confused suspicion for the whole business. I made a point of being clothed as much as possible, and looked with increasing disdain upon the paradise-seekers with whom, it seemed, I was destined to spend the rest of my childhood.

My father, in his distracted fashion, was monitoring my behavior and trying to fathom it. Somehow, it was beyond his comprehension that a thirteen-year-old boy should insist on remaining clothed all the time while on a boat in the middle of the Caribbean. Like just about everything else in life upon which he trained his attention, this apparent lack of interest had certain implications in his eyes. By refusing to parade around naked at odd and inconvenient times, and by looking askance at those who did, I was doing more than just being difficult. I was placing myself in the company of the nay-sayers: the advocates of the mundane and the ordinary, who wanted to prove that plants couldn't think, pyramids had no magical significance, and the Road was no road at all but simply a meaningless geological accident.

"You guys look like idiots running around naked the way you do. Besides, it's dangerous."

My father shook his head. "Dangerous! What an absolutely ridiculous idea. I suspect it's that school we spend so much money on that feeds you these curious Puritanical notions. We'll have to have you deprogrammed by the time you're ready to graduate."

"I suppose you think the Atlanteans all walked around naked?"

"What the Atlanteans wore or didn't wear has nothing to do with it. It's this persistent prudery of yours that I find disturbing."

My father glowered back down at the stern of the boat, his assorted worries visibly regaining their hold over him. My father was not alone, I knew, in his desire to prove that human hands had formed the great white Road, nor was he the only one to have invested a vast amount of time, money, and energy in order to examine it up close. At the moment, relations between him and some of the other Atlantis-seekers, who came and went from my father's boat and moved about on boats of their own, were becoming increasingly uneasy. Like a pack of hunting animals circling a carcass, my father and these men eyed each other with a combination of fellow-feeling and suspicion. If the Road did turn out to have archaeological significance, attention would inevitably focus on one member of this group at the expense of the others. Since each, to a greater or lesser degree, had staked his money and his reputation on the venture, a certain amount of tension was inevitable. Bad weather and endless mechanical difficulties heightened these tensions, and my father was beginning to suffer more and more visibly from them.

"Do you know what all this is really about?" my father turned and said now, suddenly refocusing on our conversation.

"All what? This boat and everything?"

"Yes, this boat and everything."

"Finding Atlantis?"

"Yes, yes, finding Atlantis, but do you know what it's *really* about?"

"No."

"It's about freedom. The freedom to do as you like when you like, and not get sucked into some artificial system of laws that tell you what to do and what not to do. That's why I'm here looking at this damn Road and that's why I've chartered this bloody boat and that's why I'm hemorrhaging money keeping all these machines running."

"Wait a minute. I get how having Betty around and being naked all the time is about freedom, I guess, but what does this stupid Road have to do with it?"

"That's just the thing, the Road has everything to do with it! Look, Ptolly: the academic establishment says Atlantis never existed, when there's plenty of solid evidence that says it did. Now just why, in the face of this evidence, should they be so intent on denying its existence outright?"

"I don't know. Maybe they just don't feel like believing in it."

"If they had the honesty to give an answer like that, I'd have a good deal more sympathy for them. In fact, you've hit the nail on the head. They *don't* feel like believing in it. Not at all. And the reason they don't is because believing in it would force them to rewrite every last one of their history books from chapter one on, and that is something they very definitely do not want to do. So rather than open themselves to the possibility that they don't really know what was going on on this planet ten or twenty or perhaps fifty thousand years ago, they simply close their ears and their eyes and cry "Bullshit" at all the evidence that's presented. Without looking at it. They're no different from a bunch of demented Dickensian schoolmasters telling you the way things are and whipping you if you point out to them that they aren't that way at all. If there's one thing I'd be happy that you took away from being around for all this crazy stuff it's the importance of that—of being free to say and do what you think, regardless of the consequences and even if everybody tells you you're out of your mind."

Most of the action on the sailboat, from gearing up the divers to food preparation, took place in the stern. That was the reason I spent as much time as I did up on the bow. There was more time to think or read or just stare idly out at the water, and less chance of being waylaid and forced into useful labor. It was unusual for my father, being director of operations, to spend much time up there himself, and one of the reasons for his doing so today was, I realized, because he was angry about the Remora. The most costly and sophisticated of the many technical devices my father had enlisted in his effort to chronicle the Road, the Remora was a sort of giant winged torpedo with a camera at its front end. It was the brainchild of Dimitri Rebikoff, the same inventor who had seen that first geometrical formation in the water back in 1967 and who had been involved in the search for Atlantis in the Bahamas ever since. Presumably, the sophisticated camera the Remora housed would allow the divers to capture the Road on film more successfully than hand-held cameras, but the more important, unspoken reason for the Remora's presence was the high-tech mystique it lent to the enterprise. Tethered to the surface by a cable that supplied its power, it glided impressively to and fro above the Road like a great mechanical fish with one or more divers clinging to its sides.

Or at least it did on the days when it worked. On this particular day it was paralyzed by some failure deep in its mechanical insides and lay at the stern of the sailboat amid a mass of cables like a captured sea beast, with Rebikoff and several of his assistants hovering worriedly over it. My father, apparently unable to look at the repair process without losing his temper, had retreated to my domain on the bow to cool off for a bit.

Nothing makes a mockery of human endeavor like the ocean. All around us, beyond the noise of the boat and the people on it, the sea and sky lay spread out in what seemed a deep and resolved indifference to the entire project. Beneath the water the white Road lay with equal tranquillity, unconcerned with the buzzing engines and laboring people, unconcerned with when the Remora would be fixed, unconcerned even with whether it itself was really an Atlantean relic or simply a natural rock formation.

"So what are you going to do if it turns out the Road isn't a piece of Atlantis at all? What if it's just a bunch of weird-looking rocks?"

"Then," said my father, "I will have laid the question to rest, and that will be the end of it. Because whatever that Road turns out to be, it doesn't take away one bit from what I just told you. The one important thing in life is having the freedom to find out what's bullshit and what's true and real, and to go after the true and the real with all of your energy. If you can't have that, there's not much point going and looking for anything else."

"So how come I'm not free to wear a bathing suit without you bugging me about it all the time?"

"You can wear a space suit and a bowler hat for all I care, as long as you're doing what you *want*—what you really want, and not what some bastard in some institution tells you you should."

"And that means I'm free to go deep-sea fishing on one of those charter boats too, right?"

"That," said my father, "is a matter not of freedom but of money, and if I weren't running out of the latter faster than I can believe, I'd rent you one of those boats tomorrow."

"So money's different from freedom, huh?"

"Ideally yes, but practically no," my father said, the specter of cash dampening his mood again slightly. "You'll understand when you're older."

Bimini is actually two islands set extremely close together. The great majority of the population lives on North Bimini, and it was here that my father had established us, on the second floor of a defunct hotel at the southern tip of the island. Wind-picked and wasted, the place had been out of use for some years by the time we moved in. The water still ran, more or less, and the glass doors that opened onto its sun-baked porches still rolled in their tracks. But everything else—from the empty pool with its cracked and faded paintings of fish and mermaids running across its floor, to the deserted thatch booth where drinks for lounging swimmers once were made—seemed like it had been out of commission for a very long time indeed. Such was the quality of pleasant, timeless exhaustion that hung about the place that it was easy to imagine that the hotel itself, at some bright and distant point in the past, had been part of the fabled lost continent.

Beyond the hotel, visible from the windows of our rooms, the chalky tombstones of a cemetery pitched this way and that in the soft island soil, the ground between them littered with coconuts and long, stiff fronds fallen from the palms that rattled high over-head in the ever-present wind. Past the cemetery, a white sand road led out to a deserted point of land, its west side forming a gentle sand beach and its east side held sharply in place by a concrete seawall. It was the job of this wall—worn and softened by wind and sand and sunlight like just about everything else on the island—to keep a steady channel of deep water flowing here, where North and South Bimini came closest.

For unknown reasons, this beautiful stretch of land served as the island dump. Empty bleach bottles, blackened banana peels, and mountains of pink and white conch shells, their inhabitants long since wrenched from them and cooked into fritters or chow-der, mingled among the sand and beach grass. Here and there a larger item, like a toilet or an auto engine, lay like a fallen satellite. Out in the water other masses of wreckage were dimly, sinisterly visible. One afternoon, sitting on the sun-warmed concrete, I was surprised to see an entire sofa, complete with cushions, float by half submerged.

There was not much to do on Bimini, especially if one was too young for the endless bars that, along with fishing tackle shops, made up most of the island's tiny main drag. On those days when no boat trips out to the Road were scheduled, or when I needed a break from the weighty and stressful atmosphere, I would head out to the seawall with a thin nylon line, some hooks about the size of my fingernail, a plastic bag of chicken gizzards, and go fishing. Surgeonfish, sergeant-majors, yellow grunts, rainbow wrasses, squirrel fish, parrot fish, angelfish, and triggerfish: throughout the long blue afternoons I marveled—like an archaeologist examining a series of living hieroglyphs—at their odd shapes and the patterns of bright color splashed across their bodies. If Atlantis did once exist, its inhabitants could not have been more finely arrayed than these modest yet grand creatures that so obligingly sucked down the little wedges of bait I offered them.

Killing these fish—as I occasionally had to do with a careful wallop to the head when they swallowed the hook and it was set beyond retrievability—always revolted and shamed me. Dropping the ruined body back into the water, I got that old feeling, experienced first on the bridge in Florida with my mother, that I was trespassing in a world that had been better off before I came along. But these crimes of destruction were the necessary price of engagement with that magical community, and I paid it. For by meddling at its edges with my tiny hooks and weights, I was allowed a glimpse into the deep and mysterious waters beyond.

The summer of 1975 was the summer of *Jaws*, when boys my age across America were initiated by the thousands into the cult of the man-eating shark. Like *Night of the Living Dead, Jaws* managed to touch with particular force that place in my mind where fear and romantic fascination met and mingled. During the film's first scene, when the invisible shark tugs on the foot of the skinny-dipping young woman who is to be its first victim, I felt the usual combination of terror and inexplicable joy that I had come to expect from this kind of film, but also a larger than usual dose of righteous satisfaction. Once again it was the old this-can't-be-happening-oh-yes-it-can sensation, but this time the victim was a nude, hippielike female—one who would not have looked out of place in my father's garden or on his Atlantean quest. Spiteful as

I knew it was, I found it wonderfully appropriate that the shark should have made this particular choice for its first human meal.

At the end of the film, as the broken body of the fish drifted down into the great gray Beyond like the beloved monsters of my childhood, all my old love and nostalgia for this magical region came flooding back to me. At the same time, all the irritation and resentment I was feeling toward the adult world came into sharp focus. What did I really want from this shark? Would I have been happy if, instead of succumbing at the end of the film, it devoured everybody in the seven seas, one after another? I didn't know. I only knew that in watching the self-satisfied little seaside community of the film turn upside down as a result of the shark's predations, I felt, one more time, that old sense of consolation at the knowledge that the secret world was still out there, waiting.

Though I hadn't seen any sharks myself, I knew that the sea around Bimini was full of them. Images of primordial, submarine-size monsters drifted continuously through my brain as I caught my bright little fish out on the seawall, and as I bobbed in the water with mask and fins above the rocks of the Road. When buying my minuscule fishing gear at the local shops, my eye would often drift down to the other end of the glass-topped display tables where the mammoth gray shark hooks lay with their chain leaders coiled beside them. Something in the bottom of my stomach would fall away as I considered the fact that someone somewhere actually baited these hooks and dropped them in the water. I imagined that a hook so absurdly large must have a sort of magical attractive power, and that one would have to be possessed of either extraordinary bravery or extraordinary foolhardiness to put that enchanted power to use.

My affection for the seawall, and the dreams of mystery and happy danger that it coaxed from me, sometimes drew me back there at night. Perhaps because of its official status as the island dump, the seawall was seldom visited by tourists, especially after dark. So I was surprised one evening, as I sat with my fishing line adrift in the darkened waters of the channel, to hear the sound of approaching voices.

"Looks like someone's here ahead of us."

Two men, each carrying a can of beer and both smoking cigarettes that brightened and faded in the shifting night air, emerged out of the darkness and stood beside me at the edge of the wall.

"How's it going, partner," the shorter and less athletic looking of the two said. "That line's a little thin for sharks, isn't it?"

"I'm not fishing for sharks," I mumbled, amazed that someone other than me was bringing up this topic. "I don't know how."

"Nothing to it. All you gotta do is drop the right kind of line in the water. We're staying down at the Angler, and a guy at the bar told us sharks cruise the inlet here at night. You might have some luck if you got the right rig."

"I'm too light to pull in a shark, even if I caught one," I said. "Maybe if I used a barrel like Quint did in that movie *Jaws*, then I could catch one and someone else could help me haul it in."

"I'm gonna take a piss over by those trees," said the taller one, placing his can of beer on the seawall. "See if you can get some more of this kid's fishing secrets while I'm gone."

"Check," said the other. "So what *do* you catch with that rig?"

"Reef fish," I said. "Mostly sergeant-majors and triggerfish. I get more squirrel fish at night. That's because they're nocturnal."

"What do you do with them?"

"Nothing. I just like catching them. I don't know why."

"Yeah," said the man, flicking the glowing butt of his cigarette out into the black slick of the current. "It's kind of weird that fishing's as fun as it is, isn't it? I don't know why I like it either—I just do."

After all my days on my father's boat, I found the bold averageness of these fellows appealing. No skinny-dipping for them, I thought.

"My name's Scott and that's Phil over there pissing," the man continued. "We flew down from Atlanta this morning. Phil was down here last year and had a bitchin' time, so this summer I tagged along."

"Are you guys going to go fishing?"

"Yup. For sharks. Phil caught a bunch last year."

"No way. He really did? How many?"

"Five."

"What kind?"

"Three black tips, a lemon, and a bull I think it was. One of the black tips had a beer can in his belly."

"What kind of beer can?"

"Bud."

"Was it full?"

"Empty."

"Wow," I said, digesting all this information as coolly as possible. "That's really wicked."

"How long are you here for yourself?" Scott asked.

"I don't know. A month. Maybe more."

"Yeah? Shit. Got yourself some rich parents, I guess."

"Not really rich, I don't think. My father's looking for Atlantis."

"No way. Like lost Atlantis?"

"Yeah. There are some rocks in the water out there off of Paradise Point, and my dad thinks they're a road or something. He and some other guys are taking pictures of them to see if it really is a road. If it is, he's going to make a movie about it."

"Hey, Phil!" Scott said to the other man, who was making his way back to us across the moon-whitened sand. "This kid's dad is making a film about Atlantis."

"He must be looking at the Road," said Phil, taking a second, more considered look at me. "Your father thinks it's for real, huh?"

"He doesn't know. He wants to find out, though. He's like a seeker of the unexplained or something. He invented that thing about talking to your plants."

"Oh, man. Your father's the *plant* guy? So what kind of boat does he have? I guess he doesn't do any fishing."

"Uh-uh. It's a sailboat and I usually can't fish from it at all because there's always divers in the water. I asked if we could go deep-sea fishing but my father says it costs too much."

"Your father has a point," said Scott. "Unless, that is, you happen to have a boat of your own. A *fishing* boat."

"Like we do," said Phil.

"Tell you what, kid," said Scott. "Day after tomorrow we're having a guide take us to a spot off Cat Cay. He guaranteed us we'll catch something there. Seeing as you're such a dedicated sportsman, it seems like a shame for you to miss it. Maybe you can come along . . . if your pop's all right with it."

"Sure," said Phil. "We can always use another steady hand."

"I'm going shark fishing tomorrow," I told my father the next morning, as much to hear how the words sounded as anything else, for, of course, there was no question of my not being permitted to go. "I met these guys on the seawall last night, and they're going to take me with them on their boat."

"Shark fishing," my father said, his eye on the Remora as it moved past us out in the water. "Now there's a vulgar way of spending one's time! Why on earth would you want to go and harass some glorious beast by dragging it up on the end of a rope? You're free to do as you like, of course, but keep in mind that there are consequences to actions. Everything produces results in life, you know—everything. Do you know what they found wrong with the Remora the other day?"

"What?"

"Nothing! Not a bloody thing. Rebikoff tells me he can't figure out why it wasn't functioning, and now it's coasting along without a hitch! Now, how do you suppose that could be. Any ideas?"

"No."

"Then I'll tell you. Vibes!"

"Vibes?"

"Yes, vibes. There's been a lot of negative thought energy on this project in the last several days, and the machines have been picking up on it. What you have to understand is that everything in life—absolutely everything—is alive and reacts to what you think about it."

"Then how come I can't make stuff do what I want just by thinking, like on *I Dream of Jeannie* or something?"

"What the hell is *I Dream of Jeannie?*"

"It's a TV show where this genie makes stuff disappear or move around just by thinking about it."

"Hmm. Well, if you really put your mind to it you could! Someday, if you read Rudolf Steiner, you'll find out that that was apparently what was going on in Atlantis. He says the Atlanteans started out with a kind of thought-energy that could affect the environment and that the misuse of that energy was what ultimately brought them to an end."

"You mean they thought the wrong kind of thoughts?"

"They did indeed. And their psychic abilities were so advanced in comparison to ours that those negative thoughts actually had the capability to alter their environment—to destroy their entire world, in fact."

The Remora, with two divers clinging to its sides and its dark power cable trailing behind it, coasted silently past our spot on the side of the boat once more, bubbles popping to the surface a few yards behind it.

"So maybe we're lucky we can't do that anymore."

"Do what?" my father said, his eyes on the Remora again.

"Make things happen just by thinking."

"That's just my point. Don't be so sure that we can't. We may not live in Atlantis anymore, but we still live in a world where actions have consequences. And thoughts are actions, mark my word."

*   *   *

The next morning, with a sandwich, an orange, and two bottles of red wine that my father had sent along as a gift slung over my shoulder, I arrived at the specified dock an hour earlier than scheduled. Scott's boat was smaller than most of the other vessels nudging together in the calm of the morning. You stepped down, rather than up, into it.

"Disappointed?" Scott called to me from the stern, where he was on his hands and knees arranging green bottles in a deep white tomb of ice. "Sharks aren't fancy fish, and it doesn't take a fancy boat to catch them. Hey, Bruce! This is our third."

Bruce, his long body bent down in the small cabin space, craned himself around and acknowledged me with a nod. I thought I recognized him, or at least the odd pink-checked golfer's cap he wore, from here and there around the island. Like the boat, he had a slightly downscale look to him—a no-frills guide ready to tackle the relatively simple job of finding some sharks.

With Scott arranging his bottles and Bruce at work in the heart of the boat, I sat, then lay, on the night-cool wood of the dock. Through a space between two planks where my head rested I could see down into the shallow water below. It was almost as clear as it was out at the seawall, so that the reef fish pausing and hurrying about on their familiar errands were sharply visible among the bottles and corroding cans. Looking down at that intimate little theater, I soon dozed off, awakening some time later to the drum of the engine. Phil was there now, and someone had scooped up my meager gear and placed it in the boat. I got to my feet and, as my first officially useful action, untied the bow line from the dock and jumped aboard.

Bruce took us out past the procession of fishing docks, the unchartered boats all crowded inside them like cows at a feeding trough. As we passed through the narrow inlet, I could see the spot where I normally sat along the seawall, which always looked small and unfamiliar from the water. In increments the landscape beneath us fell away, and soon we were cruising over the impossible, precipi-

tous darkness of the Gulf Stream. Over an all-but-invisible reef the
men caught their bait fish—seven or eight jack, all bright and
hard in the crystalline air. These were tossed into a wooden stern
compartment where they banged and flapped for some minutes,
the sound clearly audible over the hum of the engine as we made
our way again into deep water.

Twenty minutes later Bruce cut the engine and we were alone
out in the blue, the boat washing and slapping gently in the waves.
Bruce pulled a jack from the stern compartment and abruptly
whacked it in half, transforming it in a moment from a fish into
two anonymous chunks of bait. He lanced both pieces down along
one of those giant hooks I had stared at so often in Bimini's tackle
shops and hurled it and a long chain leader over the stern. A
nylon line fed gradually out, coil after coil, until Bruce at last
looped it once around a cleat. He passed the remainder of the line
to Phil, who was to watch and wait for signs of pressure.

Half an hour passed, then an hour. The men talked quietly
among themselves while I stared at the cleat, envisioning the giant
baited hook drifting in the darkness far below.

Then at last, as if responding to my wish, the loop of rope
began to tighten. Phil unlooped the line from the cleat, and he
and Scott stood one behind the other in the gently pitching boat,
their hands loosely holding the line, which continued to feed
sleepily and steadily out.

"On three we set the hook," Bruce commanded. "One . . .
two . . ."

The two men gave a tremendous yank, and the line stiffened
decisively. The hook was set. Bruce started the boat and Phil
and Scott began slowly hauling up our invisible catch. After
some minutes, the line no longer pointed down but slanted almost horizontally into the water behind us. I followed it with
my eyes until it vanished, then looked out beyond at the slow
rolling waves.

Fifty yards behind the stern a fin appeared, disappearing again almost immediately. Over the next few minutes the fin emerged, disappeared, and reappeared again, this time close enough that I could dimly make out the shape of the body beneath it. Even from a distance the shark's color was striking: not the dull, steel gray I had imagined but a warm and vivid brown. Against the sharp blue of the ocean it looked shockingly appropriate, as if selected with deliberate care by an artist from his palette. Disappearing and reappearing, the shark made its slow way toward us, drawn without much protest by the steady hauling of the two men. I kept waiting for it to leap up out of the water and gnash its teeth cinematically. But the closer it got the more it stayed under, until at last it was right up beside us, its head out in the air and its long body trailing down, completely visible in the calm water beside the boat.

What now? The situation was so much a part of my imaginative life and so removed from reality that it was hard to grasp that I was actually taking part in it. Scott broke my thoughts. "Come on down, kid. Get a good look at him!" With exaggerated alacrity, I hopped down to the stern and peered over the edge.

In the water, the animal, some six or seven feet of it, hung almost vertically, its tail maintaining this position with slow, fluid strokes. Forced into this unnatural attitude, it seemed to be doing the best it could to maintain its dignity. Its broad head sank momentarily, then once again rose above the surface, and I could see where the hook broke through the cream-pale skin of the lower jaw. I found myself tremendously impressed by the eerie nonchalance with which the shark hung there in the water. A huge and alien atmosphere of patience seemed to emanate from it—a patience that contrasted sharply with the noise and commotion on board the boat.

"Hook's set good," said Bruce. "Let's see if we can get a loop around his tail."

In a moment Bruce had formed a lasso, and with a long wooden gaff he gingerly edged it down into the water, towards the shark's tail.

"That's it. Loop's set tight. Let out that other line, we'll take him in to the beach."

With the lines slack, the shark sank down for a moment and moved off, regaining its horizontal position. Bruce pointed the boat toward a small island off in the distance, and suddenly the beautiful casualness of the fish was lost in a blast of noise and white water. Flailing and snapping, it dragged helplessly behind us as we headed for shore.

"That should drown him by the time we get there," Bruce shouted back from the helm.

"Drown him?" I asked no one in particular.

"Yeah," said Scott. "All that rushing water makes it impossible for him to breathe right. Still, he'll probably have some life left in him by the time we get to the beach."

Some fifteen minutes later, Bruce guided us into a small, protected cove on the south side of the island. The hull bumped up onto the sand, and we all hopped out, while the shark lolled drunkenly in the water behind us. Bruce secured the boat, and all three men took hold and hauled the great brown body out onto the sand.

"Brown shark," Bruce said laconically, identifying not the color but the species of the fish for us.

It was an apt enough name, slightly foolish in its obviousness. Lying on the sand like a jet taken down from the heavens, the shark glowed with a deep, living brown that faded to an equally impressive white beneath. It seemed to me that I had never seen a more perfect, a cleaner animal in my life. Its alien, velvety skin, its stiff and delicately rounded fins, all conspired to make it look as if it had come freshly minted from some incredible machine. More than anything else it reminded me of the Remora as it had looked the other day, beached amidst a mass of cables at the stern of my father's boat. Staring down at it, I realized that for perhaps the first time in my experience I was in the presence of something from the other side of life—the secret side that I had glimpsed and guessed about for so long but that had never before manifested up close, in ordinary daylight.

Bruce set to straightening and coiling the line that ran from the hook still caught in the animal's jaws, making a neat, circular heap a few feet away. While he did so, Phil dug his feet squarely into the sand next to the animal's head and began to give it a series of heavy, horrible, clunking blows with a baseball bat.

The shark at first appeared indifferent even to this insult. Beneath the blows it continued to look quintessentially, aloofly sharklike, all precision and purpose and grace. Occasionally a shiver rippled down along it, and its tail swiped absently to left and right, the lower lobe creating a clean, crescent furrow in the sand.

"Dumb sonofabitch," said Phil. "Can't tell if he even feels anything."

"Are you kidding?" said Scott. "This thing's primitive. He probably thinks he's still out in the water swimming."

Whether or not the shark was in fact under such an illusion, it was plain enough, after a minute or so more, that Phil's efforts were having some effect. The twitches and the movements of the tail died down, and suddenly blood, red and bright and familiar-looking, began to flow from the shark's gills at both sides of its head. The blood soon grew more plentiful, and Phil had to step back to avoid having it drench his white deck sneakers. After all the long commotion of the morning the four of us stood silently around the body of the fish, which though now quite obviously dead still seemed all motion and purpose, like an arrow pointing off to a realm of color and life and beauty—a realm that we ourselves would never find or enter.

Staring down at the body, I thought about my father's Atlanteans, with their sunken temples and their magical thoughts that changed the world on command, and for a moment I understood why it was that he wanted so badly to find them and show the world that they really had existed. And at the same time I found myself suspecting that if there really had been an Atlantis it was gone now—gone completely—and that nothing I or anybody else thought about it one way or the other was going to bring it back.

There's Only One Radka

"Shrines were placed in temples in which the statue of each man,
wrought in gold or silver, or carved in stone or wood, was adored
by himself. The richer men kept whole trains of priests in their employ
for the cult and care of their shrines, and offerings were made to these statues
as to gods. The apotheosis of self could go no further."
—W. Scott-Elliot, describing the decline of the Atlanteans

My father didn't find Atlantis. Some months after our initial
stay, he returned to Bimini with a crew of sober and fully clothed
geologists, who extracted a series of corings from the limestone
blocks of the great white Road. Examined microscopically, these
delivered the news that the Road was a completely natural formation, down which no lost civilizations, naked or clothed, had ever
wandered or danced. All the images of naked divers hovering and
darting about above it, all the sweeping footage captured by the
Remora as it coasted gracefully down its length, were thus rendered useless, save for their potential interest to future cultural
historians.

True to his words to me on the boat, my father took this news
in stride. Goose chases, he maintained, were inevitable when you
spent your time challenging scientific orthodoxy. The best thing
to do, when engaged in one, was to accept the fact without strug-
gle and move on. In any case, it was not as if Atlantis itself was
rendered obsolete just because the Road had lost its Atlantean

pedigree. Indeed, no sooner was it eliminated as a possible proof of the lost continent's existence than other forms of evidence began flooding in to take its place. Though he never released his film about it, my father also never abandoned his conviction that Atlantis was a reality.

Real or not, however, at the conclusion of the summer of 1975 the push to discover its remains in the Bahamas lost much of its momentum, leaving my father in possession of an island apartment, an entire house in Miami, and enough scuba and underwater camera equipment to fill both. Although my father didn't always fit in amongst its shuffleboard courts and Jewish delicatessens, he had by this time taken a liking to Miami Beach, so he and Betty decided to hold on to the house there. This didn't mean he was willing to let go of the Barn, however, and as my mother and I continued with our lives together there, my father came and went, working on one project or another and keeping his network of houses together like a harried spider tending an overlarge and ever-ripping web.

During the summer, the first shadings of adolescence had conspicuously taken over many of my school friends, and along with squeaky voices and wisps of facial hair had come a whole range of topics that were now deemed worthy of serious discussion—at least among the more forward-thinking members of my class. Rock music, marijuana, girls-as-objects-of-potential-romance—somehow or other these comical items had been transformed, while I was down among the Atlantis-hunters, into subjects to be taken seriously.

Through that transformation, I started to see just how different my home life really was. While my friends tended to live in contained, carpeted, air-conditioned environments where the vaguest hint of marijuana smoke risked making its way down the wrong vent and into the nostrils of a prying adult, I lived in a sprawling wonderland of exotic characters and risqué pursuits, all of it watched over by a bearded magus who on occasion showed up on TV for all to see, advocating things like tree hugging and sex among kindergartners. Technically, at least, it was clear that the Barn qualified as a sort of teenage dream environment.

Not that this realization of how good I had it was completely new. When spending the night at a friend's house out in the realms of bourgeois mediocrity, I was often appalled at what seemed to me to be an all-pervasive sense of limitation. There were so many boundaries, so much order—much of it depressingly arbitrary. Conversely, a sense of wonderment and dizzy relief would seize upon those friends who came to visit me at the Barn. There was both more to do, I was constantly assured by these friends, and more license to do it at my house than at anyone else's. Old cars with windows to shoot out, toys to set on fire with lighter fluid, naked garden tenders to ponder with disdain or qualified interest—something out of the ordinary could always be found to keep a ten- or eleven- or twelve-year-old entertained. In the pair of shallow ponds my father had insisted upon carving out down at the edge of the property, around the two massive concrete silos that loomed at the end of the back field, or just in my toy-crammed, waterbed-furnished room, the Barn was the place where you never got bored and never got yelled at, no matter how hard you tried.

The heroic tolerance shown me over these years came not just from my mother but, oddly enough, my father as well. Creature of melodrama that he was, my father often remained strangely calm and understanding with me at just those domestic moments when a more "normal" parent might have flown into a rage.

"Ptolly, what's happened to those bicycles I bought at the rummage sale for you? They look terrible."

"I had Theo and Bruce over last weekend and we did this thing where we rode down the hill by the silos and into the pond. We'd jump off the bikes at the last minute and see how far we could get them to fly into the water. It was fun, but they got kind of bent up."

"Bent up? They're ruined. One of them is missing completely."

"Yeah. It's not really missing, though. It's in the pond some-where. Theo made it go so far out we couldn't get it back. It looked really cool."

"I see. Well, you might try riding the next bicycles I come home with on the road. You'll get a lot more use out of them that way."

On another occasion:

"Ptolly, what's happened out in back by the tool area?"

"The tool area?"

"Yes, the tool area. There are pages from books scattered about everywhere!"

"Theo came over last weekend when you were away, and we had a book fight. You know those old paperbacks that were in all those boxes? Well, they're so old they kind of explode when you throw them!"

"Throw them! Well . . . please don't do it again. Think of the library at Alexandria! Some of those books might have been inter-esting to you later in life, and now you'll never have the chance to find out." End of lecture.

When other avenues of amusement had been exhausted, the attic of the Barn—some four thousand square feet of it, all per-fectly safe during the daytime hours—was on hand to explore. The entire space was given over to study areas, among which my father moved as mood and need dictated. Books and papers were everywhere, in lines and heaps along the shelves built into the walls and scattered across a series of overlarge tables made from barn doors set on sawhorses. Here and there, tacked up against the walls and scattered on the desks and tables, were bits of mem-orabilia from one or another of my father's books. World War II was represented by items like a Nazi storm trooper helmet, large cruel-looking boots and belts, and weapons in various states of disrepair (including an American speargun—one of the first ever made, according to my father—complete with two hefty spears that my friends and I spent many a happy hour firing into the air in the backyard). The pyramid book yielded an assortment of miniature pyramids in a variety of materials, from plastic to wood to stucco, underneath which items like carrots or razor blades, placed there once for rejuvenation or sharpening, lay like forgotten relics.

On the walls were pictures of men and women standing next to giant vegetables: submarine-size zucchini, towering squash vines, and tomatoes the size of bowling balls, all of them coaxed up out of the earth using various alternative gardening methods such as my father reported on in his books. By overcoming the tyranny of ordinary limitation that nature had imposed upon their growth, these supervegetables seemed to suggest that life could be whatever size and shape one wanted it to be, and my father had tacked them up on the walls as a source of inspiration.

Most children are familiar with the equation "more freedom = less attention," but no such trade-offs held sway at the Barn. Granted, my father was often away, and when Betty was there she had a tendency to try to impose irritating limitations on me and get me to pull my weight. But Betty as well was very often not around, and the person who *was* home—my mother—was not out to make me do any work at all. Instead, she was always prepared to cook the meals, drive the distances, and do whatever else was necessary to keep boredom at bay. After all, she wasn't just my mother but my ally—the person with whom, for years, I had faced life and all of its frights and confusions. While other mothers appeared to me to have more in common with teachers, always ready to launch into speeches and disciplinary threats, my mother was of the opinion that children should be treated not as charges but as friends. As a result, she allowed me the space to do what I wanted and trusted that the things I would come up with to fill that space would be good and not bad. After all, had I not always been, as she told me so many times, one of the good things in her life—one of the exceptions to the rule that people were not to be overly trusted or relied upon?

This sense of solidarity with my mother was a source of both nourishment and—now that I was thirteen—tension. For as much as I liked the idea that I was as superior as she always said I was, I also knew it wasn't really so. More and more, I found myself shuttling back and forth between two distinct modes. For long periods, I was the son my mother recognized from the old days, full of sensitivity and imagination and all those other good qualities she had long told me I possessed in abundance. But while at school or with my friends I now had the habit of slipping into what my father liked to call my "school valence." In this mode, sensitivity went out the window and was replaced by a penchant for cruelty and a desire to fit in that were exceptional even by thirteen-year-old standards. In the ranks of my eighth grade social hierarchy, with its new, alien rules of conduct, I hovered uncomfortably and unpleasantly in the middle, by turns obsequious to those above me and relentlessly nasty towards whomever I could find below. Whether I was slavishly eavesdropping on the conversations of the more popular members of my class or just taking time out to mock the speech impediment of someone in the grade beneath me, the spectacle I presented was a consistently ugly one. If ever there was a candidate for individual proof of the postulate that dogs were better than people, it was me while in the full grip of my school valence.

Along with the knowledge that I was becoming, as some of my friends helpfully pointed out from time to time, "kind of an asshole," there was the additional sting of knowing that I was not even developing into a very hip or cool asshole. For some reason I was unable to turn my reputation as "the guy with the crazy father" to maximum advantage. All things considered, I should have been a veritable colossus among my pot-smoking, Peter Frampton–listening friends, staggering into school groggy from experimentation with exotic new breeds of cannabis and spent from the sexual marathons I enacted with the stable of freethinking females who were forever circulating through the Barn's spacious and forgiving grounds.

Unfortunately, this was not the case. As eager as I was to score bonus points based on my enviably colorful home life, the cool stuff I got to see and do at home was not sufficient to actually transform me into a cool person. Indeed, the older I grew, the more I realized that my exceptional home setup was in many important ways wasted on me. For a child of the New Age, my tastes were stodgy and retrograde. I read too many books about sharks and listened to the wrong songs on the radio. I could not, however many times I tried, bring myself to sit through a full episode of *Star Trek* or listen to a Pink Floyd album without becoming unspeakably bored. I could only get a little excited about the skits on *Saturday Night Live,* and I was no good at doing renditions of those I liked.

Worst of all, I disliked marijuana. As prepared as I was to worship its properties in the abstract, once I had the stuff in my lungs I was invariably disappointed by the results. All the doubletakes, all the dissociation of meaning and effect, all the sudden surprise before the absurd suchness of things always ended up leaving me exhausted and vaguely depressed instead of enlightened. The jokes I made got less, not more funny, and the inane aspirations and petty anxieties that were forever circulating through my head under normal conditions only increased, their lameness more apparent than ever under the strange sharp focus provided by the drug. Far from giving me a much-needed vacation from myself, a few hits from the communal bong rendered me more stuck there than I was before.

It was during these uncertain and unpromising days that a new fellow traveler made her entrance at the Barn. One evening a slim, tan, dark-haired woman wearing white, baggy pants and a white cotton vest that made her look like a sort of holistic genie came to dinner. Upon learning of all the space available she asked if she might stay a while and was, of course, welcomed. Radka had a broad, finely featured face, a clean-but-not-so-clean-I'm-worried-about-it appearance, and the unsettling habit of looking whoever she was talking to dead in the eye for unnaturally long periods. Like those who had come before her, Radka billed herself as an enthusiast of my father's ideas—specifically, those set down in the plant book—and I at first paid little attention to her. But there was something about her enthusiasm that began to draw my attention before long. For one thing, it was not reserved for my father alone but was lavished on everyone and everything. For another, it was accompanied by a truly remarkable amount of talk. As urgent as it was abundant, this talk gushed forth in a manner unlike that of anyone I had ever met before.

"All *right!* Ptolemy's *back from school!* Got picked up in the *car* by your *mom!*"

Radka had a way of italicizing whatever she happened to be talking about. There was something scintillating and consequential, it seemed, to just about everything that entered her field of attention.

"Mm, these carrots are *gooood*, Ptolemy. *So* good. Have some!"

While she always had a ready supply of enthusiasm for things like carrots and tahini paste or the fact that I had finished my homework, Radka reached fever pitch when it came to singing the praises of our household. Thus my father was a generous and visionary soul, "a *beautiful man*," as Radka often put it. But so were Betty and my mother "*beautiful women*" who the inscrutable laws of karma had thrown together for reasons that could only be highly significant. And—not least important from my perspective—I was a beautiful soul myself: a young genius whose presence within my father's charmed circle was perhaps the most wonderful karmic permutation of all.

From the beginning of her days with us, Radka spent more time with me than any fellow traveler before or after. Though no one in that years-long procession ever had anything but kind words for me, no one else managed the feat of actually paying as much attention to me as to my father, and this did not go unappreciated. As irritating as I sometimes found her breathless and perpetual enthusiasm, the fact that a good deal of this blind and constant praise was reserved specifically for me saved Radka in my eyes. At least for a while.

"There's *Ptolemy*, down on the floor, *drawing his pictures!*" Radka would announce, sticking her head in my door without warning. And indeed, there I was. Had Radka not been there, however, I would never have realized how huge and important this fact was.

Radka had little money when she came to live with us, and one aspect of the understanding we struck up was financial. I had access, through my parents, to the odd ten- or twenty-dollar-bill, while Radka, through her little blue VW Bug, had access to the world. Afternoons took on a whole new flavor of possibility with Radka around. No longer was I marooned in my private world of television after my school day was over and my mother was tied up with housework or other tasks, for there was always the possibility that Radka would stick her ever-enthusiastic head in my doorway and proclaim that the energies were right for a trip into town—provided I could secure a little cash for the occasion.

Once we were on our way, Radka came into her own as she did nowhere else, and as she talked I listened. "It's *all* coming together, Ptolemy," she would announce portentously as McLean's distinctly unportentous shrubs, mailboxes, and little metal jockeys slid by us on either side. "This *whole thing* is all just *clicking into focus,* and it's totally, totally beautiful. You and your mom and your dad and Betty—you *know* there's a reason for all you guys being together, and you know *I'm* in your lives for a reason too. There's an energy to everything that happens, Ptolemy, and what I'm trying to do is be *present* for it, so that when it wants to it can show me the *things I need to do.* It's got some pretty special stuff planned for *all* of us, Ptolemy, and all we have to do is say

'*Yeah*' to that energy—just be there for it. If we do that, everything else will *all just happen.*"

In the beginning, Radka's enthusiasm had a fresh and energizing effect. As goofy as I thought it was, her insistence that the universe took a keen personal interest in her every move had something to be said for it. In Radka's deliriously optimistic company, and especially riding along in her little blue Bug with its eagle feather dangling from the rearview mirror and its perpetual smell of incense and clove cigarettes, I couldn't help but suspect that the universe really was rooting for me. Even a trip to the prototypical and deeply depressing shopping mall that had grown up down the road at Tysons Corner took on a cheerful consequentiality when Radka was in charge. Wandering from Waldenbooks to Sullivan's Gifts to the Magic Pan to Farrell's Old Fashioned Ice Cream Parlor with the rest of the dull and desperate inhabitants of the great suburban wasteland, I could somehow imagine, thanks to Radka's high-voltage conviction, that we were not trapped in the backwaters of the universe but at its very center. Among all these swarming souls, we, somehow, were special.

The unique brand of metaphysically charged good cheer that Radka brought to my life was nowhere more useful than at school. On the afternoons when my mother couldn't pick me up and Radka showed up instead, the sight of her little VW among all the Volvos and wood-paneled station wagons, each with its resigned and steadfast suburban mom at the wheel, was a fresh reminder of just how good I had it. Waving a final good-bye to my fellow grubby and cruel thirteen-year-olds, I would enter Radka's VW and feel myself transported from the confines of affluent, mid-'70s suburbia into a stranger, better place. Before we had passed out of sight of school, Radka would be off on one of her adamant and optimistic jags about the universe and the love and burning intentionality that percolated within it, and I would feel the shackles of my school persona falling away. With Radka, unlike with my father, there was no beating around the bush. Her monologues were free

of archaisms and hermetic references. All of it was easily understandable to a thirteen-year-old, and all of it boiled down to one
essential message: Being me, and not someone else, was not so
bad after all.

Not only did Radka make me feel better by delivering me from
the failings of my school persona; she also helped build up that
persona. Radka was twenty-four, female, and smoked marijuana
with the same openness and enthusiasm with which she did everything else. Hence she was, by my classmates' standards, something
of a walking miracle. Granted, she was a little too whole-grain in
her appearance to fulfill our *Charlie's Angels*–inspired requirements
for the Ideal Feminine, but all things considered she looked okay,
and in our circle okay was definitely good enough. It did not take
many afternoons of her VW showing up at school before my
friends started asking questions.

"Who's that girl, one of your dad's groupies?"

"Yeah. She's staying with us for a while."

"Oh *man*. What do your mom and your dad's mistress think
about her?"

"I don't know. I guess they think she's okay."

"Does she have a job? Is she, like, your dad's sex slave or
something?"

"No, she's not into that kind of stuff."

And indeed she wasn't. As far as "that kind of stuff" went,
Radka stood apart from the very start. The first thing that tipped
me off that something was different about Radka was the fact that
she insisted on remaining clothed while in the garden—and indeed
at all times. With astonishing boldness, she explained to my father
that the whole "nudity thing" left her cold, and this refusal filled
me with a weird admiration.

There is nothing like living with a sexual prophet to see just
how dubious sex is as a transformational tool. And the more
caught up in the pull of my own reluctant sexuality I became,

the more irritating it was to find myself living in the desperately sexualized microcosm of my father's world. To hear the adults around me talk, especially my father, sex was at one and the same time the most important thing in the universe and no big deal whatsoever. Lurking at the heart of most of his dinner table tirades and emerging as a topic for remark any number of times during the day, sex was close to an obsession for my father. But it was also something he never tired of criticizing the rest of the world for making too much of an issue out of. "Making love," he would often say, "should be like eating a sandwich: something one does naturally, without thinking, and which should carry no heavy charge of jealousy or recrimination. All that muck needs to be left behind, so that one can be open, loving, and free, and not have to worry about who's doing what with whom any more than one worries about who ate the bread in the freezer."

So ran the Party Line around the Barn, but to me the facts of the matter were very different. I had by this time come to the conclusion that sex was (a) anything but inconsequential and (b) a force conducive not to happiness and harmony but to disquiet and pain. Of all the blameworthy endeavors in which adults engaged, it was the most suspect, the most deserving of unmediated scorn. After all, had not all the high dramas and low disasters of recent years been a direct result of my father's quest for sexual freedom—his desire, as he had so often expressed it, to set everyone free? For all his sandwich comparisons and his talk of free, unsullied love with whomever whenever, it was simply too easy to see the wheels working in my father's head as he moved back and forth between my mother and Betty and among the other assorted females who filtered slowly through the Barn over the years. Sex had him, to use one of my mother's favorite phrases, "over a barrel," and the energy he did not expend pursuing it and struggling with its consequences he spent diligently trying to convince himself and everyone else that no such dramas were, in fact, going on.

The sexual energies that had recently surfaced in my own body were, I realized soon enough, not to be argued with. But that did not mean that sexuality itself, and especially as practiced by the adults around me, was to be trusted. As I saw it, the best strategy was to give in to my own sexual needs as vigorously and frequently as I had a mind to, meanwhile pretending to the rest of the world, and the rest of the household especially, that those needs did not exist. If I could not help being prey to sexual desire, and if I was, in fact, pursuing sexual fulfillment as desperately—in my furtive, thirteen-year-old manner—as the adults around me were chasing after each other out in the open, I could at least have a say in how much of that desire I admitted to having. And I admitted to none.

Strangely enough, everybody believed me. Of all the various cheerfully naked, patchouli-scented females who drifted through my life in those years, none, as far as I know, ever noticed that the pale, waxy-haired youth hunched over on the sidelines with his face buried in a book about sharks was, in fact, a cauldron—or at least a skillet—of fulminating and deeply confused sexual energy. Time and again, I watched in astonishment as my clumsily feigned lack of interest in all things sexual was accepted at face value.

Thus when Zaba, a young woman Betty picked up hitchhiking, sought to perform a womb-regression upon me to get to the source of my lack of sensual attunement, she never even paused to consider that I might have been too preoccupied trying to conceal the embarrassing results of her hovering, massaging presence to concentrate on what it had felt like back when I was being born. Likewise, during the Atlantean project, no one ever seemed to question why it was that I sometimes liked to sit down on the floor of the ocean in full scuba gear while a handful of female Atlantophiles were bobbing about above me. As far as everyone else was concerned, I was working on my underwater breathing skills.

Of course, the king of the clueless was my father. "I don't know what's the matter with that boy," I can remember him remarking to Betty, well within my earshot, on a number of occasions. "Here he is, surrounded with glorious nymphets, and he doesn't seem the least bit interested in them."

Betty, in turn, was not much wiser. "Ptolly, when someone kisses you hello or good-bye, you have to kiss them *back*," she would advise me, from about age twelve onward. "Your lips are a tool for showing your love for other people, and you need to become comfortable using them."

And so it went. Scowling and stuffy, I made my way through the actualized and the attuned legions around me with the pinched and scornful attitude of a visiting Anglican classics professor, and the more I scowled, the less did anyone seem to make the unchallenging psychological leap and figure out what was really going on.

It was at this point in the proceedings that Radka showed up— Radka with her bold and consequential refusal to "do the garden thing" and her equally provocative assertion that I, the pale young troll on the sidelines of my father's great parade of awakening, was some sort of an important entity in my own right. Like the "nymphets" that had come before her, Radka was given various assignments to fulfill around the house, from typing to bee maintenance, but her great talent—or the one she felt the energies urging her to make use of during her time at the Barn—was foot massage. In the evenings after I had eaten my dinner and my faithful TV was moving into its fifth or sixth hour of duty that day, Radka's smiling and mildly conspiratorial face would often appear at my door. Sitting at the foot of my bed, she would commence pressing and pulling at my feet while telling me about her day.

This foot-work had a strange effect on me. As Radka would press away and rattle on about how optimistic she felt about things, there was not much good in fighting the realization that the pressure of her hands carried a message that was larger and better than my simple dualisms about sexuality. Odd as it may sound, in a house where physical contact was trumpeted night and day as the royal road to sanity and freedom, this foot-rubbing business was the most daring and consequential physical interaction I myself had. As Radka pulled and pressed on my toes, I would make use of the information carried by the pressure of her fingers like distant signals from the alien shore of Things Female— a shore that was for me at once the most familiar and the most remote of places.

Along with foot massages, there was another occasional ritual that Radka and I practiced that gave me pause for thought. Sometimes, around ten-thirty or eleven o'clock, when I had at last turned my TV off, Radka would again appear at my door—this time with a joint in hand. I would only hold the smoke down in my lungs for a moment on these occasions—just long enough to get a small, added sensation of the physicality of my body as it lay beneath the sheets but not enough to start all the little voices and visions that my friends at school liked so much. Meanwhile, Radka would puff away more confidently, sitting at the foot of my bed and talking a little more about whatever was on her mind that evening.

Looking back, I marvel at the sexually flavored atmosphere of these evening visits, but at the same time I doubt that such was Radka's intention. For the thing about Radka was that, like my father, she was totally and entirely self-absorbed. As appreciative as she claimed to be of my supposed specialness, it was unlikely that Radka ever really paused to consider what might actually have been going on inside my hormone-addled, thirteen-year-old head. Liberated, freewheeling, emotionally plugged-in egomaniac that she was, it probably never occurred to her that the chaste but suggestive alliance she had formed with me was as disturbing as it was nourishing.

Gradually, I began to look at Radka differently. Where before

I had seen in her a redeemer of the small, stale, and cruel person I felt myself becoming, I now started to see someone else. Beyond her grand assertions about the cosmos and about me, I began to see someone who wasn't really interested in the cosmos, or me, at all. I saw someone who was interested in herself.

One morning Radka came into my room with a troubled look on her face.

"Hi, Radka. What's up?"

Radka stepped out of her flip-flops and sat down cross-legged on the floor next to me, her dark hair pulled back in a tight ponytail.

"Nothing too good just now Ptolemy, nothing too good."

"Oh, yeah? What's wrong?"

Radka looked across at me with a serious expression, and I could tell by the way she kept arching her back and moving her shoulders around, limbering her spine, that she was gearing up for something.

"You know me, Ptolemy. And you know where I'm at when it comes to what I want from life, and all the things I want to give. But it's *hard* sometimes, Ptolemy. It's *hard* to keep that energy going when the world says '*Hey*, girl, not so fast.' And that's what it's doing now. I'm getting pushed with the money thing again, and it's starting to feel real old."

Radka paused for a moment, then continued. "So what are you going to do with that check your Uncle Henry sent you for your birthday?"

"My hundred dollars?" I said uneasily.

"Yeah."

"I don't know. I was going to keep fifty of it and maybe send fifty to save the whales."

Radka's face was impassive. "What whales, Ptolemy?"

"Um, I think they're right whales. The Eskimos are killing too many of them or something. I read about it in *Defenders of Wildlife*. It's their crisis-of-the-month."

"Huh." Radka's tanned, broad brow furrowed for a moment, apparently caught up in imagining the plight of the whales. "So how many right whales *are* there?"

"I don't know. I think, like, two hundred."

"Two hundred . . ." Radka said in a singsong, contemplative tone. "Two hundred. Well, check this out, Ptolemy. There's two hundred whales out there that need your help, but there's only *one* Radka, and *she needs your help too!* Do the math and think about it. Don't you think you better give that other fifty to me?"

Radka didn't get my fifty dollars, but she did get me thinking. By promoting herself to the status of an entire species, she alerted me to what was really going on. Radka loved herself too much. A seed of total and decidedly uncosmic egotism was at work in her, and as time went on I started to notice this more and more.

The defining incident came one afternoon when the two of us crossed paths in the kitchen. "Radka," I said, before she could get going on any of the great and significant things that had happened to her that day, "have you seen the bag of M&Ms that I left here?"

"Oh, I sure *did* see them, Ptolemy," Radka responded, giving me a love-suffused expression. "I *ate* them."

"You ate the whole thing? God, that was, like, a one-pound bag!"

Radka's love-look increased by a few watts. "There were a *whole lot* of them, Ptolemy, there sure were. But that's how much I love you!"

"What the hell are you talking about," I said. "If you love me so much, how come you had to eat all my candy?"

"Those M&Ms were full of *processed sugar*, Ptolemy. I couldn't stand you taking all of that poison into yourself!"

"Oh, come on," I said. "You didn't eat those M&Ms because you love me. You ate them"—and here I paused for a moment, conscious that what I was about to say might have far-reaching consequences—"you ate them just because you wanted to!"

It was a lot of weight to put on one bag of candy, but I didn't care. From that moment on, I became open to the fact that Radka, who was so constantly and earnestly seeking my sponsorship and sympathy in her struggles with the forces of coldness and indifference—Radka the long-suffering and ever-imperiled heroine of her own personal epic—was full of shit. And once having opened the door to such a possibility, I knew that I would never succeed in getting it totally shut again. In the days that followed I found it harder and harder to be nice—or even civil—to Radka. Despite all the burnish she gave my reputation at school, despite all the trips to the mall and beyond, despite the pleasantly confusing torment of the foot massages, she had now been exposed in my eyes as a fraud, and I was not about to forgive her for it. Radka ended up giving me a vision of the dawning New Age that was to leave me suspicious of it forever after. From then on, when someone talked about love, love, love, I was always ready to suspect that they were really talking about me, me, me.

Now that I had come to understand that something rotten was lurking within my father's idealistic universe, my nose became attuned to further evidence of this rot. Other incidents from the recent past came to mind and received fresh consideration. One Saturday afternoon, kicking a soccer ball back and forth behind the Barn, a friend and I were startled by a series of loud clunks and crashes coming from one of my father's tool areas. As we approached, I saw that the commotion was being caused by a short, powerfully built man loading a number of objects into the back of a pickup truck. Looking closer, I recognized the man as Zoltan, the boyfriend of Miranda, one of my father's original garden-tending nymphets. With a swift, animallike sureness, Zoltan piled item after item—chain saws, power drills, toolboxes—in the back of the truck. So intense was his concentration that he did not see us until we were right behind him.

"Hi, Zoltan," I said.

Zoltan spun around and looked at me sheepishly. "Oh! Ptolemy! I didn't see you. I thought everybody was gone because all the cars are away."

"Peter and Betty aren't here right now, and my mom went to the store. What are you doing with all this stuff?"

Zoltan hesitated for a moment, then smiled. "These machines," he said, warmly and with a touch of sadness, "are *broken*. I'm helping your father by taking them to the shop to be repaired."

"All those screwdrivers and wrenches are broken too?" I said, looking over the items visible in the truck behind him.

"Oh, no. Those tools belong to me. I've been lending them to your father for a long time but . . . now I have to take them back. Well," he continued, shutting the back of the truck and moving quickly around to the driver's door, "time for me to get going!"

This was a very familiar scenario. My father, in the course of his grand and energetic pursuits, attracted opportunists like an old man with a bag of bread attracts pigeons. Dishonesty and betrayal followed, and after the inevitable bad ending, all was covered over with the same thin veneer of good intentions that my father tended to use when covering up his own more questionable actions. Whatever high-sounding reasons were cooked up to justify the naked facts, what it boiled down to was that the M&Ms were always missing, the cereal bowls were always full of shit, and no one was around to own up to the damage.

Sometimes, thinking about all the punishment my father suffered at the hands of his various hangers-on over the years, I would find myself wondering how much of it, karmically speaking, he really deserved. To hear him talk, all he ever wanted to do was help everybody. He certainly spent enough time telling my mother as much, but both she and I knew, even when we pretended otherwise, that things weren't as simple as that. Perhaps it was only fair, then, that an endless parade of opportunists should file through our lives, piling up my father's belongings and driving off with them while shouting over their shoulders that it was for his own good. In the last analysis, maybe this was the very least of what he deserved.

Throughout the peak years of his paradise fever, I had watched as my father schemed and skirmished in a thousand ways to coax the universe into becoming the larger and better place he wanted it to be. And all along, I had quietly nursed my own dreams and guesses about that universe—dreams and guesses that were sometimes similar and sometimes very different indeed from my father's.

It still remained to be seen which one of us was right.

Stairways to Heaven

"The word 'lost' is indeed the keynote of all Atlantean mysticism; it is full of the pain of longing for the unattainable and yet contains the irrepressible hope which refuses to recognize the destructibility of beautiful things; for if the substantial forms of beauty pass beyond human perception, their shadow may still be felt lurking in the folds of dark secrets."

—James Bramwell, Lost Atlantis

My father gets joy out of whatever he builds, but staircases have always been his favorite project. In the course of our years at the Barn he put up no less than five, for the sheer ramshackle enormity of the place was such that for a long time he could always find another stretch of floor in which to cut a new one. Sawing and hammering in a frenzy of purpose, he could produce a gaping new hole and at least the beginnings of an accompanying flight of steps almost overnight. Like a cornfield worked by an overzealous groundhog, the second floor of the Barn became, as a result of his efforts, a hazardous place to walk. Dinner guests, taking in the cavernous generosity of the attic after a few drinks, risked making a wrong turn and vanishing down a freshly sawed hole.

Even when he had time to finish them, these jiffy staircases could prove problematic. In his haste to construct one of them in the laundry area, next to my room, my father wedged a nearby refrigerator underneath it as a structural support. Some months later, after its supportive role had been forgotten, the refrigerator was pulled out and carted off for use in another of my father's houses. Without the refrigerator to hold it up, the staircase came crashing down one morning soon thereafter, bringing my father with it. Though not hurt in that particular fall, he wasn't always so lucky. Toppling absentmindedly down another staircase at the rear of the house during his writing of *The Magic of Obelisks,* he ended up with a fractured spine that forced him to write the final chapters of the book on his back.

Being around my father meant risking injury—and not just from staircases. This was because my father's world, like the houses he lived in, was full of unfinished spots. There were great gray areas in the Larger Life he was always at work on creating, and if a person wasn't careful he could stumble into one of those unfinished spots and be swallowed up.

The dangers of my father's paradisal project were never out in the open and never predictable. Like the lurking monsters of my imagination, they showed up disguised, in places people didn't expect to find them. And, like those various movie monsters, they had a habit of picking on the people you didn't expect to get picked on. So it was that the one to suffer most in the course of the great search that informed and animated the years of my youth was not my long-suffering and patient mother but that grinning, self-assured woman who, so many years ago, had marched into our lives with the stated purpose of changing them for the better.

The robust dislike that I had developed soon after Betty entered our lives had continued for the first four or five years of our relationship, interrupted by the occasional moment of empathy. The more I got to know her, the more it seemed to me that she had some nerve rolling into our house, all smiles and golden assurance. Though my father had dropped the business about her being my poetry coach after her first evening with us, for months and even years afterward he persisted in maintaining that she had been brought in not just for his own good but in order to "broaden all of our horizons."

The horizon that stood the most chance of broadening was, it was often suggested, my own. As my father explained to both my mother and me time and again, Betty was chock-a-block full of culture, the kind of culture that a boy like me would benefit greatly from being around. "You know how you are," he would say to my mother. "You hate museums, parties, things like that— you're a loner. How is Ptolly supposed to learn about the world and all the things it has to offer just by going off to that wretched school every day and coming home to his television? Betty writes poetry, has a real knowledge of literature and art, and knows all sorts of people in those worlds. With her around, all kinds of doors will open up to him that would have remained closed otherwise."

As it turned out, he was right. Betty did end up teaching me about those books and paintings he was always mentioning, along with all sorts of other things. She was, in fact, the blessing to my life she was advertised to be. But I did not find this out until much later. For those first years together, she impressed me as little more than an inexplicable and supercilious nuisance, sent by the forces of disquiet to boss me around and cause my mother unhappiness. And she, in turn, thought little better of me.

Then, little by little from the time I was fifteen onward, it all changed. As the fury of my father's paradise fever began to wane, Betty and I became less of the pinch-faced adversaries that we had been throughout all our Atlantean and post-Atlantean adventures and more like allies. If, as I suspected more and more, loving and admiring my father meant knowing when to stop taking him too seriously, Betty was the one who taught me how best to strike this balance between humor and respect. "Well," she was fond of re-marking to me when life with my father was at a particularly difficult or troublesome pass, "you chose him." This half-sarcastic reference to the New Age tenet that people choose their parents before being reincarnated was her little way, it seemed to me, of admitting to her part in the Great Plan and all that it had wrought. For Betty knew full well that, karmic forces or no karmic forces, it was she who had done the choosing, and she who bore responsibility for much of the mischief and misery that had unfolded in the course of those early years.

When I spent time at Betty's house in Sagaponack in the later years, she and I would often go to the beach in the afternoons. On weekends and holidays, the beach road was lined with parked cars on each side far back from the entrance. If I was driving I would usually pick a space far back rather than trying for one up close. Betty, however, always drove all the way up to the front, her theory being that if you had the proper attitude a space would open up at just the right moment. Very often, a space would indeed appear, as if on command, and at these times we would strike up a conversation about the significance of the event. Did the world react to positive thinking? Did it care? Betty always believed it did.

In 1970, when she took up with my father, Betty already suspected she had the beginnings of breast cancer, and her decision to be with him reflected the attitude she wished to adopt toward her condition. My father maintained from the beginning that following the instructions of "the surgeons" was foolish, and Betty felt the same way. After all, if attitudes toward life were really to change, did this not involve risks as well as sacrifices? And so Betty said no to the surgeons, hoping that her condition was either not as bad as they said it was or would improve as a result of the approach she took to it.

As time went by, though, this didn't happen. For the first seven years of her life with us Betty's illness was never openly discussed—though the fact that something was amiss became gradually apparent to me through stray scraps of conversation. As a child with a sharper-than-average sensitivity to secrets and a firm belief in the idea that invisible destructive forces constantly threatened the fabric of ordinary life, I found these sotto voce discussions the adults had around me intriguing. Something *was* wrong after all!

For a long time, though, I couldn't figure out what it was. Finally, walking along the beach one day with my father when I was about fifteen, after Betty had been out of sorts and she and my father had been silent with each other for some days, I asked him if there was something wrong.

"Betty has a lump in her breast," my father said simply. And then he lapsed back into silence—a silence that continued for several more years, with only a few overheard words or inexplicable actions every now and then clueing me in that something was still very wrong.

In the spring of 1980, when I was in my senior year at the Washington high school I attended and Betty was spending a lot of time at the Barn because of a show on arts and culture she had started doing for National Public Radio in Washington, she and I took to discussing *Zen and the Art of Motorcycle Maintenance*. The previous summer it had become my favorite book, and Betty, impressed with how much I liked it, had reread it herself. Over the past weeks, the two of us had established a continuing investigation of the book's ideas during those odd moments when we found ourselves together.

I don't remember the fine points of these discussions, but I remember the feeling of excitement as I described one or another of Robert Pirsig's notions, and saw in turn that Betty understood what I was talking about. As we chatted back and forth, the world around us seemed to grow bigger, the possibilities it contained more rich. On the edge of adulthood, I was experiencing the sensation of being on the trail of totally new ideas and ways of making sense of life, ways that *had no negative side to them*. All the sharks, ghouls, and zombies of my childhood had been left behind, and in their place the hints of a new understanding were making themselves felt: an understanding in which the world could be huge and deep and infinitely mysterious, without being terrifying at the same time.

One morning Betty and I were talking in the laundry room while she folded some clothes in preparation for a car trip to New Mexico. As I took advantage of her willing ear to ramble on about some new aspect of Robert Pirsig's theory of quality that had occurred to me, she interrupted me and gave me a strangely urgent hug. An hour later she left on her journey to New Mexico—to take part, I assumed, in yet another spiritual retreat. Why, in the midst of a perfectly normal talk, had she gotten all serious and teary? I only learned the reason years later. The lump in her breast was growing more painful, and Betty was going to see another in a long line of holistic healers in an attempt to reverse this increasingly dire situation.

A few more years went by. Then, one afternoon in 1982 when she was leaving a restaurant in New York City, Betty fell while descending a short flight of stairs and broke her hip. At the hospital, the doctors who operated on her told her that the break in her hip had been the cause, not the result, of the fall. Bone cancer—originating in the lump in her breast that had been there throughout the days of the Great Plan and the Atlantis quest—had rendered it so weak that it had simply given way under the weight of her body.

In desperation, Betty and my father journeyed to Canada to visit the clinic of Gaston Nassens, a controversial French biologist with a new and purportedly effective cancer treatment. My father had only recently heard about Nassens from Christopher Bird, his collaborator on *The Secret Life of Plants*, who was later to write a book about Nassens's phenomenal success treating a wide variety of cancer patients. Nassens turned out, over time, to be one of the authentic amazements in my father's long career of anomaly hunting. His simple treatment—which involved little more than a course of self-administered injections of a paraffin-based formula—appeared to be the alternative to "the surgeons" that my father had always hoped and expected was out there somewhere. Like most other people my father tried to tell about Nassens, I assumed he was a crackpot, but after watching an extraordinary number of people lose their symptoms under his treatment I eventually came to believe that there really was something to what he was doing.

Betty was not to be among those whom Nassens's treatments saved, but they did appear to give her a second lease on life after her fall. Under his care, Betty recovered and eventually got to the point where she could walk almost normally. She began to smile and joke again, as she had in the days before her fall, and would show the enormous scar across her thigh where the doctors had installed an artificial hip joint as if it were no more than a reminder of a menace now long passed.

Then the menace returned. In the summer of 1984, while visiting Europe with my father, Betty had another fall. The cancer had come back—presumably too deeply entrenched for Nassens's treatments to have a lasting effect. Without admitting it, at least to the outside world, Betty was entering her final days, and as she did so, I noticed a change come over her. The person I had known for the past four or five years—the one who had given me the right books to read at just the right moments and who had taught me to love my father even while laughing at him at just the right times—began to fade away and another person to take her place. This "new" Betty was serious and sober. She didn't joke around as much, and she had the irritating habit of judging the people around her and taking them to task when she felt they weren't behaving up to her expectations. This new Betty, I began to suspect, was actually not new at all, but rather the old Betty—the bossy and supercilious presence of my younger years—returned with a vengeance. Her illness, and the fear it filled her with, was bringing out Betty's least desirable qualities and sapping those other, better ones that had come to endear her to me so much.

I was in my early twenties by this time, and had been away at college for a few years. Consequently, I was no longer the naive, enthusiastic almost-man Betty had grown to like in the calm and happy period of my late teens when the dramas of the Great Plan had died down and everybody in my father's world had started to get along. I was an adult now, and had a whole arsenal of fully formed opinions that I had concocted out beyond the borders of Betty's and my father's world, and that didn't always jibe with theirs. Other factors were also entering into the equation—specifically, alcohol. I had by this time made the very important discovery that when I drank the world changed and I changed along with it. And I liked that change intensely. No more did I feel, as I had for so much of my adolescence, that my place was on the sidelines, watching as the alternately curious, fascinating, frightening, or irritating spectacle of life slid by, just slightly out of reach. With alcohol I was led, easily and naturally, to the center of things—the place where life was actually happening. And once there, I got the surprising sensation that I was as welcome as anybody else.

The more comfortable I became in the world outside the borders of the Barn, and the more impressed I became with the things alcohol could do as far as situating me within that world, the more suspicious I became of the cautious, self-consciously spiritual domain that Betty inhabited. As she grew weaker, I grew bolder, more sure of myself, and more indifferent to the complaints that any adults on the sidelines had about my doing so.

For some years now Betty had been a Sufi of sorts, spending a lot of time at Sufi retreats and seminars and consorting with people with names like Atum, Shams, and Latiffa. Betty took a Sufi name—Tarana—and went by it whenever possible. Betty and her fellow Sufis were probably not really such a bad lot, but at the time I couldn't stand them. With their soft clothing, their abnormally hushed voices, and their seeming obsession with herbal tea, they struck me as having a more-spiritual-than-thou attitude made all the more odious by the fact that it masked itself in an atmosphere of ecumenical humility. Sufis, to hear Betty talk, were distinguished by their open-mindedness toward other traditions, other ways of approaching the world. But as far as I could see, boisterous and relatively constant inebriation was not on their list of acceptable paths. With my bottle of beer, my cigarette, and my freshly minted sense of intellectual superiority, I was Sufi anathema, and it was a status I was more than happy to accept.

Meanwhile, my mother had moved into a small, two-room house on the edge of the field behind the Barn, near the ruined silos and overlooking the twin ponds. This little house had sheltered a number of fellow travelers over the years—usually the ones who really got on my father's nerves and needed to be kept as out of the way as possible. After shuttling from one room to another in the Barn, my mother moved out to this little house in order to "get away" from things. Once there, she transformed the place from a slightly sinister shack into civilized living quarters, and from then on it became a sanctuary—a place that was set pleasantly apart from the dramas of the Barn but connected to it nonetheless. Though still in my father's orbit, my mother established an existence of her own out there, and during most of the '80s she held a mid-level office job and lived like a more or less conventional person, even as my father's ever-unconventional world continued to spin and rumble just a stone's throw away.

When I returned to the Barn on vacations during this time, I tended to spend most of the day shut up in my room reading, then head out to the little house at the edge of the field to while away the early evening with my mother and her dogs. After a few hours out on the periphery lounging, smoking, and making jokes at the expense of "the honeymooners"—as my mother had long referred to my father and Betty—I would weave across the field and sit down to dinner with the two of them.

Compared to the cheerful, hectic atmosphere out in my mother's house—with its TV, drinks, cigarettes, dogs running around, and all the other "dumb stuff" that was so familiar and comfort-ing—the atmosphere at the honeymooners' table struck me as pre-posterously somber and self-important. What a gloomy and grandiose pair they are, I would say to myself while pouring a big glass of my father's wine. By the end of the meal, I would often have so appalled Betty with my new, blisteringly unspiritual attitude that she would get up from the table early and leave my father and me staring at each other. On a really good night, I would still have enough vinegar left in me to drive my father away as well. Then I would sit back, light yet another cigarette, and revel in the feeling of having the table all to myself. My days of noncommittal silence were over at last.

Betty was by turns friendly and irritatingly cold and judgmental toward me in this final period, first reaching out to me as she might have done just a few years before, then withdrawing when she did not like what she saw. The more she shrank into her illness and tried desperately to cope with the fear it engendered through willed spirituality, the more contemptuous I grew of what I saw as her phony sanctimony and Sufi seriousness. When I thought back to those conversations we had had about *Zen and the Art of Motorcycle Maintenance,* I realized that the weird dizzy optimism they inspired had been dishonest. The book itself had been full of darkness, yet somehow or other, in our talks about it, that darkness had been covered up. This, I now realized, was because Betty herself had feared that darkness—that shadow-side to life that I had spent such a long time watching both as a child and an adult. She wanted to pretend it wasn't there, and the fact that I wouldn't buy into this denial angered and frightened her.

The fact that Betty was dying and therefore due a little patience and compassion did not do much to temper my thoughts about her during these days. As an adult at last, with a fledgling mem-bership in a world truly outside my father's domain of concerns, I felt it my duty to point up all the hypocrisy I saw at work behind her veneer of rarefied spirituality. If she was afraid of the dark after all, I would be the one to call her on that fact.

Once years before, during a tour of Yucatan and the Caribbean that my father had organized, he, Betty and I had gone with some friends of Betty's to a remote beach on the coast of Haiti. While the adults lounged on the sand and my father talked excitedly about purchasing the entire beach along with a nearby structure that had apparently functioned as a brothel centuries before, I waded about in the water looking for fish. After we had been on the beach for some hours, a boatload of four young locals spotted us and paddled in. When the boat reached the spot where I stood in the shallows, one of them held up a very young sea turtle about the size of a Frisbee.

I stared at the little turtle for a moment, its front flippers flapping like those of a mechanical toy and its head craning about feebly, then shouted for my father to come down and look.

"It's a hawksbill," I said as he waded out to us. "It's a real endangered species."

"Poor brute," said my father. "I suppose they're going to eat it."

"You can't eat this kind, I don't think. You can only make stuff out of the shell. Like that big comb Betty has. That's why they're endangered."

"We'd better help this one get another chance," said my father. "*Combien?*"

One of the other boys spoke a few words of heavy Haitian French to my father.

"Well?" I asked. "How much do they want for it?"

"About five dollars."

"Can't we get it? Please?"

"All right. Go and have Betty get some cash out of my bag."

I ran up onto the sand and curtly told Betty to give me the Haitian equivalent of five dollars.

"Five dollars? Are you buying that animal they've got down there?"

"Yes."

"Why?"

"Just because! C'mon and find the money!"

Betty hesitated, then silently rooted around in Peter's bag until she found the cash. My father gave one of the boys some crumpled notes, and the one with the turtle passed it over to me. Then all of them watched with puzzlement as the rich American waded out into deeper water and let the turtle go.

On the way back to the hotel, Betty, her eyes obscured by dark glasses, shook her head and said "Someday, Ptolly."

"Someday what?" I said irritably.

"Someday you'll learn that that's just not how life works. You can't go around spending five dollars of your father's money every time you see some animal you don't want to get hurt. It isn't realistic."

All the dislike I had ever felt for Betty seemed to awaken in me afresh when I heard this remark. I said nothing back to her—preferring instead to simply stop speaking altogether for a few days, as was often my habit—but I committed her words to memory. For I knew—or at least I hoped—that they would come back to haunt her.

And I was right. As cruel as it may have been of me, Betty's illness and her seeming inability to suffer it gracefully struck me as a perfectly reasonable—indeed, practically a choreographed—response on the part of the universe to remarks like the one she had made after our time on the beach that day, and countless other ones besides. Karma—that word that both Betty and my father had loved to toss around over the years—had won out at last. The days of parking spaces opening up at just the right time and certainty that the universe was going to administer preferred treatment were over. Betty was going to die, and on some level both she and my father knew it. But they were not being "realistic" about this fact at all. Instead, they seemed to be engaged in an elaborate attempt to prove that such a fate was beneath her—that she was, in fact, too good for death.

During these days of increasing fear and uncertainty, ever more Sufis came out to the Barn. Over tables of herbal tea and sugarless biscuits, they would tell Betty again and again that things were not going to go as she feared. "You can't possibly leave us now, Tarana," I remember one of these smiling, white-clad visitors telling her. "You still have so much to teach the world." It was all so familiar, this pose of indifference to the possibility that the hidden side of the world was darker and wilder than expected. And for the first time in my life, I could see with adult eyes that the adults really didn't know much about that hidden side after all. From the very beginning, it had all been a sham. For all the confident assertions, for all the belief that good things came to special people and bad things didn't need to be worried about, the adults were in the dark too—only they were afraid, or simply unwilling, to admit it.

Ever since the end of sophomore year the previous spring, my then girlfriend Sarah had been staying with me at the Barn. Not long after Betty entered into the final phase of her illness, the two of us decided to move out to the Midwest together. My father—then in the middle of one of his periodic financial slumps—didn't have enough money for me to return to college, Sarah's financial aid had fallen through, and with little idea of what to do with ourselves, we decided that this modest geographical change might help us better get a handle on being adults. My father took me down to the used car lot nearest the Barn and helped me find a cheap vehicle, gave me a check for rent, and Sarah and I drove off into the snows of January, clueless but hopeful. Meanwhile, Betty, with the help of her two sons, Nicky and Alexander, moved to an apartment in Georgetown. It was her hope that, away from the perennial distractions and dramas of the Barn, she could better concentrate her energy on coping with the illness that she no longer had the option of ignoring.

Sarah and I stayed away for only six months before coming to the conclusion that life in the middle of the country was no less confusing than it was back east. On the last day of the summer writing class I was taking, we climbed into our car and drove sixteen straight hours back to the Barn. Neither of us was sure what we were going to do once we got back there, though I suspected some more weeks of hanging around reading and having drinks out in my mother's house on the edge of the field would eventually yield inspiration.

During the whole time we had been away I had not spoken to Betty once, and the handful of friendly letters and postcards she sent had gone unanswered. Something in me had shut down, and I was not going to pretend I felt differently about her than I did just because she was going to die. That kind of pretense I would leave to her legions of New Age friends, who didn't seem to mind pretending they felt one way when they really felt another.

At some point during the long drive home, the reality of Betty's situation closed in on me. I not only realized for the first time that Betty's death was an imminent reality rather than an abstraction, but also that I would now have the opportunity to talk to her one last time, before death closed our relationship down in the midst of our impasse.

By the time we pulled up in front of the Barn, Betty was much on my mind. My mother, with her four dogs of the moment, was there to greet us, and after a short bit of talk I asked her about Betty.

"She's still alive, from what I gather," she said in a removed, vague voice. "It really has nothing to do with *me*, you know. But Nicky's in the Barn right now, looking for some things of hers. You can ask him."

I walked into the low, dark, deeply familiar living room at the eastern end of the Barn, grabbed a beer out of the refrigerator, and walked through the rooms until I found Nicky, bent over a chest of drawers, sorting through some of Betty's things.

Nicky was in his early thirties, and had a "path" of his own that he was following. The path was Tibetan Buddhism, and he had recently gone so far as to take the vows of monkhood and join a Tibetan monastery in the south of India. His initial ten-year phase at the monastery had only recently begun, when his mother's worsening condition forced him to set up residence in her Georgetown apartment in order to look after her. Alexander, Nicky's brother, had for years been out of the picture as a result of his involvement in another spiritual organization called the Inner Peace Movement—an involvement that kept him off in Europe and Australia, far from the gravitational field of the Great Plan. He too, in response to Betty's illness, had returned and set up camp in Georgetown.

Alexander had managed to distance himself from my father's world so early and so successfully that I didn't really feel like I knew him, but I knew Nicky very well indeed. The two brothers had been teenagers when the Great Plan came along, and in many ways they had suffered more heavily under it than I had. Rather amazingly, both of them—Alexander from a distance and Nicky from close up—had come, after a time, to accept my father's presence in their lives, and Nicky had even been on hand for many of the adventures of the Atlantis era.

Nicky's entrance into monkhood paralleled Betty's illness in my mind, in that both events seemed like indicators of a change in the general mood of my extended family. Did life, as the cliché suggested, really have seasons, and were the colors of a whole group of lives capable of going from bright to gray together? Nicky himself certainly didn't look at his abandonment of his old, decidedly unmonklike ways in such grim terms. But there was something about the sobriety of Nicky's Buddhism, and Buddhism in general, that had come, after an initial period of interest, to repel me. While on one hand I found Nicky's new life-is-suffering perspective refreshing (no smiley New Age optimism for him), on another level it made me just as suspicious as Betty's Sufi enthusiasms did. In spite of all the respect and affection I had for Nicky, there simply was nothing storm-tossed and apocalyptic about the new religious perspective he had adopted, nothing that to my eyes was sufficiently dramatic and mysterious.

It also seemed to me that there was something less than totally human at work in the grave, karma-conscious rigor of Nicky's Buddhism, just as there was in Betty's cheerful Sufism. All these transplanted spiritual disciplines, with their different-colored robes and their assorted ideological trappings, had an *Invasion of the Body Snatchers* feel to them. Thank heavens I had beer, which no matter what the circumstances always resoundingly increased my sense of humanity and brought me back to my own, deeply felt center. There was peace of mind in this—peace of mind and a sense of personal power more intimate and immediate and charged than anything I saw at work in the various transplanted faiths taking root around me.

Reserved as I was about certain aspects of Nicky's new spiritual calling, there was something in his Buddhism that I did admire without qualification, and that was the honesty that seemed to go along with it. This willingness to face life on its terms was apparently serving him well in the situation currently at hand. Of all the people close to Betty in the days of her illness, Nicky struck me as being one of the least ruffled by it. This was not to say that it caused him any less pain, but the pain was something he seemed to be interested in confronting rather than hiding from or chasing away.

After some brief preliminary talk, I asked Nicky about his mother. He always had a slow, mannered way of speaking, and fledgling monkhood appeared to have accentuated this.

"She had a bad night," he said in his whimsical, measured, Manhattan-socialite-turned-Tibetan-Buddhist manner, "but she opened her eyes this morning and said 'Still here.' "

Nicky spoke with a touch of his old humor, and for some reason this made me a little more conscious of what had been going on in my absence and how horrible it must have been. I tried to picture Betty, whom I had not seen in six months and who had looked more or less normal at that time, waking up and surprising her son with the words that she was "still here." It sounded like the kind of light remark she might have made in the old days, when we had gotten along.

"Well, if she's alive, I guess I better go and see her."

"I can call ahead and tell them you're coming."

"You mean right now?" I said, flushed throughout my entire body. "I don't know . . . I just drove sixteen hours and I'm a little tired. How about tomorrow?"

Nicky smiled—a genuine, unphony smile. "If I were you, and I wanted to see her, I'd go now."

After unpacking a few things and having another beer, I got back into the car with Sarah and drove the thirty minutes to Georgetown. Cruising slowly by the front of Betty's apartment building, I waited for a parking space to open up at just the right moment, but it didn't.

"She's probably not going to want to talk too long," I said nervously to Sarah. "Maybe I'll just double-park and you can sit with the car while I go up."

The building was new and immaculate—the antithesis of the kind of place my father would have chosen. Up on the fourth floor, Alexander opened the door for me, and I was further surprised at the apartment's neatness. Betty's things—Moroccan masks, African prints—were hanging on the walls and displayed on the furniture, with no hint of my father's presence. Not a hammer, not a TV with a coat hanger stuck in it, not a floral print easy chair from some rummage sale was to be seen. Though my father was in and out every day and slept there much of the time, the place was truly Betty's. At long last, with the help of her two sons, she had managed to claim a space that didn't bear his mark.

"She's down there," said Alexander, pointing towards a long hallway leading to a closed white door. "She's getting a foot massage from Lena."

God, I thought to myself. Foot massages again. Lena was one of Betty's Sufis. She was small, delicately built, spoke with an unnatural softness, smiled frequently, and I couldn't stand her. I walked to the end of the hallway and knocked. "Come in," came a voice that sounded like it might be Lena's. I walked in.

In the white room, sparely decorated with more paintings and artifacts familiar from her Long Island house, Betty lay with her head propped up against a group of big, equally white pillows, her curly, blond-gray hair spread out on it like a small halo.

She was unrecognizable. The disease had taken all the body fat from her face, giving her the appearance of an impossibly old woman. Were it not for her familiar hair, there would have been nothing truly identifying about her for me to latch on to.

Lena was sitting at the foot of the bed rubbing Betty's feet, the toenails of which someone had taken the trouble to paint with red nail polish. She gave me one of those broad, warm, Sufi-like smiles I had grown so suspicious of, and said, "She's tired, but she's been waiting for you."

With that, she got up and left the room. From Nicky back at the Barn, to Alexander at the door, to the just-departed Lena, everyone around me was embarrassingly natural and at ease. It was only I—the champion of honesty and brave acceptance of the worst that the world had to dole out—who was uncomfortable. In the face of Betty's disease and what it had done to her, it appeared that I was being knocked off a pedestal made up of smug, uncaring arrogance as bad as any I had ever accused Betty of. I had not slept for thirty-some hours, and my fatigue, in combination with the two beers I had drunk before coming out to Georgetown, helped blunt my discomfort. But it was very much there nevertheless.

I sat down on the bed, wondering what to say or do next. With great difficulty Betty addressed me. She spoke in a whisper that was low and far away.

"How are you?" she said.

How was *I*? It was a surprising question coming from this new, unrecognizable person.

"I'm okay," I said, then, idiotically, "How are you?"

Betty gave me a look of infinite weariness. "Not very good. I'm tired, Ptolly. Oh, I'm so, so tired."

Her thickly clouded eyes drifted off to the side and she said nothing more. From the moment I entered the room, I had noticed something unusual in the way I felt—something that didn't have to do with either my exhaustion or my guilt and embarrassment. In Betty's presence, my body—my hands and my arms, my back and my head—somehow felt more solid, more consequential. I found myself suddenly conscious of the space I took up as a flesh-and-blood creature, and the life and consciousness that set me apart from all the other objects in the room. With shock, I realized that this new, mysterious sense of my physicality and aliveness was coming to me as a direct result of seeing Betty. On the verge of leaving her body, Betty was bringing the physical world around her more intensely to life. Everything was a little clearer, a little sharper, a little more in focus—even to me, with my protective screen of fatigue and alcohol. For all the discomfort of sitting there in front of Betty after her months of misery and my months of unforgiving silence, some part of me felt comfortable, and almost grateful, to be there.

It was precisely the kind of new sensation that, a few years before, as a seventeen- or eighteen-year-old, I would have looked forward to discussing with Betty. In those days, I would often discover what I thought about new ideas and experiences as we talked—a phenomenon that puzzled me because I didn't under-stand how it was possible to know what you thought yet not know it until you heard the words actually coming out of your mouth.

"It takes work to know what you think," Betty had told me

once, when I had brought up this curious fact. "The work of talking or—if you're an artist—the work of writing or painting or
whatever it is you do. Otherwise, the things you really think and
feel can just stay locked away somewhere with no way to get out."

It occurred to me now, for the very first time, that Betty's and
my days of talking about such interesting ideas were over.

Betty regained her focus. "You look different," she said slowly
and vaguely.

Another strange thing to say. I was the one who looked different? For a moment I thought that she was referring to the consider-
able amount of weight I had put on in Iowa, where I had done
little but sit at my desk, drink beer, try to write, and contemplate
the unfairness of becoming an adult while Sarah supported us
both by working at a restaurant in town.

"Your hair," she said. "What's in your hair?"

For some time, this being the early '80s, I had been in the habit
of putting a great deal of gel in my hair so that it stood up in
spikes. When I was thinner, the effect had been satisfactory
enough. With the extra weight I had put on, however, the look of
all this gel was altered. My hair, standing straight up over my
beer-rounded face, gave me a bizarre, slightly cartoonish appearance, like that of someone who has just seen a ghost.

"Oh, it's just got some stuff in it so it stands up."

Carefully, as if it were some recalcitrant mechanical device she
had to use a lot of concentration to control, Betty raised her arm
and brought her hand up above my head. She patted the spikes
a couple of times and put her arm back down on the bed. Then,
somewhere beneath all the sheets, her body stiffened.

"It hurts."

"Maybe I should go," I said.

"No," she said. "Stay a little more. Tell me—why don't you
tell me what you're going to do."

"Do? Um . . . you mean do for my life?"

"For your life."

I looked at Betty, beneath her halo of hair, in her body that was scarcely even a body anymore, and found myself amazed at how much of her was there in front of me. With her physical being washing away and almost gone completely—weighing nothing and so close to death I could not believe that it had not come and taken her already—the real Betty had come back. All the moments of bullshit and nonsense, all the petty complaints and competitiveness, all the judgments and resentments on both her part and mine, had slipped away. And in their place there were only these few, simple questions—about my hair, about what I was going to do in my life.

"I guess I'm going to try to be a writer," I said, wondering at how stupid this sounded.

"What are you going to write about?"

"I don't know."

"You don't know?" She sounded surprised.

"Not really."

"I'm sure you'll find out. In time."

"Maybe. I hope so."

I sat for a minute more, but Betty said nothing, her breath coming in and out of her with a low, difficult rasping that seemed like it might come to a complete halt any moment. At length I thought she was asleep, but as I stood up, she spoke again.

"You're going away," Betty said.

"Yeah, I think I'd better go. Sarah is downstairs in the car. She's double-parked. Do you remember Sarah?"

"Sarah." Betty seemed to be trying out the word. "I like Sarah. Can she come and talk to me?"

"Yeah. Okay. I'll send her up. I'll go down and get her."

"Good. Good. Come again tomorrow," Betty said.

"Okay."

I walked to the door and opened it, turning to look one more time at the white bed and the small, incongruous body lying in it. Betty's hand was in the air now, hovering strangely. At first I thought she was gesturing for me to come back, that she needed me to tell Lena or Alexander something. But then I saw that she was waving.

"Bye. Good-bye," she said, just audible above the sound of the traffic outside and the air conditioner and all the other little sounds of the August day.

"Good-bye," I said, and closed the door.

Betty died the following day, and a few days after that I went to her funeral. I had had quite a bit to drink the night before, staying up late and talking with my mother and Sarah out in the house on the edge of the field, and as a result I was sweating very heavily all the way through the service, the gel in my spiked hair running down the sides of my head and dampening the tie that hung desperately around my recently thickened neck.

For the service my father read a poem by Rumi, and one of Betty/Tarana's Sufi friends spoke. The Sufi friend was of the stamp that I found especially irritating. With his wise, all-knowing smile, his beard and robes, and his talk of Tarana's deep spirituality, he called to mind every half-baked, softheaded, smugly self-assured seeker who had ever filtered through the doors of the Barn and my life over the years. Nursing my sweaty drink and listening to the man go on about Tarana's specialness, it occurred to me that many of the people at the service—the friends from Betty's old, prespiritual life—must have felt deeply uncomfortable listening to all his confident, tranquil talk. Hadn't the long hell of Betty's disease proved exactly the opposite of all this man was saying? Hadn't it shown that Betty was, in fact, and in spite of all protest to the contrary, not so special after all? If being special meant being somehow different or better than the rest of humanity—if it meant avoiding the fate of getting ground up and plowed under in the "world of shit" that everybody, myself included, wanted so much to escape, then why hadn't Betty's willed spirituality served her better? It was all so unrealistic, all so far from the ways in which the world really worked and the things the world was really capable of doing to a person.

In the weeks following the funeral, a sort of intermission fell over everyone's life. During this time my father was, as usual, taken up with this or that project, but his activities were subdued in comparison to times past. Sarah and I spent much of our time hanging out with my mother and her dogs in the little house in the back, while my father stayed up in his enormous attic, moving quietly from one desk to another. One afternoon during this time my father took Sarah and me to a diner a short drive from the Barn. All of us were in an inexplicably cheerful mood, including my father, who was going on about the quality of the food to be had at this particular diner and how it outshone all the others in the area.

"Betty and I came here after our wedding," he said finally.

I remembered Betty telling me once how she had been particularly charmed by my father's decision to visit a diner after the brief courthouse wedding they had taken part in some two years previously. When first told about it, I had been surprised and puzzled at this ceremony. After all, "Who needs weddings?" was a refrain I had heard a lot over the years.

As it turned out, my father and Betty needed one. On a deep level, perhaps, Betty had known she was dying, as had my father, and the wedding, it occurred to me now, was a demonstration of their solidarity in the face of that fact. After a decade of rule-breaking and institution-mocking, the two of them had taken it upon themselves to enter into the very institution they had started out by mocking most of all.

Looking around that afternoon at the Greek columns and polished chrome, I understood for the first time that my father had lost his wife. As he went back to his food, I pictured the two of them coming to the diner after the ceremony. My father no doubt went into an overdetailed consideration of the quality of the food they ordered, much as he was doing now, and Betty no doubt listened, with a combination of affection and exasperation, just as she always did.

On another day, toward the end of this period and just before Sarah and I moved up to New York, I heard hammering at the east end of the Barn near the tool area where Zoltan had loaded up his truck so many years before. Walking over, I saw my father down on his knees among a mass of boards of various lengths freshly purchased from the lumber store. With no room for any more of them inside, my father was installing one more staircase—this time on the outside of the Barn.

Watching him at work on this stairway-to-nowhere, I found myself struck by the poetic quality of the scene.

"What the hell are you looking at?" my father said when he finally noticed me standing behind him.

"I'm looking at you building a staircase that doesn't look like it's leading anywhere."

"Well, of course, it doesn't lead anywhere now, but it's *going* to lead somewhere!"

"Oh, yeah? Where?"

"It will lead to a *platform*."

Unsatisfied with this answer, I pressed further.

"And what's going to happen up on the platform?"

My father paused for a minute under the low and leaden McLean skies, and I could tell he was thinking. At length, his muse of purposefulness did not let him down. With a certain undisguised pride he replied: "Dances. We'll have dances up there."

As my father returned to his hammering, I found myself regretting that he probably would soon be distracted by some other task, and was unlikely ever to complete this platform, much less put it to the fanciful use he had just outlined. For it was perhaps from such a structure—raised slightly but securely above the limitations and disappointments of the ordinary world—that he could at last find a way to accept those limitations and live at least somewhat comfortably within them. In a way, that was really all he had been looking for throughout those long and eventful years of my childhood: a place above, from which the landscape below might suddenly slide into focus as it never had before.

What I didn't realize then was just how much I wanted the same thing myself.

THREE

Never Again

"Whatever the causes of the Fall, its effects are described similarly in almost all traditions. With disobedience, attachment, and forgetting come the loss of contact with the sacred Source; death and the necessity for reproduction; and limitations of various kinds, such as the loss of luminosity and the abilities to fly and to communicate with the animals. Human beings must now labor to obtain what they need to survive, must invent technologies to compensate for the diminution of their various natural abilities, and must wander through life unaware of their real nature, purpose, and collective past."
—Richard Heinberg, Memories and Visions of Paradise

"YOUR crown chakra," Michael the aura reader said. "There's something wrong with it."

The crown chakra is a point of subtle energy at the very top of the head. The highest of the seven chakras of yogic physiology, it is said to be the contact point of the celestial cord that invisibly binds the incarnate, earth-bound soul to the heavens. When the crown chakra is fully awakened, it whirls like a bright pinwheel, scattering light and drawing in the energies of the universe. The halos of Western art and the golden rays of light emanating from the heads of Buddhas and bodhisattvas in Eastern art are depictions of the crown chakra as it appears to the eyes of clairvoyants, who can see the spiritual essence of a person glowing behind the dense curtain of his or her physicality. Even to clairvoyant eyes, the crown chakra is only highly visible in individuals who have achieved a state of enlightenment. In ordinary, unenlightened people, this chakra has a muted quality, like that of a flower not yet open.

It was August 1995, I was thirty-three years old, and I was not at all surprised to hear that there was something wrong with my crown chakra. It was more puzzling to me that I should have one at all. I was sitting in one of the first-level bedrooms of a large tin-roofed, cinder-block structure known informally as the Milk House because of its former capacity as a milking station for cows. The Milk House sat atop a stretch of rambling hillside property in northern West Virginia, about two hours away from Washington, that had replaced the Barn as my father's mission control. My father had moved himself and my mother out there in the late '80s, and by now it was as familiar to me as the Barn itself.

I had arrived about a week before, and from the moment I walked in the door it was apparent that, as my mother put it, something was "off" with me. During the days I stayed for unnaturally long periods in my room, either sleeping or just lying silently with *Cosmic Memory*—Rudolf Steiner's book on Atlantis and its sister continent of Lemuria—propped up in front of my face in case someone stuck his head in to see what I was up to. But from hour to hour, the page of *Cosmic Memory* seldom changed, and when I came out in the early evening it was only to sit silently at the dinner table as my father came up with stray bits of conversation that faded away soon after he introduced them. When dinner was over, I would make a feeble gesture toward helping out with the dishes, then stagger back to my room and my bed.

Every other day or so, after a brief and unimpressive showing for lunch, I would emerge from my room at around four o'clock with my wallet in my pocket and a look of purpose on my face and zip into town for supplies. Once back from this exhausting, fifteen-minute pilgrimage, I would go straight to my room, choke down a few inches of the bourbon or vodka that I had bought, stick the rest in my sock drawer, and head out to the west side of the house to join my mother for the drink hour. On the way, I would grab a beer from the small store of them my father usually kept in the refrigerator and nurse it in civilized fashion while watching the sun go slowly down through the trees.

In past visits this would have been the best time of day—the time when the gravity and dullness that clung to the ordinary hours fell away and all things seemed energized and celebratory. But something had gone wrong with me—something I didn't understand—and for the past year or so things in my life had gradually stopped working. Not even the drink hour offered much relief.

That was why, on this windy and overcast afternoon, after a few clandestine hits of vodka to get my energy up, I was sitting in the guest room where Michael was staying, listening to him tell me about my aura. Michael had arrived the day before and was to leave the following morning, on the way from his home in the Carolinas to a New Age convention of some sort in New York City. He was a longtime friend and associate of my father's, and I had submitted to the reading not because I expected to get anything from it but because I liked and trusted him. Though he practiced what I tended to think of as a flaky line of work, he himself was not a flake.

"Something's wrong with my crown chakra?" I said, still wondering at how Michael could make out anything of my aura at all given my wretched state. "What exactly?"

Michael paused and rubbed his short black beard. "It's dented."

"Dented! I didn't know you could do that kind of thing to a chakra."

"Well, that's just a way of putting it. Did you ever have a bad fall onto the top of your head, perhaps as a young child?"

"Yeah. . . . It's funny you should ask. I fell from the top of a staircase in one of my father's houses. This weird old place on the river in New Jersey across from the city. It used to be an organ factory before my father took it over. The main staircase in the place didn't have a railing. I was only three years old or so, and I was always being told to stay away from the edge or I'd fall off. So I'd spend a lot of time up at the top, really close to the edge, shouting to everyone how I was going to fall. To get attention, I guess. Anyhow, I did fall eventually. I landed right on the top of my head and got knocked out for a while. Or so I'm told. I don't remember any of it."

Michael continued rubbing his beard and staring at me. I thought he was going to say something more about the dented chakra, but instead he changed the subject. "Do you know anyone named Larry?"

"Like a close friend or something? No."

"I've been watching this figure move in and out of your personal field for the past half hour or so. A thin, balding guy."

"My grandfather's name was Laurence. He was pretty thin and bald the few times I met him as a kid before he died. But I didn't really know him. Generally speaking, I wouldn't say he makes up a very positive image in my mind."

Michael sat back in his chair and shook his head. "Oh, this guy's not positive! Not at all."

I had refined my drinking habits to the point that I no longer went through the standard drunk-hung over-drunk pattern that had characterized my early, novice years. These days I was typically neither drunk nor sober but something in between—a twilight condition made up of periods of greater or lesser clarity, greater or lesser periods of nausea and exhaustion, and occasional, fleeting runs of weird, hallucinatory euphoria. During these moments, I enjoyed the rushes of certainty that had been commonplace in the past, when drinking was the great and secret treasure that set me above and apart from the rest of the world instead of the plain affliction it had now become. In those old moments, I had known what it meant to win and to lose, and knew as well that I was made to win—that the world around me was, in fact, a vast and elaborately constructed amphitheater in which that slow but inevitable victory would play itself out.

This was not one of those magical interludes. Sitting uncomfortably on the straight-backed chair that Michael had pulled up for the reading, I imagined how I must appear to his supersensitive eyes. A ladder of glowing orbs of color, blackened and smudged here and there from booze and drugs, with the one at the very top sputtering and flickering feebly like a damaged streetlight, still on the fritz from my fall off that staircase so long ago. And moving back and forth around this dim ladder of lights, the sinister, balding specter of someone named Larry.

Michael's expression lightened. He seemed to be relaxing his gaze, giving himself a break from the unpleasant spectacle in front of him. Outside, a chill, unnaturally fall-like wind was blowing across the tin roof far above us, making a moaning sound that mingled with the occasional, clattering bursts of rain. Moving underneath these gentle sounds was another, heavier and more insistent sound, coming from closer by: the sound of hammering. Beneath the shelter of a wall of trees that crept up almost to the back of the house, my father was at work on a small wooden staircase.

The Milk House, though big and Barn-like, had much less space than the original Barn had, and outfitting it with extra staircases was a more difficult prospect. Nevertheless, my father was doing what he could to indulge his desire to create them. He had recently installed a raised pool on the grass out back and had built a raised wooden deck to make it blend in with the rest of the Milk House. It was that deck he was now outfitting with the staircase.

"What's your father building out there?" said Michael.

"A little wooden staircase that he's going to attach to that tacky instant swimming pool he bought this spring. I told him how ugly I thought the pool was, and he said that by the time he'd finished with it I wouldn't recognize it. Actually, I have to admit it *is* starting to look okay now that he's put that deck around it."

"I don't see where the staircase is going to go, though."

"Oh, he'll find a place for it. He can always find a place for another staircase."

Michael sat and said nothing for a moment, his mind apparently on something else, the dim pattering of the rain and the thuds of my father's hammer continuing behind him.

"Never again."

"What's that?"

"Never again," said Michael. "It's what I'm getting from the psychic space around you. Over and over, those two words."

"You mean I'm saying them?"

"Some part of you is, yes."

"Why?"

"I'm not sure. It's keyed into a past life, I think. Something happened to you at some point long ago—something bad that you haven't forgotten about. It slows you down. Especially on a day like today, when your energy is low."

"Bloody fucking Jesus!"

From outside came the result of what I suspected was my father's hammer coming down on one of his fingers, as it often did thanks to the habitual if pointless urgency with which he worked.

"When we come back in a new body," Michael continued, "the things that happened to the ones we lived in before come with us too, and they nag at us. In this case, 'never again' might be tied in with some specific past life situation, or it might be a more general reference. It might suggest you'd had enough knocks in your life before this one and didn't want to come back at all. The material dimension—this whole frightening, frustrating, disorganized testing ground we've all found ourselves in—might have exhausted your patience the last time around. Maybe you wanted to stay in the higher worlds and keep away from all this confusion and pain, and something in you is still angry that you didn't."

A few more hammer blows sounded in the background, followed by a long howl, like that of a lost soul suffering the torments of some lower hell.

"Sounds like he hit the same finger again," said Michael.

"He has a tendency to do that."

"So do most of us," said Michael, seizing upon the analogy with satisfaction. "In life after life we come back and bash the same finger we did the last time, right at the spot where it's the sorest. I think that's what's going on with the 'never again' script. I'm getting the picture of a situation that's repeated itself over and over again in your previous lives. It's a situation you know on some level that you still have to get right. You have to go through it and be done with it once and for all, but that frustrates you. You're tired of repeating the script."

I had to admit that this scenario of grim repetition that Michael was painting for me made a certain amount of sense. It had been my general experience that past lives, when recounted by the assorted seers and psychics that had drifted through my father's life over the years, were often too grand and exotic, with little connection to ordinary life. More than anything else, their talk of previous incarnations seemed to be a way of making the people they were talking about feel important. I thought in particular of a woman who spent a long time trying to convince my father that he had been King Henry VIII in a previous life and she one or another of his ill-fated wives. From the psychic perspective, there didn't seem to be many run-of-the-mill, humdrum past lives. I decided to ask Michael for more specifics and see if, according to his vision, I had been Alexander the Great, an Egyptian high initiate, or perhaps Shakespeare during my previous stint on earth.

"So when and where exactly did this situation happen last time?" I said.

Michael closed his eyes and furrowed his brow. "I'm getting an atmosphere that feels like it might be ancient Rome. I sense you were a Roman yourself, and that there was some conflict between you individually and the state or some other larger group. I'm not sure if it was political or religious, but it ended without a resolution. It's definitely something you know you still need to resolve, but you have a strong desire not to bother. It's like a higher part of you is saying 'Oh God, not *that* again.' You've definitely had enough."

The scream of a circular saw now replaced the hammering that had been accompanying us up to this point. "I hope your father takes more care with his fingers when he's using the saw than he does when he's hammering."

"That's an interesting point," I said. "You'd think he'd be lopping off fingers right and left, but he never does. He saves the self-mutilation for the less dangerous tools like hammers."

I expected Michael to come back with another neat analogy, perhaps along the lines of "We all do that, hammering our fingers but never going so far as to actually cut them off," but he didn't. Instead, he stared across the room, apparently lost in thought, at a bookshelf that held a jumble of worn titles that had washed up there from previous houses my father had owned over the years. I followed his gaze as it traveled along the shelf, recognizing many volumes that I had previously seen elsewhere as they shuttled from room to room and house to house. *Occult Magic*; *Flying Saucers—Serious Business!*; *Practical Astral Projection*; *The Hollow Earth*. Such titles alternated, as they did throughout my father's houses, with others on more down-to-earth subjects: *Yes I Can! The Story of Sammy Davis Jr.*; *The Girl Scout Handbook, 1954*; *Gentlemen Prefer Blondes*; *The Catcher in the Rye*. Armies of such titles drifted back and forth, none ever judged so useless or outdated that it was consigned to the trash.

"Your father never throws anything away, does he?"

"Not really, no. It's part of what makes him who he is."

"Mm. Let's get back to the figure moving around you. To Larry. I still want to find out who *he* is."

"He's still there?"

"Very much so. Listen, is there much of a history of drugs and alcohol in your family—perhaps with your grandfather, for instance?"

"With my grandfather?" I said, surprised. "Actually, yeah, there is. He liked pills quite a bit apparently. 'A pill to get up and a pill to go to bed.' That's how my father described him to me once. And his wife—Peter's mother—oh boy. My brother and sister lived with the two of them for some time when they were kids, and they saw quite a bit. My brother told me that my grandmother would start her day with a glass of Ballantine scotch with a raw egg in it and a Seconal. When she was young she spent a lot of time hanging around with famous people—George Bernard Shaw and James Montgomery Flagg, the guy who painted the 'I want you' Uncle Sam posters. Anyhow, people paid a lot of attention to her, found her charming and stuff. Then she got older and lost her looks and she sort of went to seed, lying around all day with her Seconal and her scotch, a detective novel, and a box of chocolates. Pathetic."

I had managed to work myself up a bit in the course of this story, and Michael noticed my interest in the subject. It appeared he had found what he was looking for.

"Stop me if I'm getting too personal," he said, "but you enjoy getting away from life through drinking and things like that yourself, don't you?"

"Drinking?" I said through the merciless blanket of sick fatigue that lay over me like a urine-drenched sleeping bag. "Yeah. I'd have to say that's the case. Though I would qualify 'things like that' and say that I don't like pot or hallucinogens. I like the soft-focus stuff—alcohol and pills."

"Like Larry."

"Laurence. He went by Laurence."

"Right. Whatever. Anyhow, I think we've ID'd this figure. He's not really your grandfather, of course, but there's something of that whole complex—your grandfather, your grandmother, your feelings of disdain for them—at work in him. He's a real *figure*, but he's an amalgamation at the same time. Of people, of issues in your life. And substances—alcohol, pills—are definitely a part of it. Is any of this making you uncomfortable? Because we can stop this whole investigation any time."

"Oh no," I lied, trying to affect an air of scientific dispassion. "It's very interesting."

"Okay, good. Then let me ask you a little more about your own tastes. You like pills, downs. Anything harder than that?" Michael seemed to be looking for something more, as if someone had hammered up a large billboard behind me that he could read and I couldn't.

"Well, heroin, of course. That's really my favorite."

"Mm," said Michael. "Heroin. No big surprise there. I can see it, as a matter of fact. In your aura. Heroin has a very visible effect on one's subtle body. At least it does in my experience. You haven't had any for a little while though, have you?"

"No," I said. "That's more or less why I came down here, to get away from it. I was doing a lot in New York, because I had stopped drinking for a while and I fell into it as a substitute. Then I realized that I'd come to like it better than drinking. My fiancée, Rebecca, was really getting on my case about it, and I hadn't seen my parents for a while, so I thought it might be a good time to come down here to sort things out. The trouble is, once I arrived, I kind of started drinking again—this time as a substitute for heroin, I guess. One of those stupid back-and-forth things."

I paused and sat forlornly in my chair for a moment, my chakras all spinning slowly and soddenly like old carnival wheels in an amusement park destined never again to re-open. "I guess the trip isn't really working out the way I wanted it to."

"So how much longer do you think you're going to stay down here?" Michael asked.

"I don't know. I should be getting back to New York pretty soon, I guess, but Rebecca is really being a pain. She says she doesn't want me back unless I give up everything, and I told her she could forget about that. We have these phone calls at night where she just sort of nags at me and I get irritated and hang up. None of it leads anywhere. It's nice spending time with my parents, even though I'm not much company in this condition. They're pretty oblivious, but they're bound to catch on to what's wrong with me sooner or later. Then I don't know what I'll do."

"Did they know you had stopped drinking?"

"Oh, yeah. The whole reason I stopped was because I got the D.T.'s while I was visiting my mother a year or so ago, when she was up in Vermont. I was in my room for three straight days—shaking, hallucinating. It was horrible."

"So your mother saw all this?"

"Yeah. I mean, sort of. She was in the living room watching TV most of the time and didn't really get how sick I was until I told her later."

"Well, don't your parents think it's a little odd that you've started again? Doesn't that worry them?"

"You know how parents are. They're not used to thinking about things that way. I can walk around with a butcher knife and Mickey Mouse ears, and as long as I show up for dinner on time, they think I'm okay. Actually, that's not completely true. My mother notices other, little things, but the drinking stuff seems to pass her by. She drinks herself obviously, and she's never had any problem with it. I don't think she wants to think of me that way, so she just doesn't. And my father—well. He's always got a lot on his mind and . . . it takes a lot to penetrate it, to get his attention."

"It's pretty interesting, from my perspective, that you should end up being your father's son, because the two of you have a way of approaching the world that's sort of a mirror image of each other. It's the same thing almost, just reversed. You can actually see the reversal in your auric field."

A long, unnerving blast of screaming circular saw penetrated the cinder-block walls of the room and brought Michael to a halt for a moment. He seemed to be focusing his soft, small eyes on a point over my right shoulder.

"You don't really trust the world of things. You don't like them because they're too solid. Too . . ."

"Too *there*," I said with enthusiasm. "I don't know about ancient Rome, but you've definitely hit it on the head with that. I think that's always been why I've used alcohol and drugs as much as I have. They make the world weigh less—make it all a little transparent for a while. I guess that's not a very original reason to like them . . ."

". . . but it's valid," said Michael, finishing my thought. "It's why a lot of people drink and take drugs. In their way, these substances *work*, that's the thing. For a while they actually change your etheric and astral makeup, and they do it in such a manner that you get taken away from the garbage that comes along with life in the body—just lifted right out of it. It's not just your imagination that it's happening. You *are* getting better. For a while at least. But, as you've obviously discovered, it doesn't last. In your case, I can actually *see* that it isn't working as well as it did in the past at all. But I can also see the desire for it anyhow—the need to get out, up, *away* from it all, in the colors of your field. It takes the form of a wall of bright color energy meeting with another, darker one that mutes and kills it. Now, with your dad, that's not the case. You don't see that kind of dynamic at work in his field at all. In fact, you see the exact opposite, as I mentioned. With him, the dynamic isn't between the psychic energy moving up, trying to escape from the physical and getting blocked. Instead, his field is all about collision in the horizontal dimension."

"The horizontal?" I said, following with interest but difficulty as exhaustion, and the feeling that I could use another inch or two from the bottle in my sock drawer, pulled at me.

"Yes. In other words, he's not trying to get *out* of this dimension, out of the physical, the way you are. He likes it down here. That's why he spends so much time building things, fixing things, messing around with them in general. Physical objects don't make him suspicious the way they do you. He likes to get right down into the physical world and wrestle with it. For better or worse, just like he's wrestling with that staircase out there now."

Outside, the power saw screamed into action again, the sound rising and falling as the blade charged into and retreated from the wood. With a particularly angry acceleration of the motor, Michael's bedside light flickered for a moment, threatening to go out. I felt a sense of gratitude at being in there with Michael and not outside, where the danger loomed of being roped into the staircase project myself. Now as in childhood, I was wary when my father was at work on one of his home improvement projects. Not that I was ever much use when he did manage to enlist my aid, for such help as I provided was limited significantly by my habit of keeping one hand in my pocket at all times. This detail struck me as significant, so I sent it by Michael.

"That racket Peter's making, and this stuff you're saying, reminds me of all the times he's tried to get me interested in things like carpentry and how cars run and stuff like that. You're right—he's so comfortable with the world in a way, for all his cursing and howling. When I was younger, he always used to yell at me about my hands. 'Jesus, Ptolly, take your hand out of your pocket!' I heard that a million times, because I have this habit of keeping one hand in my pocket even when I'm busy doing something. It's half laziness, of course, but there's something more to it too. Whatever I'm doing, like washing the dishes or helping him while he's building something, there's this bit of noncommittal spirit in me, like I'm determined not to get too involved. Sort of like Bartleby in the Melville story. 'I would prefer not to.'"

"Always one hand in your pocket," said Michael. "That's perfect. It's the 'never again' script in a nutshell. It seems to me there might be a money factor in there too. How do you feel about money?"

"Oh, man. It's the same thing, really. I've never had any, never known how to get any, and in a way I've spent the past ten years trying to escape from having to think about it, either by hiding out at home or taking stupid jobs."

"Are you saying you're lazy?"

"Lazy? I'm not sure. I don't think I'm lazy, actually, as much as it sounds like I am."

"You've done some good writing, published a few things, right? Writing's hard work."

"Oh, yeah. Definitely. All those times I spent at home with my parents I was always up to something—some writing thing or other. But financially, I could never really make it *work*. It was always a little half-baked, like even though the writing work I was doing was okay, I was still hiding from the outside world. I think I'm a hider by nature. One of the reasons I became a writer is because it allows for that—the disappearance from regular life for long periods. I even used 'Bartleby' as part of a pseudonym for a book of nature trivia I wrote. I'm an 'I would prefer not to' man through and through. I remember in my late twenties when I was living with Sarah in Massachusetts, doing research for a writing project, she looked at me once and said, 'My God, all you really like to do is read and drink!' We were having a fight at the time, and I think she meant it as an insult, but I couldn't help taking it as a compliment."

"But you don't live with Sarah anymore."

"No. We broke up finally. I met Rebecca a year or so ago and now I live with her . . . in New York. And it's like, suddenly I'm not in my twenties anymore. She has two kids, she's older than me, she supports herself, and I don't know. You know how New York is. Even if you have a job—which I don't—it's easy to feel useless there. Somehow all the other towns I've bumped around in over the years—they were always pretty humble spots to begin with. I didn't feel like I needed some legitimizing kind of job in those places because most of my twenty-something friends didn't have anything of that nature going either—they were all free-floating bohemian flotsam like me. Now I'm living with this older woman, she has these two kids, I decided I wanted to get married. It's almost . . . "

Michael interrupted me. "It's almost like you're supposed to be an *adult* now, right?"

"Exactly. It gives me the creeps."

Michael sat back and slapped his knee.

"Good! Fine. I couldn't agree with you more. Why *shouldn't* becoming an adult give you the creeps? For that matter, why shouldn't being born in the first place give you the creeps? Listen, I can promise you that a lot of this isn't so unusual, and while you may think you're experiencing it late in life, I think you're just about on schedule. But there *is* something a little bit unusual about your style of retreat from the world. It's not just a passing phase but something that's really ingrained in you—something you believe in and are invested in, in more ways than you even know. Whatever you're doing, one part of you is always working on stopping and crawling back out of the world, out of all this noise and confusion and bullshit. Of course, all of us want to do that to one degree or another. Freud would say you want to go back to the womb. I'd say you're just smart enough to remember there's a bigger, better world that we left behind to enter into this one and that you want back. On a certain level, you're obviously right to do so—to want to flee back up into the spiritual dimension. The hard part is coming to accept that there must be a reason we're stuck down here in the tar pit. That we have something to gain from wading through the material dimension."

I didn't know how much energy aura reading took out of a person, but it seemed all of a sudden that Michael was getting a little tired. As for me, I had been exhausted from the start. Noting with relief that it was a little after five, I suggested that he had done a good enough job and that it might be time to go relax on the front porch—perhaps with a beer.

"That's okay. I'm going to meditate a little before dinner. I'll see you then."

"Listen, do me a favor and don't mention any of this stuff to my parents, will you? I don't want to alarm them."

"Oh, of course not. I'll be off tomorrow morning anyhow. I hope things work out, though. Keep 'never again' in mind. I have a suspicion it has a lot to do with all of this."

Leaving Michael in his room, I stepped into the long, book-lined hallway cutting down the center of the Milk House—a space that had once been full of milling cattle—and pondered my options. Relatively forthright as I had been with Michael, appearances had nevertheless demanded that I pretend to be at least a little less sick and desperate than I really was, and all this acting had tired me out. Evening was approaching, and though I had a few inches of vodka left in my sock drawer and could avail myself of two or three beers from the refrigerator, these wouldn't do the trick. The other alcohol to be had in the house—a couple of bottles of wine bought by my father and a bottle of bourbon from which my mother made her nightly drinks—were strictly off-limits. I needed a new personal supply—preferably of hard alcohol—to get through the evening, but I didn't know how I was going to get it. My body was probably giving off more of a scent of alcohol than I was aware of, which made me leery of driving to town. In any case, I didn't relish the task of maneuvering my car the half mile there and back, negotiating the four-way stop, and dealing with any small talk that might arise with the counter person at the 7-Eleven. It all sounded exhausting and extraordinarily complicated. Still, something had to be done.

Looking through the glass doors at the end of the hall, I could see my father, in a dusty brown pair of corduroys, a T-shirt, and the down vest that he seemed to wear at all seasons these days, down on his knees before a long wooden picnic bench. On the bench lay a broad, white length of wood that he was cutting into one of the base lengths of the small stairway that was to dignify his instant swimming pool. Quickly, before he had time to see me and wave me out to assist him, I stepped across the hall and up a set of steps leading to the Milk House's second level.

The top half of the Milk House was my father's domain—as the tops of all the houses he had owned over the years tended to be—and I knew that as long as I heard the occasional sounds of the power saw it was safe to walk around up there undisturbed. I didn't think there was any alcohol to be had on the upper level— I had already checked a few days before—but looking one more time couldn't hurt. Perhaps my father had stored a bottle of wine, or something better, somewhere and forgotten about it, and I had missed it on my previous investigative trip.

After the short walk up the staircase I was coated with sweat, and my heart was pounding desperately in my chest. Not since my bout with the D.T.'s had I felt quite this bad for quite this long. It was not only unnerving but extremely irritating. Here I was, far from the meddlesome intrusions of my fiancée and free to indulge in whatever substances came to hand, but no substances, other than alcohol, were coming to hand, and thanks to my declining condition, even that was becoming difficult to procure. For all this, of course, I had only myself to blame. Why on earth had I not brought any heroin down with me from New York? Somewhere in the back of my mind, the memory that I had, in fact, left New York specifically to stop taking dope occurred to me. But the thought was alien and somewhat preposterous now, and I didn't know what to do with it. The long and the short of the situation was that it would be dark in a few hours, and I was in trouble.

Continuing to catch my breath at the top of the staircase, I took in the room before me. Books and papers lay everywhere, as they always did in my father's work spaces. Many of the shelves on the second floor held books dealing with ancient Egypt, and I absently scanned some of them as I pondered where first to search for the saving bottle. *Serpent in the Sky: The High Wisdom of Ancient Egypt; Her Bak: Egyptian Initiate; Incidents of Travel in Egypt; Egyptian Magic; Pyramid Power; Harnessing Pyramid Energy; The Secret Books of the Egyptian Gnostics.* Assorted suitcases and bags, each with their own half-vomited cargo of clothes, books, and papers, slumped and sagged wherever they had been dropped upon my father's return from various trips. Several rumpled pairs of brown corduroy pants also lay about, marking the spots where my father had stepped out of them. Over in the corner, a cardboard case that had once housed a happy army of wine bottles sat opened, the neck of one last bottle visible inside it. Though never a heavy drinker himself, my father was as fussy about his wines as he was about food in general, and boxes like this had been a familiar part of the houses we lived in throughout my childhood. I recognized this particular bottle from previous investigations, but I decided to take another quick look at it anyhow, in the event that I had incorrectly assessed its contents or it had perhaps transformed itself into something better since I last looked at it.

Pulling it out by the neck, I noted unhappily that its contents was unchanged: about three inches of pale, brownish, unappetizing-looking liquid. The bottle had originally contained tequila, but I had long ago drained it of that, replacing what I had drunk in increments with tap water. The unhappy results of this process sloshed about in the bottom of the bottle, taunting me. Why on earth, I thought to myself now, hadn't I done something about this sooner? Why hadn't I had the presence of mind to replace this bottle with a fresh one, which I could have easily bought when last in town? Had I done this, I would be able to avail myself of some of the fresh supply now—only this time I would not be so foolish as to take as much, having discovered that water and tequila don't mix very convincingly. The problem with playing absurd little household games like this was one never knew what had been seen or not. Had my father picked the bottle up recently and noticed its peculiar contents? Certainly the stuff in there now looked nothing like tequila. Better no bottle at all than this, I found myself thinking, and before I knew what I was doing I had uncapped the bottle and drained the grim brown mixture, my stomach seizing up painfully as soon as the tequila-scented swill hit it.

I replaced the cap on the now-empty bottle and placed it back in the box. Next time I was in town, I would buy a full bottle and complete the replacement. In the meantime, I wouldn't worry about it anymore. Back to the situation at hand, which was now, thanks to my having swallowed the tequila-water, even worse than it had been before. There was just enough tequila left over in the mixture I had consumed to ensure that anyone within three feet of me, including a patrolman leaning in through the window of my car, would smell it. My trip to town was an even worse idea now than it had been before.

What I needed—what I really needed—was a bag of dope. Simple, odorless, with no bulky bottles and little in the way of stomach upset, heroin was the substance for people who wanted to feel as good as possible with minimum fuss. How many potions and unguents, teas and tonics, homeopathic powders and realigning rubs I had been given or offered over the years, and how little they had ever done to set things right. Heroin wasn't like that at all; it did as advertised, driving to the heart of the problem in a few short minutes and eliminating it completely. You didn't even need to shoot the stuff to achieve the effect either. Just dump the contents of one of those likable little wax paper bags with dark and mysterious names like "Sudden Death," "Lights Out," or "Black Horse" onto a smooth surface, roll up a dollar bill, and inhale. In a sea of false promises and weak antidotes, it was the good medicine that really came through.

These wistful thoughts reminded me that there was still one more possibility—one other fleeting chance of freedom. During this visit I had not, thus far, subjected my father's bags to a really thorough search for painkillers. Now in his late seventies, my father was forever being prescribed them by one doctor or another for a variety of petty ailments, and he inevitably forgot about them soon after. Bottle after bottle tended to sit, tucked in odd corners of the house or in the bottom of some half-empty suitcase, waiting for me to come along and avail myself.

I took in the large, cluttered floor before me and tried to decide which of the bags might hold the saving orange bottle somewhere within it. I picked up the one nearest me—a big canvas bag with a collection of coats in it—and gave it a good shake. Nothing good in there. I tried a smaller, leather one and it rattled promisingly. A quick search disclosed, to my great disappointment, a bottle of vitamins. Another bag yielded a harvest of suspicious herbal potions, several blue-green algae capsules that I remembered my father had sworn by for some time, and a packet of bee pollen.

With my heartbeat more or less back to normal and the whining of the power saw reassuring me that my father was not going to be coming up and surprising me any time soon, I sat down on the floor and tried to imagine the spot where the saving bottle—of pills or booze or whatever—was to be found. From that perspective a little more of the floor was in my view, and looking across it, my eye came to rest on the big burgundy BarcaLounger in the middle of the room that I used to like to come up and work in during better days.

Something was lying underneath this chair—something orange. Not bothering to get to my feet, I crawled quickly over to take a closer look, and the closer I got the more it looked like what I wanted it to: a large orange pill bottle. I reached under the chair and, slumping against it to catch my breath, looked at the label. There was the familiar red sticker with a sleepy-looking eye that told me whatever the contents of the bottle was, it made the taker groggy. Scanning the label further, I zeroed in on the name of the contents: Roxilox.

The name was unfamiliar but promising. "Roxi" was a prefix I had had good luck with in the past. Opening the bottle, I was encouraged to find that it was almost full to the top with large blue-and-yellow pills. I shut it again and studied the label further. To my delight, next to the sleepy-eye sticker, I found the magic words: "Take every four hours or as needed for pain." Bingo.

After an uncomfortably long period of silence, the scream of the circular saw once again cut through the afternoon air. I hopped to my feet and made my way down the staircase and back to my room—suddenly full of energy as I had not been for days. Shutting the door, I went over to my suitcase and rummaged through it for my copy of the *Pill Taker's Bible*. Buying this book had been a major admission of the importance that drugs of one sort or another had taken on in my life. For a long time I had just gone down to the bookstore to visit it, but ultimately it had proved so useful in allowing me to separate the wheat from the chaff when puzzling over bottles found in my father's medicine cabinet or elsewhere that I had given in.

I looked up Roxilox in the index and was overjoyed to find it listed under the oxycodone group: Percodan and its relatives. I shook out two of the pills, swallowed them with the aid of the last bit of vodka in my sock drawer, and was disappointed to see that the bottle's contents had gone down appreciably with just these two gone. These things were big—which I hoped meant that they were reasonably strong too. While far less potent than even a weak bag of heroin, painkillers like this, if taken in the right combination with alcohol, could still raise me a few inches above the ordinary world. And a few inches, at the moment, was all I was asking for. I walked over to my bed and dumped the rest of them out to see just how much time I had bought myself with this little discovery.

There were sixteen pills left. Three or four days of mild euphoric interludes, if I was careful. Though I would have preferred three at a time, I would take only two in order to prolong the effects. For now, though, I decided to celebrate with something a little more robust. I swallowed another, and again counted my supply. Fifteen. Five times three. Or seven times two, plus one. Or six times two plus three. . . .

Continuing these silent calculations, I scooped the pills up, dropped them back into the bottle, stuck the bottle under my mattress, and headed back out into the central hallway. Though it would be a good half hour before the three I had taken would start to do me any real good, the psychological benefits were rolling in strong already. Suddenly, the remainder of the long summer day spread itself out before me with a tremendous and completely surprising promise—a promise that must have been there, hidden, all along, but which I had somehow failed to notice. Things weren't so bad! Indeed, the day was a sea of possibility.

Looking up at the wall of books before me, I spotted a volume from my childhood: *The Natural History of Sharks* by Backus and Lineweaver. What a wonderful book that had been! Perhaps, I thought, it still held some of the magic it had when I was younger. Pulling it down, I made my way to the front of the house, where I expected my mother was probably feeding her dogs.

I sauntered into the kitchen area and pulled a beer from the refrigerator, opening it and enjoying my first swallow as if I were just a normal, thirsty person enjoying a refreshing beverage at the end of the day. That, it occurred to me, was the thing about alcohol: You could take it or let it alone, provided there were other, better substances on hand to back it up and keep it from becoming a lifeline to sanity. I knew that I would have no trouble holding myself together for dinner that evening, because the magic of the Roxilox would make liquor a secondary matter. I was back in my old form, freed completely from the desperation that I had labored under earlier in the day. Liquor was no longer a precious necessity but merely a psychic condiment—something to flesh out and enhance the sense of well-being I obtained from my pills. Perhaps now my family visit and the rest, relaxation, and clarity I had been hoping to gain from it could begin in earnest.

I brought my beer out onto the porch and sat down on a long wooden benchlike structure set up against the cinder blocks of the Milk House's front wall. Put together by my father as one of his afternoon carpentry projects a few years before, the structure had a cushion made of a single slab of foam rubber covered by a length of brightly colored cotton fabric. My father had been a great believer in foam rubber during the '70s, constructing a number of fanciful, amoebaelike couches around the perimeters of the Barn's living spaces. Examining a portion of the cushion where the covering had slipped off, I saw that age had cured the foam rubber to a deep, mustardlike yellow.

Looking more closely, I thought I recognized gouge marks that I had made in it years before, as a child on some idle afternoon, when the slab had helped furnish the Barn. These marks in turn reminded me of a small, Sunfish-like boat my father had once purchased as part of a years-long and consistently unsuccessful attempt to interest me in the world of sail. About twelve feet long and just big enough for two people, it was made entirely of Styrofoam, and during outings in it I would stab and gouge at it as assiduously as I did at the foam cushions around the Barn. "Stop picking at the hull!" my father would bellow suddenly as we waited out on the water for the breeze to rise.

I ran my finger along one of the deeper gouges in the foam rubber slab, restraining myself from continuing the work begun long ago, and looked out at the world around me. The rain had slackened completely at some point during my pill hunt, and the sun, absent for the long, dull hours of midday, had sunk beneath the mattresslike cover of clouds and was now illuminating them from underneath, making the landscape all around look like the lit interior of some enormous room. Out on the lawn that ran down from the Milk House, a single tree stood in the deepening rays of the suddenly powerful sun. Beneath it was a chair, and in it, I now noticed, sat my mother, a drink and a cigarette in her hand, her four dogs stationed around her. The proudly solitary tree with its lengthening blanket of shade and the relaxed but watchful group of animals beneath it gave the whole scene a kind of Serengeti feel that went well with my new feeling of tranquillity and triumph.

The power saw still whined intermittently from the other side of the Milk House, and it occurred to me that I would like to be a little farther away from it still. With my beer and my shark book in hand, I got up and headed down towards my mother. Rudy, a black, barrel-shaped miniature poodle, and the most active of my mother's current collection of dogs, rose from the shadow of the tree and came toward me, an old gray tennis ball in his mouth.

"Hi, stranger," my mother said when I drew near. "You're looking a little better this evening."

"I'm *feeling* a little better too," I said, sitting down on the grass among the dogs and nestling my bottle of beer into the grass so that it wouldn't tip over.

"We'll have to see if it lasts. If it doesn't, I'm making an appointment with Dr. Quail. I've been to him twice this year and he's terribly nice."

"Dr. Quail?" I said, half amused and half irritated by the notion that I should be needing a doctor. "Why on earth would I want to see Dr. Quail?"

"So he can give you a checkup," said my mother. "It's not natural for a man your age to be so tired all the time. I think there might be something wrong with your blood."

"Don't be ridiculous. There's nothing wrong with my blood. I feel fine. I've just been a little run-down, that's all. You don't know how it is for me up in New York. There's a lot of stress involved in living there these days. I have a lot on my mind."

My mother looked dubious. "You shouldn't have so much on it that you have to stay in bed all day!"

"Just don't worry about it. You'll be seeing more of me from now on. I guarantee it."

"I can't help worrying," my mother said, taking a sip of her drink. "I'm a worrier. *And* I'm your mother."

"Worry if you have to," I said, lighting a cigarette. "But for the moment you'll just have to find something other than my health to lose sleep over, because I'm fine."

Rudy the poodle nosed the tennis ball firmly against my foot and emitted a short, exasperated bark. Rudy was "ball crazy," as my mother called it, and had been trying to get me to play with him ever since I arrived ten days earlier. Thanks to the strange case of exhaustion that had been wearing at me on this visit, I had not been of much use to Rudy. His passionate fixation depressed me, and I would manage to toss the wet, foamy ball only a couple of times before a feeling of pointlessness would overtake me, and no amount of whimpering and wagging on Rudy's part could get me back at it.

I picked up the ball now and hurled it across the lawn into the tangled line of trees at its perimeter. Rudy took off, his tail bobbing straight up behind him like the antenna on a radio-controlled robot, and stopped at a stretch of grass some yards short of the spot where the ball lay, zigging and zagging across the grass with his nose to the ground.

"Rudy!" my mother shouted. "He'll never find it, Ptolly. You shouldn't throw it so far."

"Oh, he'll get it eventually. The challenge is good for him."

In complete contrast to the previous days, the sight of Rudy's rotund, furiously single-minded little body charging back and forth across the lawn now struck me as cheering. Somewhere inside me I felt a dim humming and bustling sensation, as if I were an enormous house that had been closed down for a season and was now reopening. In room after room, boxes long closed were being pulled open and all kinds of wonderful nostalgic objects were being unwrapped and placed on the tables and the window-sills. The pills were beginning to work.

It had been a long while indeed since "drink time" had felt this way for me. In the old days, before the whole drink time concept had been smudged out by the fact that I drank constantly, the time between five and seven o'clock played a specific and crucial role in my life—especially when I traveled home to spend time with my mother. Whether she thought of them this way or not, it was very clear to me that the drink hours were a kind of escape hatch—a time when it was possible, for a moment, to climb outside of our lives and look back down at them from a slight remove; a remove that made all that had happened, both good and bad, equally acceptable.

My mother had always distrusted people who didn't like to get "a little tiddly" at the end of the day, and I was the first to agree with her. Perhaps the biggest indicator that something new and terrible was afoot with me these days was the fact that there was now no common area in which my mother and I could come together and talk about the life each of us had lived and was living, laughing at some parts of it and seeing others in the full light of their sadness. Once my mother and I could sit down and find ourselves remembering all sorts of long-forgotten episodes and alarms from days past, but my newfound numbness and sickness now rendered this kind of discourse impossible. For some mysterious and apparently implacable reason, I was turning into a genuine drunk, and with this transformation a distance—small but unmistakable—had grown up between my mother and myself. It was as if, without really intending to, I had stepped aboard a ship, and that ship was pulling away towards some unknown destination leaving my mother, with her dogs and the fellowship we had enjoyed since my earliest years, behind on shore.

Such, at least, had been the case yesterday, and even a few hours earlier. Now, thanks to a few blue-and-yellow pills found by chance under my father's burgundy BarcaLounger, I felt myself moving back into that old sense of ease and good humor. I was myself again—whoever that was—and it seemed to me that my mother knew it.

"I think I'm going to have my hair cut off," my mother said in a cheerful, singsong voice. "*All* of it. Just an inch long all the way around."

"You did that two summers ago and you hated it, don't you remember? You said you couldn't wait for it to grow back because it looked so terrible."

"Did I?" My mother thought for a moment, sitting erect in her chair. Her childhood among an endless procession of harsh governesses and schoolteachers had given her relentlessly good posture, so that like a rabbit or some other prey animal she always had an air of alertness to her, even when relaxing. "Maybe I'll do it again anyhow. It'll give me something to look forward to."

"What do you mean, something to look forward to?"

"Waiting for it to grow back again!"

"That's ridiculous," I said just as Rudy came gasping back with the ball. I picked it up and heaved it off into the woods again.

"Well, that's your mother—a little ridiculous, right?"

I picked up *The Natural History of Sharks* and started leafing through it absently, stopping at a photo of two dead great white sharks with a man holding a harpoon leaning against one of them. The photo was in black and white and grainy, so that the huge creatures looked like figments from a dream.

"When is La Belle Lena arriving? Has Tompkins told you?"

"Not this weekend, I don't think."

Lena, Betty's old Sufi friend, was now my father's long-term woman-friend, and she often came out to the West Virginia property from her house in Washington on weekends. I had witnessed the ecstatic arrivals and tearful departures of a good number of women over the years since Betty's death, watching with my mother from the sidelines. While I never knew what my mother *really* thought as she watched "the only man she ever loved" go through his deeply familiar motions with these women, the two of us tended to look upon the whole business with a decidedly jaundiced eye. We rarely missed an opportunity to make a little fun of my father as he attracted, then drove to a state of ragged distraction, one woman after another.

"God," I had once said to him. "What is it with you and women? All you do is scowl and grumble about how the CIA is committing crimes that only you know about, or how no one really understands you, and these females just follow you about like you were Svengali himself, loving every minute of it."

"Don't ask *me*, Ptolemy!" my father had replied, somewhat winningly. "*I* don't know what they see in an old man like me. They see that I love them, and they respond to it. Women respond to love, even if it comes from some creepy old ogre like your father!"

When Lena had first started making regular appearances in the late '80s, gazing rapturously at my father as he groused about the food in various restaurants or reprised some all-too-familiar World War II narrative, I had found her more contemptible, if that was possible, than I had when she was one of Betty's Sufis. But after a while, and against my better instincts, I had come first to tolerate her, then even to genuinely like her. Ultimately, Lena had become one of my most valued friends, and though my mother said she was fond of her too, I wasn't really sure about their relationship, just as I never was completely sure what my mother thought about any aspect of my father.

"What have you been doing this afternoon with that young man?" said my mother now, changing the topic.

"Michael? I was having my aura read."

"Your aura? Is that what he does for a living?"

"That's all. I guess you were in Vermont when he came to stay the first time. He's a nice guy, actually."

"What does he want from Peter?"

"Nothing. He just likes him. I think he does pretty well for himself with his aura reading, so he's not looking for free food and lodging or anything."

"How much longer is he staying?"

"Just tonight. It's too bad. He could have had a look at your aura too."

"That's all right. I don't need to know anything about my aura, thank you very much."

"You never know. You might learn something. As it turns out, I have a secret fear of a man named Larry."

"Larry? Who's Larry?"

"I don't know," I said, throwing Rudy's ball again, this time farther into the bushes than ever, "but I'm afraid of him."

"That's your father's real name, of course."

"Peter's name is really Laurence?"

"Yes, originally. He changed it a long time ago, when he was little."

"Huh. Just like you did. What was your name when you were born?"

"Lucy Eleanor." My mother sat up a little straighter, like a fussy school teacher. "Lucy Eleanor Talbot Smith. Yuck!"

"Pretty goofy. But it's weird Peter did the same thing as you, changing his name as a child. Why do you think he did?"

"Oh, I don't know. 'Laurence Junior.' He just hated the *sound* of it probably, like I did with Lucy Eleanor. He was only four when he did it."

"Four! Molly and Laurence let him change his name when he was only four years old?"

"Oh, sure. He could do whatever he wanted as long as it didn't involve getting in their way. He went with Shaw and Molly to a production of *Peter Pan*—it may have been the premiere—and Peter liked it so much he decided then and there to become a 'Peter' himself."

"Wow," I said absently, impressed as always with my father's astonishing consistency. "I would have mentioned that to Michael if I had known."

"But why on earth would that man think you're afraid of your father?"

"He didn't say for sure who it was. Just *someone* named Larry. It's mysterious."

My mother took a puff of her cigarette and sat thoughtfully as I went back to the pictures in my shark book.

"There's nothing to fear but fear itself," she said after a moment. "That's what my father always used to say."

"I guess that's what made him think it was okay to throw you off that boat."

When my mother was two years old, her father, to win a bet that all children know how to swim automatically from birth, had tossed her off the side of an ocean liner while it was at sea. The ship came to a stop, and my mother stayed afloat long enough to be rescued, winning my grandfather's bet for him. In the course of their travels from one political post to another, my grandfather was forever dragging my mother off on courage-testing, generally unpleasant, masculine adventures involving tremendous physical exertion and danger—apparently in a fruitless attempt to turn her into a boy. Mountain climbing, high diving, marathon hours of tennis; my mother had hated all of it but persevered out of a grim sense of duty no doubt instilled in part by all those stern governesses.

Further burdens and traumas were provided by my mother's mother, by all accounts a cold and professionally unhappy woman who played the role of an American diplomat's wife with a cruel and resigned determination. My mother had told me many a bizarre story concerning this woman, who, like her father, had died some years before I was born. There was the time my mother had stood by helplessly as her mother, the spirit of indignant American colonialism, threw one of her Chinese nursemaids down a staircase as a punishment for "laziness." Or the time when, pregnant by her lover, she had made my mother, then only twelve, stand by her side holding her hand during a home abortion.

Then, of course, there was the piano episode. Laboring under the theory that all proper young ladies should "excel" at something, my grandmother set my mother, at age sixteen, to practice at the piano for twelve hours a day, with a half-hour walk in a garden with her governess as her only break. This schedule resulted, after a few months, in a nervous breakdown that had left my mother with a facial tic that lasted for a year and a dislike of the piano that stayed with her for the rest of her life. As fondly as she often spoke of her parents, there seemed little in my mother's life with them that had not left her with a phobia or aversion of one sort or another. If it had been her parents' intent to teach my mother that there was nothing in her life to fear but fear itself, their attempts had been stunningly unsuccessful.

Similar criticisms could have been leveled at my father's parents. A trust fund bohemian with artistic aspirations and a Georgia debutante eager to break away from the rigidities, if not the comforts, of her Old South background, Laurence and Molly spent most of my father's early years in Europe. Child rearing soon proved to be a less diverting adventure than they had imagined it would be, and young Peter was dispatched at a very early age to what would prove to be an endless series of boarding schools. It was in these unremittingly grim and repressive institutions, subsisting on half-cooked horsemeat and enduring endless threats of hellfire, that my father learned his first great and abiding lessons about the world of Authority and the need to undermine it. These schools were also, most likely, the places where he hatched that other defining insight around which he had built his world-vision: Life—the Larger Life that people long to live in their heart of hearts—is going on elsewhere. "All I ever wanted," I had often heard my father say, an amused, forgiving, but nonetheless very sad expression playing across his face, "was to be with the

adults—to feel like I was *part of what was going on*. And unfortunately, all my parents ever wanted to do was get rid of me!"

The most lasting insult came in my father's ninth year, when
his parents were living in an island villa on Lake Maggiore, in the
north of Italy. Learning from the servants with whom he spent
most of his time that he would go to Hell for eternity if he did not
become a Catholic, my father was persuaded to enter the Collegio
Rosmini, a miserable monastic boys' school directly across the lake
from his parents' villa. Pleased to have him out of their hair, and
impressed by the cost of tuition—the Italian equivalent of fifty
dollars for a year—Laurence and Molly plunged their son into a
medieval round of prayers and punishments about which they
remained happily oblivious, despite being less than a mile away
across the lake. The close-yet-distant house of his parents was
visible to him throughout much of the day, and from the window
of his dormitory my father could see, each night, the lights of the
Larger World twinkling just across the water.

Looking out at the tall trees on the lawn's periphery, all on fire
now from the sun behind them, my mother said, "The two of
them should never have had any children."

"The two of who?" I said.

"My parents, that's who. My mother couldn't bear my father,
really, and the only people who should have children are the ones
who *love* each other. Just *adore* each other."

My eyes dropped to follow the small, distant figure of Rudy,
still searching for his ball after my last throw. I imagined my
maternal grandfather, with his vacant, nothing-to-fear, American-
style disdain for all the mystery and terror of the world, pitching
his two-year-old daughter off the side of a ship into the dark
waves below. Then I saw my nine-year-old father, pausing amid
some hideously barren school lesson or at prayers before his cot
in the evening, stealing a quick look out the window and across
the water toward the world of the adults, with all its untasted

freedoms and adventures. Then I took another swallow of my beer.

"They fuck you up, your mum and dad."

"What's that?" my mother said.

"It's a line from a poem."

"I guess Peter and I fucked all of you up, didn't we, you children."

Neither my sister nor my brother were currently speaking to either of my parents. The issues were complicated, ambiguous—and tiresome. Who didn't love who enough, who did who wrong, who let who down. By all accounts, Timothy—or T.C., as he liked to call himself, taking part in the family tradition of altering one's given name—had had the worst of it. Sent to live with his paternal grandparents at age seven, he developed symptoms of malnutrition and grew accustomed to returning home from school in the afternoons to find the lights out and my grandmother unconscious on the couch from her breakfast of scotch and Seconal. His childhood, and Robin's too, had been unarguably miserable, the two of them suffering from a lack of interest on the part of our parents that was in direct contrast to the enthusiastic reception I had received.

My mother, my father, my brother, my sister: sitting beneath the tree in the fading light I saw them all before me as the children they had once been. My father, a precocious but lonely little boy in search of a world of love and belonging from which he was inexplicably barred. My mother, an equally lonely little girl, unfairly forced to witness an array of adult dramas and unhappinesses, and thrust by an unthinking father into a world of competition and aggression she wanted no part of. And then their children, born too soon to parents who had in certain ways never stopped being children themselves.

What a lot of wounded children! And, sorry as I felt for the whole bunch of them, I longed to have no part of it. Why, I wondered to myself, couldn't everybody just count to three and *get better*? From my present, chemically aided vantage point, it seemed to me that all these recriminations, resentments, and assorted unhappinesses were nothing that the right combination of drugs wouldn't put right. No doubt I was not the Messiah-like prodigy my parents had taken me for when I came along, but at least I had the right idea about what to do with this miserable mass of familial failure, disappointment, and dysfunction: Get *out*—out of all of it, in whatever manner and with whatever tools were at hand.

"Everybody fucks everybody up," I said grandly to my mother now. "Your parents fucked you up with all their bad behavior, Peter's did the same to him, and sure, you and Peter fucked Robin and T.C. up when they came along, whether you meant to or not."

"But that's just it, Ptolly, we *didn't* mean to," my mother said, leaning forward in her chair. "We loved them! Now you, *you* speak to us, and you had to put up with Betty moving in, with Peter's and my fighting all the time, with all the yelling. Robin and T.C. didn't have any of that."

"No, but they had other problems. You know what Robin says. However much you may have loved them in principle, you weren't there for them. You were too young, too interested in other things—yourselves mostly. With me, something was different. Even though you were fighting with Peter and there was all the stuff with Betty, you were still always worrying about me before anything else."

"That's true," said my mother. "I guess when you came along I was really ready to have a child. Robin remembers all those details—'You didn't do this, you weren't there when I needed that.' *I* don't remember what happened, but maybe we really were as terrible as she says we were."

Though T.C. had been out of the picture for some time, Robin had only recently stopped speaking to my mother. My parents' strange post–Great Plan relationship, in which each swung back and forth, in and out of the other's gravitational field without ever really coming together or separating, was something that my sister had long played a part in—"rescuing" my mother when things were going badly, only to find her returning to my father's orbit shortly thereafter. It was, of course, to my sister and brother-in-law that my mother had fled upon Betty's arrival, and it was to them that she had retreated again, a few years back, when life on the West Virginia hillside was proving too much for her. Just a few months previously, my mother had abruptly fled the house in rural Vermont that Robin and her husband had bought for her in an attempt to help my mother achieve a little distance from my father. My mother was back with my father once again, and it was the last time, Robin had sworn to me recently, that she would play any part in the drama. She would leave them to their gravitational dance and not open herself up to any further insult from either of them.

My mother and I had been over all this family history before, on any number of evenings like this. But it was always comforting to go through it one more time, like watching a movie one knows by heart—and especially now, as I was feeling so much more "myself" than I had in such a long time.

"But you all get on," my mother said now. "You and Robin and T.C. Right?"

"Oh, sure. Robin's terrific to me. Stuart too. I talk to T.C. on the phone a lot as well."

"That's good," my mother said. "Even if they don't like the parents, children should get along." She had offered this bit of homespun wisdom many times before, and now as always she gave her words a gravity that made it seem as if she had read them somewhere.

"She called this morning," I said.

"Robin? Here? Who answered the phone?"

"Peter."

"Peter! Did she speak to him?"

"Not really. She said, 'I'd like to speak to Ptolly,' and he said,

'Wouldn't you like to speak to me?' and she said, 'No, I wouldn't,' and Peter got really sort of hurt and hung up the phone. I happened to be out lying on the couch in the living room for a minute and saw the whole thing."

My mother shook her head. "Jesus. And you called her back?"

"Yeah. She said, 'Why should I pretend I want to talk to him when I don't?' Anyhow, the only reason she called is because she's worried about me."

"She is," my mother said. "Because of your health?"

"Yup," I said, somewhat dismissively. "She thinks I'm an alcoholic and I'm going to die or something."

"Going to die!" my mother said.

"Yeah. Rebecca told her I'm drinking again and she's all in a tizzy about it. But don't worry about it, she's just being overdramatic. It's true, I shouldn't drink. That's probably what's making me tired all the time down here."

"But you're not drinking that much, are you? I only see you having some beer or wine in the evening, and you never have any of my bourbon like you used to."

"Well, it's complicated," I said, wondering where I was going with this peculiar mix of honesty and outright lies. The thing that made talking to my mother about my problems a relatively safe enterprise was that she inevitably came up with some reason of her own for worrying about me: a reason that usually had nothing to do with the problem at hand. Though I felt uncomfortable bringing up my drinking dilemma at all, I was confident that before too long the conversation would lead us down some blind alley that was safely distant from the whole drinking issue.

"You remember," I continued in my best professorial tone, "when I was visiting you in Vermont last year and I got the D.T.'s?"

"Do I ever! Jesus, what a business. You were really sick."

"Right. Well, theoretically, I'm not supposed to touch any alcohol at all anymore. Once you get the D.T.'s, drinking just isn't the same ever again."

"But you said you're not drinking that much now," my mother said.

"No, but Robin's worried anyhow. You know her, she's a *therapist*. She has her official view on these kinds of things because of all those schools she's been to, and her official view on my drinking is that if I drink anymore something horrible is going to happen to me."

One of the stranger qualities of addiction, I had started noticing recently, was the way it made a person capable of believing his or her own fabrications and falsehoods. The more vociferously I critiqued my sister's concern with my drinking, the more I believed what I was saying—despite the fact that I knew Robin was most likely right. The whole process—the way I could now so easily get in the swing with my own lies—was so interesting that I was tempted to bring it up with my mother now, but I restrained myself.

"It's not worth worrying about," I said, deciding to wrap things up before they got too much more complicated. "Robin and T.C. both mean well, at least toward me. As far as you and Peter go, there's not much I can do to patch things up."

"Water under the bridge," said my mother, invoking one of her favorite expressions. "It's all water under the bridge. But I'm still worried about your blood."

The Orchard and the Ice Age

"In actual fact the father was able to transfer his gifts to his son by educating him in such a way that he handed over his personal accumulation of life pictures and made him instinctively rather than intellectually able."
—James Bramwell in Lost Atlantis, describing occult theories of Atlantean education

T HE power saw had been quiet for some time, and from behind the distant swimming pool my father now hove into view and made his way down to us. Carrying a large, rusty machete and limping slightly from a bad hip that had been troubling him more and more, he had about him the air of a warrior emerging from a long and exhausting battle.

"Anyone for a walk?" he said when he drew close.

Though generally speaking he, like my mother, was remarkably well preserved, my father was at the point where the first real marks of old age were starting to show. He had for some years been engaged in a gradual and most welcome mellowing process, and now only rarely metamorphosed into the grandiose hot head of my younger days. He was also skinnier now—though he had never been fat—and moved about the property more and more slowly as a result of the problem hip.

Looking at him as he limped ever closer, I realized that the bottle of pills I had just pinched from him had probably been prescribed for his hip condition. This flooded me with an annoying feeling of guilt that overcame my desire to stay just where I was.

"Sure, I'll come."

"That's the stuff! About time you got a little air in your lungs."

Stretching out behind us on the hill was an apple orchard owned by a local farmer. My father's property began right next to it, the measured fields of apples giving way to a brambly forest of weeds, small trees, and blackberry bushes. A path, cut by my father on one of his battery of sit-down lawn mowers, wound up through this thick growth, paralleling the edge of the apple field. We started up this path now, me taking my customary position behind my father as he set a limping but determined pace, head down and shoulders hunched.

Looking at him moving ahead of me down the path, swinging his machete at the occasional overhanging branch, I began thinking back over the years and wondering at how much time I had spent in just such a position, following my father and studying him as he both marched ahead and stewed in a soup of his own preoccupations. The path today reminded me of those long subterranean walkways joining the stacks at the Library of Congress, where my father had spent so much of his time during my childhood. It had been some time since my father and I had visited the library together, but the basic structure of our relationship had altered little since our very first trips there. Physically and metaphorically, my father took the lead and I followed in his wake, sometimes attentively and sometimes not, sometimes full of admiration and fellow-feeling and sometimes loaded down with unspoken scorn.

"Ptolly," my father said, stopping in his tracks and turning back to me when we were only about twenty yards down the path, "I've been thinking."

If any words could snap me out of my private reveries and get my guard up, it was these. Without a trace of doubt I knew, in the way that forest animals know it is the first day of hunting season, that a scheme was about to be unveiled—a scheme most likely involving two very familiar elements: a book idea and my spare time.

Most writers have pet projects that they hope to turn into books but somehow never get around to. My father, in keeping with his general philosophy that more is better, had dozens. Like old cars or furniture, book projects were something he collected, and just as he rarely let go of physical objects no matter how long they had been hanging around, so it was with intellectual property. Ideas hatched in the '40s or '50s and even earlier continued to incubate in my father's mind, awaiting their day in the sun. Sheltering these nascent ideas for as long as he did, my father inevitably experienced the frustration of seeing them hatched and brought into the light by others before he got around to it. "Scooped!" he would shout when coming across some plot or premise that had occurred to him in some blurry, yet-to-be-realized form decades earlier.

If my father suffered from frustration at the fact that books took years and not just minutes to write, and that he could not some-how or other get behind every idea that came into his head and sponsor it on its journey toward public awareness, the fact that he now had a son who was a writer was a potential consolation. Along with a bewilderingly vast and cluttered physical inheri-tance, I lived now beneath the shadow of a perpetually looming intellectual patrimony in the form of these unrealized ideas for books. I had long taken care, when staying with my father, not to present myself as having too much in the way of time to burn, because inevitably one or another of these projects—begun long ago and placed aside to ferment in the attic of one or another of his houses—would be recommended as a solution for my spare time dilemma. Obviously my unprecedented lassitude on this visit was to blame for whatever subject my father was about to bring up now.

"An idea," I said, inflecting neither up interrogatively nor down declaratively, but hovering somewhere in between.

"Yes," said my father. "You realize"—and here he began walking again, his steps timed to the cadence of his speech, with me still following a step or two behind—"that there's a gold mine waiting out in that barn for you."

"A gold mine." Again, neither a question nor a statement.

"I'm absolutely serious, Ptolly. Now listen. It's only a matter of time before someone produces a book giving the full story on the Piri Reis map and the others like it. One reason—perhaps the most important one—why such a book hasn't been produced yet is that I have some of the most crucial documentation on it out in the barn. The stuff was put together by my old friend Mallery, and the evidence is incontrovertible. It proves beyond a doubt that the whole business is for real."

"That's good news," I said. "So you can get to work writing it as soon as you're finished with the projects you're working on now."

"That's the problem, Ptolly. I'm totally over my head as it is. And this book is just waiting to be written. It will practically write itself!"

The Piri Reis map was created in 1513 by a Turkish admiral of the same name, who, in putting it together, used a number of other, now-vanished maps dating back to ancient Greek times. The map had been rediscovered in the '50s by my father's now deceased friend Arlington Mallery. He and a group of other researchers had believed that it, along with several other ancient maps discovered subsequently, held a revolutionary significance for the understanding of world history. Many of them depicted a body of land at the southernmost point of the then-known world that looked very much like Antarctica—the same Antarctica that today was buried beneath miles of ice, the detailed geography of which had only recently come to light as a result of new sound-scanning techniques. The various ins and outs of the land, its mountains and valleys—all were represented with uncanny accuracy in these ancient maps, along with a water level that, according to the latest geological speculation, probably existed more than several thousand years ago, before the mass of glaciers that cover Antarctica today had built up. That suggested that someone had been on hand thousands of years before the beginning of our era with the ability to map the dimensions of the ice-free Antarctic continent.

We were reaching the end of the mowed path now, and my father took off to the right, wading among a mass of thin, ropelike trees and thigh-high bushes. We climbed a short hill, took turns slipping through an ancient, rusted barbed wire fence, and came out in a corner of the apple field. Row upon row of trees spread out before us, some of them with tapering, slender-topped ladders leaning into them in preparation for picking time. My father stopped for a moment and took the whole scene in.

"Can you imagine, Ptolly, that this field—this *entire* field—is alive with nature spirits? Not a leaf or a blossom or a root is left out. There wouldn't be a single apple this fall without them. And on top of that, they can see us too—they're watching every move, even picking up on our feelings. I think it's bloody extraordinary."

My father had been working for some time on a book about the nature spirits—sylphs, fairies, undines, brownies, and the like—that esoteric tradition maintained invisibly populated the natural world, their secret ministrations allowing all the myriad processes of growth, fruition, and decay to unfold. My father couldn't see the nature spirits himself, and I certainly couldn't either, but the farther into the book he got, the more fervent would be his occasional eruptions about them in the course of our nature walks. Today, the trees and the grass and the sky looked as opaque as ever to me, but I was happy that the conversation was at least veering away from the Piri Reis book.

We passed the remains of a small gray bird, its feathers scattered on the grass around it, that had probably been killed by one of the semiwild cats that lived in the area.

"Do you know that the soul-essence of birds, when they die, rises up and actually feeds the astral realm?" my father continued, drifting even further away from his pitch for the map book. "I've been reading about the whole process today, and it's absolutely fascinating. Anyhow, I wish you'd give some thought to the map book. Out in the barn there are a couple of boxes with most of the material in it. I came across them just the other day while I was looking for something else, and got sucked right in. The bloody bays and hills of Antarctica, with portions of the Americas to boot, just as they appear in a modern atlas!"

As unwelcome as it was at this particular moment, my father's suggestion that I look at his abandoned map project was not really so unrealistic. For reasons that I had long since stopped trying to understand, many of the occult-style topics that I had spent my childhood rolling my eyes at now interested me as well. It is always a jolt to find that we have anything in common with our parents, and for years I had greeted the realization that I had inherited many of my father's interests with the enthusiasm of a young vampire discovering that he carries the family curse. More recently, however, the similarity of our interests had started to strike me as not so much disturbing as puzzling. Were those bland psychological theories about the centrality of parental influence really correct? Did I like the things I liked not out of any real and elemental affinity, but only because, like some imprinted goose in a behaviorist's experiment, I had spent so much of my childhood watching my father obsess about them—and had finally just fallen into line behind him?

Whatever else one thought about him, the sheer force and pervasiveness of my father's influence was undeniable. Love him or hate him, it was hard, if you were anywhere in his vicinity, not to feel the effects of his presence. This, of course, applied doubly to his children, as my sister Robin's life most clearly demonstrated. In recent years, Robin's "square" husband, Stuart, had been earning larger and larger amounts of money, and the two of them had recently constructed a second summer house in Vermont, down the road from the quarters they had purchased for my mother. Designed by Robin, the place was not really a house so much as a *very large barn* with *two small ponds adjacent to it*. No step in the creation of this enormous structure had been undertaken in a manner remotely like my father would have. The best, most expensive materials were used, and each and every detail was carefully thought out and then rethought, with not a hint of the slap-it-up-and-have-it-running spirit that informed my father's construction projects. The reversal of strategies was total, down to the positioning of the structure at the bottom of a hill, where my father, a lover of sweeping vistas, would never have dreamed of building anything. The place was, in fact, a sort of anti-Barn—a complete and unilateral statement of my sister's desire to be and act other than my father.

And yet, as I had pointed out to my sister and she had acknowledged, it was still a barn. That was just the way it worked with my father. For those who ran at top speed from him as for those who sought out his company, being touched by him in some way was unavoidable.

As for me, I had no desire to make any such efforts to escape my father's influence. This was not only because I realized it was impossible but because I loved and, for all his idiosyncrasies, admired him. The problem of influence in my case was more a professional one. It would have been better, from a strictly practical point of view, if the debunking spirit flowed in my veins. If, like his legions of detractors, I thought my father was nothing more than a self-righteous old crank, then I could easily set about creating a contrasting persona for myself using his flamboyant interests as a background. But I did not. The older I got, the more of my father's passions—from ancient Egypt to Atlantis to the writings of Rudolf Steiner—began to interest me too. Though some of his areas of specialization remained reassuringly dull to me—I cared as little about George Bernard Shaw and the intricacies of World War II, for example, as I ever had—the commonalities far outnumbered the differences. This being the case, it was becoming more and more difficult to determine where I began and he, the creator of this whole sprawling network of odd and urgent concerns about the secret nature of the world, left off.

If I ruled out the option of fleeing my father's influence entirely, as my siblings had done, I seemed to have two choices. I could find a place *beside* my father, far enough away to breathe and grow on my own but close enough for communication—or I could remain completely in his shadow. To do the latter, I suspected, would only be a mistake, for sons who spent too much time in the shade of their fathers ended up not as trees but mushrooms— pale, bloaty, and ready to fade back into the earth at the first sign of direct sunlight.

Following Betty's example, one of the more effective methods I had developed for coexisting well with my father was by taking time out, every now and then, to laugh at him. Between the extremes of pure veneration and pure hatred, love and respect— with a good healthy helping of humor thrown in too—was the recipe I strove for.

In my adult years, I had always done best at maintaining this delicate balance of respect and indulgent humor when there was plenty of alcohol and drugs of one sort or another on hand. Thanks to my new pill discovery I felt ready now, as I hadn't for days, to plunge into a discussion of the map book and all the old familial baggage that went along with it. After my long days of incubation in my room, I was full of energy and eloquence, and ready to plunge into the mix of dependence and independence, humor and seriousness, respect and scorn that made up my relationship with my father.

"Look," I said now, my new, bold, and bouncy sense of self evident in the timbre of my voice, "all this map stuff sounds perfectly interesting, but I can't write some book you want to write yourself just because you don't have the time. It's sick! I think it's great that we have all these interests in common, but you have to draw the line somewhere. Do you really want a son who's nothing more than a half-baked clone repeating all the same old opinions you've had for years?''

"This isn't a matter of opinion!" my father shouted, neatly missing the point. "It's a matter of evidence, pure and simple. Look," he continued, slowing his pace and limping a little more emphatically, as if supporting the burden of my willful indifference. "I'm not trying to tell you what to do. The last thing I have any interest in is controlling you, you know that. I'm just bringing up the map material because it's what I have to offer and it's for real—totally authenticated stuff and a great opportunity for somebody. And it's all *right there* . . . out in the barn, just waiting for someone to come along and have a look at it. As you're here and appear to be up in the air as to what you're going to do next, I thought I'd offer it as a possibility to investigate. That's all."

The guilt feelings were coming in now, swirling like vultures and settling, one after another, on my shoulders. But the pills were there too, doing their good work within me, and I still felt up to the challenge. I changed my tack.

"Well, I tell you what. I'll look at the map material, but I don't think I'm your man for writing a book on it. I'll look at it because it kind of relates to another topic that I've been considering trying to write about."

"What's that?"

"Atlantis."

"Atlantis!" said my father, plainly surprised.

"Yeah. What I've been thinking about recently is all that material left over from the film you made down in Bimini. There's something in all that stuff that I'd like to investigate—in my own way, though, not necessarily the way you'd want me to. I think there's a story there that I'd like to tell. I'm not exactly sure how it all falls together yet, but I think it's there for me to find if I look around a little."

"Atlantis," my father said again, brightening by the minute. "That sounds great to me. You know you can do whatever the hell you want, I'm only here to make a suggestion if it comes into my head. But I'd love you to look at the Atlantis stuff. Maybe you could get the story right."

Oh, boy. Get the story right. What was I doing? Maybe I had already hit that point where the happy new chemicals coursing through my brain were affecting my judgment. Perhaps three pills were too many? Also, I was still shaky after all those days in my room, lying there with *Cosmic Memory* propped open on my face. This was a lot of conversation to be entering into so quickly.

"Well, remember, I wouldn't be telling *your* story, I'd be telling mine. In fact, it might not even be about Atlantis at all in the way you think of it."

"What do you mean, the way *I* think of it?" This kind of vague talk irritated my father to no end. As someone used to dealing with truths, not opinions, and more often than not truth in bulk form, my father felt that too much talk of one person's views versus another's could mean only one thing: a willful refusal to embrace the actual facts. This refusal always came, when all was said and done, from the same source: bourgeois timidity in the face of the hidden side of the universe and what really went on there.

"It wouldn't be about any of the usual Atlantis stuff," I continued. "I wouldn't bother with all of that business about pole shifts and weather changes and geology and where Atlantis was and when it sank. Instead, I'd be looking at the *idea* of Atlantis—why it is that anybody's interested in it at all. Sort of a mythological perspective."

My father always bristled at the word *mythological*. To his way of thinking, talking about the mythological aspect of something was equivalent to a waiter's regaling a hungry patron who has ordered a steak with a long description of what the steak might look and taste like if he actually had one. It was gobbledygook—or, to be more precise, "academic gobbledygook."

"Look," I continued quickly, before he had a chance to say

anything in reply. "I know you've always been interested in proving that Atlantis existed. There has to be a real Atlantis, with real
Atlanteans, otherwise the whole thing is useless to you."

"Of course it's useless!" said my father, vehemently swinging
his rusty machete at an overhanging branch. "What good is a lot
of academic gobbledygook full of polite literary theories in the
face of the fact that the evidence points to Atlantis as a very real
place. Now, when I went to see my friend Cesare Emilliani, the
geologist in Miami, after the Bimini business fell through, he
showed me the readings in the geological record! A dramatic rise in
the water level, eleven thousand six hundred years ago, throughout the entire world. The evidence is simply there to be examined.
When you have solid, indisputable data like that, why you have
to spend your time over in the English department is beyond me.
You've got the geology, you've got the clairvoyant record, you've
got Plato's myth—and it all fits! Take a look at the material yourself and you'll see. Emilliani has taken the measurements down
to a hair. Then you have Plato very clearly giving the statement
by Solon's Egyptian informants that Atlantis sank nine thousand
years before his time. An exact fit! And as if that weren't enough,
there's the Russian material, with coral fossils being dredged up
from the bottom of the Atlantic—coral that no one can account
for other than through the existence of very shallow waters there
at some point in the past. Add to that Hapgood's theory of earth
crust displacement, the Piri Reis map and the others like it, the
new notion that Atlantis might have actually been Antarctica itself
before glaciers covered it, and it seems to me you have a pretty
interesting story. Certainly more interesting than a lot of bloody
English professors arguing about who came up with the *myth* of
Atlantis."

"Fine, fine," I said, a little shaken by the whole business and
reassured to see the Milk House coming into view. "But all that's
still *your* story. I want to tell my own."

"I've got to go into town to pick up some supper," said my father, abruptly changing the subject. "Want to come along?"

"What market are you going to?"

"The Food Lion, then to the 7-Eleven to pick up a newspaper."

"The 7-Eleven? Um, sure, I'll tag along. I've got some stuff I need to get anyhow."

Out behind us, the trees of the orchard, lit by the falling globe of the sun, glowed like the fields of lost Atlantis or the green fields of Antarctica—six thousand years ago, before the glaciers came.

Rummaging Among the Ruins

"On awakening from his dreams, the Atlantean was convinced of having entered a higher world and of having held intercourse with the Gods. For he remembered, although he often confused his dream-life with his waking life. To him the Gods were protectors and companions whom he met on a footing of friendship. Not only was he their guest at night, but they often appeared to him in the daytime also. He heard their voices in the winds and in the waters; he received advice from them; his soul was so suffused with their influence that he sometimes felt them within himself, attributed his actions to them, and believed himself to be one of them."
—Edouard Schuré

"Ptolly!"

I opened my eyes and looked at my watch. Eleven o'clock!
"Ptolly!"

My father's voice sounded again. Why was he calling me like that instead of just knocking on my door? I lurched up out of bed, fully clothed and ready for the day, and stuck my head out the door. My father was at one end of the central hallway, down on his knees in front of the double doors leading out to the new pool.

"Come help me with this door, can you?"

"In a second. Let me go freshen up a little."

In the bathroom, taking a quick look in the mirror, I tried to focus my mind and situate it as best I could. After our walk the previous evening, dinner had been comparatively uneventful. My mother had questioned my father as to when Lena would be out to visit, and my father had complained at length, as was his habit, about the food he himself had cooked for us. Michael had confined himself to a brief discussion about the relative merits of intestinal cleansers, and my father had forgotten about the disappointing food long enough to tell a familiar story about his encounter with coffee enemas in Florida back during his Atlantis days. I had done the dishes, and after an hour spent watching TV with my father upstairs in his study, retired to my room.

Once there I moved without much ado into a tranquil hallucinatory state more or less resembling sleep, courtesy of my newfound pills. I had managed to buy an especially large bottle of bourbon the night before at the 7-Eleven while my father was out by the gas pumps checking the oil, but I had scarcely put a dent in it, so good a job did the pills do. This new bottle, still all but full, now slept among the socks in the drawer across from my bed. Without the pills' residual labors on my behalf, the small, subtle, but all-important sense of well-being I now felt would be gone, and I would be prey to the army of anxieties waiting to ambush me. On the way out the door, I swallowed two more.

"Why are you down on your knees like that?" I said, ready to be of help.

"Didn't you hear that wind? Someone left the door half open and it's blown off at the bottom. I've got it all lined up but I need you to hold it so I can get the screws in straight. Hurry, would you? My back's killing me."

Throughout the course of a life spent down on his knees tinkering with things, from plumbing pipes to lawn mower belts to circuit breakers, my father has always worked better with someone standing behind him—a sort of gentleman-in-waiting, handing tools to him when asked and otherwise just guarding the periphery and lending silent emotional support. Though it was my general policy to avoid this position when possible, I had been so singularly useless up to this point on my visit—unable, with the exception of the previous night, to even add to the dinner conversation or do the dishes afterwards—that it now seemed, given my newfound pharmaceutical fortitude, I should keep up my good behavior for as long as possible.

"Okay," my father said as I came up behind him, "grab the top of the door and hold it very still. The wind tore the hinge right off the wood, and all the holes for the screws are stripped out. This electric screwdriver should do the trick, but I need both hands to steady it."

"When was all this wind? Last night?"

"Shit, didn't you hear it? It was howling for a long time."

"I must have slept through it," I said vaguely.

"Amazing," said my father. "All that noise. You're quite a sleeper."

I knew that my father, oblivious as he was to most of the smaller details of my life, was well aware of my tricky relationship with alcohol and drugs, and that sleeping through a big windstorm and waking only at eleven o'clock might well be chemical-related behavior. I suspected he probably understood perfectly well that alcohol or drugs were behind my poor performance on this visit, since I had mentioned these problems to him in passing many a time. While not unconcerned, my father did not really know what to do with this information, and his tendency was to either ignore or discount it. Dyed-in-the-wool utopian that he was, my father was a firm believer in the idea that all problems in life had solutions. If drugs or alcohol presented a problem, a magic-bullet-style cure no doubt existed—one that conventional science had intentionally ignored—and the only problem lay in finding it.

As a matter of fact, the cure for drug addiction had indeed already been found, according to my father. "You know, Ptolly," he had said to me the previous year, shortly after hearing of my bout with the D.T.'s, "I know a German fellow who can take us to see a shaman on the Amazon who will give us a complete yagé ceremony. He assures me you can cut right to the heart of your desire for alcohol with it, and all other drugs as well."

Yagé, or ayahuasca, the drink brewed from the famous hallucinogenic vine of the South American rain forests, had recently become a favorite topic of my father's. In the course of researching his book on nature spirits, he had decided that among all hallucinogens, ayahuasca was the one that gave a person the most genuine access to the spiritual dimension. He had gone so far, in the pages of his new book, as to sing the praises of the drug as a sort of all-purpose visionary tonic, capable of conferring semiinstant, authentic spiritual insights upon those who spurned more lengthy and labor-intensive methods of spiritual discipline.

This enthusiasm had struck me as peculiar from the start, considering the lack of interest my father had shown for other drugs throughout the course of my life with him. Even in the drug-saturated '70s, he had remained so indifferent to marijuana that he uprooted a massive cannabis plant growing behind the Barn and tossed it in the compost pile thinking it was a weed. As for ayahuasca, my father had tried it only once, at a ceremony in Holland organized by a group of Dutch Rajneeshians. Among all the white-garbed, vomiting participants in the ceremony, he was apparently one of the least affected, not even getting nauseated from his dose of the stuff. Despite this disappointment, his faith in the "visionary vine" was undiminished.

I had declined my father's invitation to travel to the rain forest or to Holland for the cure, but his faith in its efficacy allowed me, it seemed, to be as much of a mess as I wanted around him, for in his head the problem was already solved.

"Okay, here goes," my father said now, as I stood precariously over him holding the wind-broken door. "Hold it steady."

My father pulled the trigger of his screwdriver gun and the silence of the morning was broken by a short, ugly, mechanical growl, followed immediately by a rattling noise as the screw my father had meant to drill into the wood shot out and bounced along the concrete floor.

"Shit!" said my father. "These screws are too big. They won't make it through the hole in the hinge."

"Why don't you get some smaller ones?"

"Because I can't find my screws! I had three or four jars with screws of every bloody size and length imaginable, but that fucking T.L. has made off with the whole collection. Nothing stays where it's supposed to. I mean, it's unbelievable!"

Around my father's house it was customary to have what I liked to call a tool scapegoat—someone who could be blamed when various items (generally tools) disappeared without explanation. For years, my father's right-hand man, T.L., had filled this role admirably. Like so many of the pivotal players in the dramas that unfolded at the Barn, T.L. had been picked up while hitchhiking, and since his entrance into our lives some seventeen years ago he had been on hand, on and off, with more consistency than perhaps any other fellow traveler.

T.L. had grown up in the Roxbury area of Boston and had a distinct biker look to him. He had lived an active life before showing up at the Barn—including two stints in jail and a stretch as the proprietor of a bar in central Florida, where the customers carried guns and on occasion even used them. In a word, T.L. was tough, and I for one admired him for this. None of the other visitors circulating through the Barn had tattoos on their arms or had done jail time. None had had guns pointed at them or been knocked unconscious in fights. To me, T.L. represented the darker side of life, yet managed to do so in a light, well-meaning manner in sync with the highest New Age aspirations. It had seemed to me from early on that T.L. had something on most of the other fellow travelers who came before and after him, and over the years I had stuck to this opinion.

T.L. was everything my father needed in a single package—carpenter, general assistant, sympathetic ear—but his role as tool scapegoat was central. Almost from the moment of his arrival, T.L. was blamed for everything that went wrong around the Barn with the possible exception of the weather. "Where's my fucking tape measure? I just bought it yesterday!" my father would howl. Then, following a brief pause, like the one which separates the dropping of two shoes: "That fucking T.L.!" After a while I took to calling T.L. "T.F.," in recognition of the frequency with which my father introduced his name with this epithet.

For all the criticism my father could heap on T.L., their relationship was anything but one-sided. If my father used T.L. as a catch-all for blame and general abuse, T.L. wreaked abuses of his own upon my father. He did, in fact, steal stuff—though not necessarily with the constancy and abandon my father accused him of. It was a give-and-take situation, and as with most stormy relationships, the blame lay on both sides. At some point during our long friendship, T.L. had told me of a psychic he had questioned about his relationship with my father. The psychic had confidently responded that this incarnation was not their first meeting. In a past life, she said, my father had been T.L.'s wife. In repayment for his abusive treatment of her, T.L. was slated to spend the majority of his present incarnation as his former wife's general caretaker and servant, suffering a menu of abuses similar to those which he had once dealt out to her.

It was an intriguing picture, but if T.L.'s present life assignment was, in fact, to establish a harmonious and healthy relationship with my father, he was not living up to his end of the bargain. For T.L. had drug and alcohol problems of his own, and had only just left the West Virginia property after a long series of confrontations with my father. During one of my father's prolonged absences, T.L. had gone on a terrible binge using thousands of dollars from my father's local bank account. Returning to find the Milk House a shambles and a massive new debit at the bank courtesy of T.L.'s "emergency withdrawals," my father was in a position to have T.L. put away for some time. Angry as he was, though, he had not done so. "If he goes to jail," he had said to me, "who profits? He made a mistake, and he knows it. I'd get no pleasure from knowing he was suffering in some cell."

The whole business had upset everyone, including me, for I still counted T.L. as a friend and was saddened, in a comfortably distanced sort of way, to see what sort of wild mistakes could be born from affection for a particular drug. Thank heavens I was above such things myself.

"Goddamn that fucking T.L.," my father intoned one more time, down on his knees before the blown-off door, with an inevitability to each syllable that bordered on the liturgical. Hovering above him, my hands still steadying the door, I was starting to feel signs of fatigue. How did my father manage to fiddle and fuss with all these mundane details and not become hopelessly dragged down by them as I did? Light sockets, door hinges, wax toilet washers, floor tiles, two-by-fours, roofing brads, copper washers, soldering spools—I had spent my life watching my father purchase and play with an endless procession of such items, happy and content with the whole business for all his muttering. Meanwhile, through all those years and all those trips to the hardware store, where he would pick item after incomprehensible item from the bins that lined the aisles, I would wander a few steps behind him, my thoughts ever more distrustful and disdainful of things material.

That was, perhaps, the great difference between my father and myself: From the location and climate of lost Atlantis to the interactions of the etheric and astral energies of sylphs and brownies, he was all "hows." Knowing how things worked, whether in the material or the spiritual dimensions, was mysteriously nourishing to him. I, on the other hand, couldn't seem to get past the "why" aspect of any of these things. Time and again my father would attempt to interest me in plumbing or carpentry or auto repair, and time and again I would find my mind skating off into the distance even as I tried to pay attention—until I gave up trying at all. Eventually, my father had realized that there was no hope—that as far as the manipulation of mundane objects for practical ends went, his son was a resounding wash-up. But that did not stop him, as now, from occasionally soliciting my company while his romance with things material continued.

I handed the screw back to my father. With an impatience so palpable it made me itch, he lined it up against the hinge, braced himself, and pulled the trigger on the screwdriver gun a second time. Once again the snarl of the motor and the delicate clattering sound of the screw followed. The screws were just too big for the holes.

From his position down on the ground, my father stared at the hinge of the door for a moment, like a samurai warrior whose opponent has just performed a new maneuver that he knows he is incapable of countering. After another moment he slowly stood up, dusted himself off, and took the broken door from me.

"Well, there's no way it's going to work with these screws. We'll just have to keep this door shut and be careful not to use it until I get to town and pick up some that are the right size. Are you ready for some breakfast?"

Breakfast. In the real world it was a logical enough question, but I had just swallowed two of my precious pills, and the last thing I wanted to do was mute their effectiveness with any unnecessary food.

"That's okay. I've wasted so much time sleeping, I think I'll go out to the storage barn to look for those boxes you mentioned last night. I'll wait till lunch to eat."

"Great!" my father said. "The ones I'm talking about are in the clear area over by that bloody potter's wheel T.L. made me buy. You might bring them into the archives if you're feeling up to it."

"I sure will," I said, heading toward my room. The "archives" were two walls of boxes set up in a small storage shack on the lawn near the front of the Milk House. In these boxes, each carrying labels with captions like "Pyramid notes," "OSS," "Tinelli," and "Shakespeare," were the collected materials for my father's entire universe of interests. Constructed at Lena's suggestion a few years before, they were slowly and steadily growing into an uncharacteristically orderly nerve center for my father's projects. My father was forever finding boxes of materials here and there on the property to add to the archives, and in better days I would help him carry them into the little shack out front. So far on this visit, I had moved down one box half full of papers from the top floor of the Milk House, and the effort had left me out of breath for a good ten minutes afterwards. Perhaps today I would be able to do a little better.

Leaving my father to ponder the door some more, I stepped into my room, shut the door behind me, and went over to the sock drawer. Amid the socks, the bottle of bourbon lay like a magnificent sarcophagus, the riches it held within looking inexhaustible. Staring down at it, I had an idea. Getting on my knees, I looked under my bed and found an empty pint bottle from a previous visit to the 7-Eleven. This I uncapped and filled with bourbon from the sarcophagus bottle. Then I slipped the smaller bottle into the shorts I was wearing, which conveniently had extralarge pockets. It occurred to me that I could enjoy this smaller bottle out in the storage barn, where I was sure to be undisturbed by my parents or anybody else.

With my hand in my pocket to steady the bottle, I went through the kitchen and out the front door toward the storage barn, a swarm of familiar thoughts buzzing along behind me like meddlesome but basically harmless insects. The map book. Atlantis. My future. The inescapable influence of my father in all I thought and did, and my ambiguous feelings toward that influence. How could my father possibly expect me to write a book that was so completely in his sphere of interests? When, if ever, would I arrive at the right relationship with him? Then again, why was I worrying about any of this? Shouldn't I, instead of feeling put upon by my father's interest in my intellectual affairs, be grateful that I had a parent with whom I shared so much in common? Still, the map book was too much. My father's urgency about "getting the book out" was well meaning, but it didn't mean I had to succumb to it. Let someone else do that work.

Crouching like a predator in the long grass, an old Triumph Spitfire that T.L. once had ideas about fixing up eyed me with the broken shells of its headlights as I approached the storage barn's huge sliding doors. Beyond it, a series of lumpy, semihealed scars in the lawn marked the spots where various attempts at organic gardening had unfolded over the years. My father's houses were always halfway along on some holistic makeover or other, with greasy buckets set aside for compost and receptacles for plastic, tin, and paper products lined up next to them. The trouble was that these projects never really took off. Absentminded and taken up with multiple projects as my father always was, the depositing of a particular piece of trash in the right receptacle was not the sort of activity that he could manage to stay focused on for long. On visits, I was forever pulling pieces of plastic or Styrofoam out of a heap of wet spinach and chastising him for not paying attention to the regimen he himself had instated.

My father's chief method of coping with all recycling problems was, of course, to avoid classifying anything as trash. Nowhere was his defiantly charitable attitude toward the discarded things of the world more evident than in the storage barn. At the high-water mark of his property collecting, my father had owned some seven different houses, or collections of houses, all in widely scattered locations, and when they had passed out of his possession, much of their contents had ended up right here. Picnic benches, painting easels, stone dead or spark-spitting toasters, lawn mowers, shadeless lamps, lampless shades, frames without paintings and paintings without frames, doors, windows, carpets, lumber fragments, Easter baskets, hair dryers, and mattresses; in the end, it had all come to a rest at this single spot.

The majority of the stuff had come from the Barn when my father at last decided to sell it in 1987. As hard as he had tried to find a willing buyer, no one with taste along my father's lines and money to back it up had appeared to take the Barn off his hands when he needed one to. So with great reluctance he had sold it to a developer, and it was knocked flat shortly afterward. Moving the contents of the Barn was a nightmare project, but my father would no sooner have parted with the booty that larded its rooms than he would have torn up the check he got for selling the property itself. Nothing that stood even a remote chance of being useful was left to the bulldozers. Not only were old lamps and threadbare rugs carted off to safety, but windowsills, toilets, and kitchen sinks as well.

Hired on for the mighty task of transferring the Barn's insides to the West Virginia property was T.L., just back at the Barn after a prolonged absence, and his friend Monty. My father, busy with other things, had waited until the last minute to get out, and there wasn't time to pack everything carefully. On one particular day in this three-week marathon, I remembered looking down at a box that was waiting to be loaded onto the truck and registering its contents: a stack of yellowed file folders, three or four volumes from an old encyclopedia, a salad bowl that still held oil and a few flecks of lettuce, and, inside the salad bowl, a telephone without a receiver.

The same urgency that characterized the packing of this box presided over the entire move, and the end result of this exodus now lay before me as I pushed the storage barn's great sliding door to one side and entered. High up in the rafters, a pair of pigeons stirred, settling down after a moment near a *papier-mâché* owl strung up long ago to frighten them away. All about me, the assembled wreckage of the past lay heaped up, some of it covered by dusty, pigeon-spattered tarpaulins and some of it open to the air. Here and there, the shifting heaps of junk had been wrestled into makeshift lines, with avenues of more-or-less-open space between them. These cleared-out lanes were wide enough to walk down, but one needed to take care where one put one's foot, because there were large gaps between the planks and a person could fall into the lower level—a muddy, primordial wasteland where T.L.'s two horses had until recently been stabled.

I made my way down one of these clear alleys, stopping in front of a wheelchair—one of several to be found here and there among the storage barn's holdings—that looked like it might be in good enough condition to hold me. I settled myself in it and found it remarkably comfortable. Then, looking around in that absentminded way that shoplifters do before they pick up an item of merchandise, I pulled the bottle of bourbon from the pocket of my shorts and drained about half of it. The bourbon made its way down to my stomach, ran into the pills already there, and the two began organizing a deal together. As they did so, I contemplated the absurd yet somehow miraculous profusion of objects that surged around me. Lugged from one place to the next, breaking and getting fixed, passing from one hand to another, they had all at last ended up here—each of them, no matter how small or dusty or broken, a reminder of the intractable solidity of the material dimension.

As the pill-enhanced bourbon flooded my nervous system, I took in the wall of goods directly across from me, idly registering each item. A snowplow blade for a sit-down mower, a torn trampoline, three half-empty sacks of concrete, a red velvet easy chair, a large cage with the warning "Live Animals" written across it, a baby's crib, the bottom half of a rocking chair, an ice cream maker. . . . Thanks to the pills and alcohol, I found myself looking upon this mass of wreckage—this terrifying residue of my father's sloppy odyssey through the world—with a charitable, almost loving eye. Each item, in its bruised particularity, seemed to give off atmosphere the way a chunk of dry ice gives off smoke, and I was in just the right condition to appreciate it. Sober, the storage barn depressed and exhausted me: I was, after all, no longer the naive child I had been in the attic of the Barn, to whom this kind of crazy profusion of objects could seem harmless and even fun. But under the influence of the right chemicals, I could still find it in myself to appreciate the storage barn as a unique microcosm of waste and disorder. To me it was the "world of shit" itself, all concatenated and concentrated into one single, remarkable place.

Minutes went by, and at length I found myself emerging from my slow, bourbony inventory and returning to the task at hand. Rousing myself from the wheelchair, I made my way over to T.L.'s massive pottery wheel. Near it, a collection of boxes destined for the archives sat amid the surrounding disorder like a cluster of wagons at the heart of a wild forest. The words "Map Book" were scribbled in hasty black letters atop several of them. The word "Atlantis" was written atop one of the others. I decided to bring this latter one back to my room. As I hefted the box the dust on it rose, much of it settling on my sweat-dampened skin. It was heavier than I had expected, and for a moment a wave of sweet, bourbony nausea passed over me. Then it was gone, and I made my way unsteadily down one of the open alleys and back to the relative order of my room.

A Memory of Snakes

"The primitive Atlantean, who used stone-pointed arrows, had a slender body, more elastic and less dense than ours, with more supple and flexible limbs. His sparkling, serpent-like eyes seemed to see through the soil and the bark of trees, and to penetrate into the souls of animals. His ear could hear the grass growing and the ants walking."

—Edouard Schuré

AFTER depositing the Atlantis box on my floor, I still felt like I had enough energy to transfer the half-dozen remaining boxes to the archives as my father had asked. By the time I was through with that, the breakfast hours had been left behind and it was time for lunch. My father whipped up an omelet for me, which I ate swiftly while sitting a few feet away from him at the dining table in the hope that the smell of bourbon might not reach him. Then I ducked back into my room to work on my Atlantean studies until drink time.

Sitting on the floor with the door shut and the stereo tape player running, I looked through the contents of the rescued Atlantis box. The tape player was one of my father's, and it was of poor quality. It had a bewildering number of controls on the front, most of them purely decorative. As Sinéad O'Connor sang "The Last Day of Our Acquaintance," the little numbers on the three-digit counter were frozen at zero. Out of the box came page after page of typed notes; newspaper clippings; water-warped notebooks full of my father's pale, spidery script; and loose, age-curled photographs, many of them featuring the massive rocks of the Bimini Road.

Down at the bottom I found a number of magazines as well. Among these were two issues of the *New Atlantean Journal*, dating from the mid-'70s and apparently put together by someone outfitted with nothing more than a copy machine and a stapler. On the cover of one issue a primitively drawn flying saucer hovered over an outline of the state of Florida. The other issue featured an equally crude drawing of three pyramids with what looked like cosmic rays shining down on them from the sky. Opening this one, I flipped through the pages, stopping here and there.

SHADOW PYRAMIDS AND THE CRYSTAL FROM THE TRIANGLE! shouted one headline. The article turned out to be about Ray Brown, an adventurer who had rescued a mysterious crystal ball from a chamber inside a sunken pyramid that he maintained he had encountered one day while diving off the coast of Florida. I knew this story of the pyramid and the crystal ball very well, as Brown had spent a good amount of time at my father's Miami house.

Flipping through a few more pages, I came across articles on the coming ice age, tracking past lives, cattle mutilations, giant dinosaurlike birds flying over Texas, and one titled simply INVESTIGATION REPORT—VENICE, FLORIDA.

On the evening of June 10, 1975, at about 10:00 PM, Ronnie Steves was in his room when he heard a commotion in the duck pen directly outside his room. He looked out his window and saw this large whitish thing within his pen chasing his ducks. He yelled out for his parents and this apparently frightened the "creature" and it left the pen. When Ronnie looked back out in the pen nothing could be seen but his ducks.

He got dressed and went outside to check them and saw that none were hurt but that the pen was covered with feathers. He then proceeded to go around the house to check his other pen in front. When he walked up to the pen he saw this "it" about six feet tall, leaning against the fence. He became frightened and ran back to the house and when he looked out again it was gone.

The article went on to suggest that the mysterious "it" was the Floridian version of Bigfoot, and attempted to tie the event, along with a host of others like it, in with a series of UFO sightings that had occurred in the same area.

It seems to me that there is more than one type of creature. There seem to be at least five different types: The whitish creature; the clean and well groomed "Yeti"; the standard smelly creature, the tall, humpback creature with the glowing eyes, and the short creature. Of all these different creatures only one type has actually been seen chasing animals, the whitish one. There is also another disturbing fact: that is that most people have assumed that the two different creatures Ronnie saw were one and the same. This does not seem possible because the whitish creature jumped the fence surrounding the duck pen, but the other creature did not even move when Ronnie yelled and walked up to it at the other pen! If it was the same creature why didn't it also run? Maybe in the months ahead we might learn the answers to these questions. . . .

Reading along, I was reminded of the mysterious "Larry." Michael and I, in our short tour of my aura, hadn't gotten to the bottom of who this figure was. I imagined a standard psychological interpretation would identify him as the shadow figure of my father. Certainly the fact that my father's name originally was Laurence supported this, for I might have retained this piece of information subconsciously from childhood. Still, this straightforward interpretation didn't satisfy me. Like Ronnie Steves, I was being trailed by mysterious presences whose true identity and intentions I might never uncover but who seemed to be especially interested in me during this stay on the hill.

Tiring of the *New Atlantean Journal,* I pulled out a fistful of yellowed articles clipped from various newspapers. ATLANTIS—FOUND?; BIMINI WATERS YIELD SIGNS OF A LOST WORLD; ANCIENT RUINS FOUND IN ATLANTIC NEAR BAHAMAS. Next to a headline reading FOUND: OLD 'MAYAN' TEMPLE IN BAHAMAS, FLORIDIANS SAY was a photo taken from a plane of a dark square on a stretch of shallow, sandy water typical of the Bahama banks. This was the Andros Island structure, discovered around the same time as the great white Road. I had had a chance to see this structure up close toward the end of the Atlantean adventure, when my father visited it in a chartered seaplane.

As my father saw it, the temple did not have much in the way of Atlantean potential, being more likely the remains of a large storage bin for sponge hunters—which is what locals from the nearby island of Andros said it was. Nevertheless, my father thought some reasonably cinematic footage might be milked from the structure by showing a group of scuba divers making their way out to it in an inflatable Zodiac. The problem was that the water was so shallow that the boatful of divers ended up looking ridiculous on film. This was exacerbated by the fact that most of the shots also featured me in the background, wading in the two-foot-deep water looking for fish.

As far as the Atlantis film went the whole visit was a bust, but looking at the aerial photo now, in my semiinebriated, opiated state, that didn't seem to matter. So what if this dark square, lying on the sandy ocean floor like a giant tattoo, was built in a few weeks' time by a couple of Bahamian fishermen in the 1930s? Like the junk out in the storage barn, it radiated mystery. In the right frame of mind—the one I was in right now, for example—nothing was mundane. You didn't need Atlantis to find the world uncanny and miraculous. A few chemicals and the right attitude would do the trick just fine.

"Ptolly!"

My father's voice brought me out of my meditations.

"Yeah!"

"Ptolly!"

The voice came closer.

"What!"

My father's head appeared in my door. "Come out to the back of the house. Quick!"

"Why? I was just getting settled into some Atlantis material here."

"Atlantis will have to wait. Come on!"

Strong words, I thought to myself. My father's head vanished from the door, and I dropped my handful of clippings back into the box and stood up, losing my balance a little as I did so. Whatever was happening, I hoped it didn't involve driving, for I was in no shape for it. Thanks to the pills, which were continuing to buffet and soothe my nervous system, it was hard to tell how drunk or sober I really was. I had taken a few further pops from the big bottle in the sock drawer after lunch, and although I felt on top of things, I knew also that the pills were probably fooling me, making me think I was in better shape than I really was. Caution was essential, lest I make some gaffe that would force my father to address my condition.

I went over to my sock drawer and took another quick pull off my bourbon bottle to steady myself, then stepped out after my father. I was about to charge through the door leading to the pool, but remembered just in time that it was broken. Walking around via the front, I found my father at the back of the house by the pool. With a worried look on his face, he was staring at a thick black electrical cable coming out of a crack in the wall near the broken double doors. Looking a little closer, I saw that the cable was not a cable at all but a snake—about three feet of it twisting down the wall. The entire outside of the Milk House was painted a bright, unlikely shade of pink, and the animal's dark body stood out surrealistically against it.

My mother is terrified of snakes. So intense and crippling is her fear of them that it has sometimes seemed to me as if she sees their existence as a personal betrayal on the part of nature—the same nature to which she has always looked for consolation in the face of all the wrongs and disappointments she has found among humans. If my mother had long ago decided that only the space, peace, and essential goodness of nature were to be trusted, then snakes were the great and troubling footnote to this trust. By their very existence they seemed to suggest that there was nothing in life that might not ultimately let her down.

My father, in his inimitable way, had long held to a simpler explanation for my mother's snake phobia. Convinced that it was the result of a traumatic event such as being thrown into a snake pit in some previous incarnation, he had spent a good deal of time and effort in years past trying to "get her over it" with E-meter readings, past life regressions, and other such esoteric techniques. But to no avail. Egyptian snake pits or no, my mother's fear was personal and immediate, and bound very much to this, and not some previous, incarnation. Nor was it going to go away just because someone—even my father—told it to.

Given these facts, the West Virginia countryside was a singularly inappropriate place for my mother to have ended up. Rat snakes—long, black, and highly sociable—thrived in the area— and especially, it seemed, on our hill. So plentiful were they that it sometimes did appear that, as my mother said, they "had it in" for her. On one occasion a female gave birth to a brood in the hollow area above the Milk House's kitchen ceiling, and for some time afterwards the youngsters had dropped down out of the ceiling cracks and light socket holes at unexpected moments. On another occasion one of them had leapt out at my mother from a desk drawer when she was reaching for some paper. By this point, my mother was never totally at ease on the hillside in the summer months, for there was always the chance that just at the point that she really relaxed and forgot about them, another snake would show up.

"Wow, that's a big one."

"What is it," said my father, "another rat snake?"

"Looks like it to me. My *Peterson Field Guide* says they get to be eight feet sometimes. This one must be close to six."

"Your mother's in town at the market," said my father. "We've got just enough time to get this one out of here before she gets back."

"It's a losing battle, you know," I said. "If she's going to live here, this snake thing is going to have to be solved somehow. She's just going to have to get used to the fact that this whole place is lousy with snakes and that she's going to be running into them no matter how many we cart away."

"I've tried everything, Ptolly. It's no use. You know that. It's clearly a past life recall, and at a deep level she can't get over it."

As we were talking, the extraordinarily large specimen before us was slowly making its way farther into the Milk House. It was hard to see just how it was accomplishing this, as the opening did not appear wide enough for it to fit, but the body was definitely growing shorter and shorter.

"Shit," said my father. "He's going in fast! We've got to get him out now. A little further and we'll never budge him."

"I don't think we can do anything about it. He's more than halfway in already. Why don't we just leave him be?"

"Your mother just can't take it, Ptolly. If he gets in he'll show up later on the floor of the kitchen, or in her bedroom. We've got to get him out and off the hill now."

Snake catching was one of the few activities that my father and I shared where he took a back seat. Though he didn't fear them as my mother did, he was not extremely keen on picking them up. This was fine with me because it gave me a chance to make up, at least to a small degree, for my general uselessness in other areas. If I was no good at driving a nail or changing an oil filter, I was at least the one to call when you needed someone to pull a snake out of a hole.

I stepped forward now and took a gentle but firm hold of the snake at the point where its body disappeared into the side of the house. The part of the animal still outside the wall promptly wrapped itself around my arm like a vine around a tree, and I felt the snake's mysterious muscles tighten. I gave a tentative pull, and the snake tightened its grip further. I had a quick moment of dissociation, seeing the action unfolding from a slight remove. Neither the snake nor I knew what to do next, and the situation appeared to be degenerating into a standoff.

"What should I do?" I said to my father. "I don't think he wants to come out."

"Just ease him out slowly," said my father, trying his best to maintain a supervisory tone. At any moment my mother might return, and if she came around to the back for any reason, the jig would be up. Realizing that the next move was up to me, I decided to just begin pulling and see what happened. To my surprise, the snake began to reverse out of the house, inch by inch.

"That's it, good work," said my father.

"What do I do when I get to the head?" I said, realizing as I spoke that this event was just moments away. And indeed, before I got an answer, the head of the snake emerged and began flailing about, its jaws open and snapping desperately.

"Grab its neck!" my father shouted.

"*You* grab its neck!" I shouted back, holding the looping, twisting body out toward him. Each time I tried to get my hand around the animal's neck, I would miss and receive a glancing, painless, but still unnerving bite. Finally, on the fourth try or so, I succeeded in grabbing near enough to the head that it could no longer reach me with its mouth.

"Okay, now what?"

"Come on, let's take it down the road," said my father.

We walked around to the front and my father started up the truck while I eased into the passenger's seat with the snake. It was so big that there was no hope of my keeping track of every inch of it. Before I knew what was happening it was wrapping its lower half in the springs underneath the seat.

"Watch it," said my father. "If it gets lodged under there we'll never get it loose."

As we rumbled down the hill in the truck's small cab, I cursed myself for taking that last pop of bourbon. Surely I smelled like a still, and even someone without my father's sensitive nose would have been unable to ignore the fact in these cramped conditions.

"Jesus," my father said, firming up my suspicions, "what on earth have you been drinking?"

"Bourbon," I said, following my own words with interest. "I had one of those little airplane-size bottles in my room. I drank it just now to steady my nerves. I figured this was going to be another snake adventure and I didn't feel up to it."

Whether out of innocence or courtesy, my father accepted this tale. Giving me a mischievous sort of smile, he said, "Not much fun, staying with the parents."

"How far are we going?"

"Just to the top of the hill up here, then we'll let this fellow go."

"Mm-hmm," I said dubiously, looking down at the still-squirming snake in my lap. "It should take him at least half an hour to get back from there."

"Maybe, maybe not. Perhaps he'll find a better home for himself."

As we rumbled up towards the top of the hill, I took stock of my situation. All things considered, I was doing well. What a difference from this time yesterday! Where before I had been languishing in my room with an unread book across my face, I was now a fully functioning member of the household—indeed, an essential one. Still, it was a hollow victory and I knew it. By this time tomorrow, or with the greatest of restraint the day after, I would be out of pills, and who knew what would happen then? Like the snakes that my father was forever taxiing away from his property, my old problems would soon crawl back and be waiting, coiled, in the same old places they had been before.

When we got to the top of the hill, I hopped out and walked over to a stretch of long grass and gave the snake a gentle heave. For a moment it lay there, and I was afraid that I might have harmed it in the course of wrestling it from the side of the house. Then, suddenly, it regained its senses, and in a moment it was gone. Driving back, my father and I saw my mother's small Toyota pull into the long driveway just ahead of us.

"Shit," said my father. "How's that for timing? Good work."

Messages from the Ants

"They despised everything but virtue, not caring for their present state
of life, and thinking lightly on the possession of gold and other
property, which seemed only a burden to them; neither were they
intoxicated by luxury; nor did wealth deprive them of their self-
control; but they were sober, and saw clearly that all these goods are
increased by virtuous friendship with one another, and that by
excessive zeal for them, and honor of them, the good of them is lost, and
friendship perishes with them."
—Plato, describing the Atlanteans in the <u>Critias</u>

"How's it looking?"

"Still down."

"Oh, Jesus. How far?"

"The same as yesterday. Maybe a little worse."

"Oh, fuck, I can't believe this."

"Look, I'm telling you, it's going to go up. I know this stock.
This stock has never let me down."

"But when's it going to do it?"

"I don't know. But I know it's going to. I told you when you
got in that it was going to be a rough ride. You just have to
sit tight."

I was back in my room, lying on my bed, talking on the phone
to my friend Elliott the stock whiz. About three weeks earlier,
when I was still in New York, pondering my future and arguing

with Rebecca about my growing predilection for heroin, my father called me with some good news. He had just sold one of the last of the properties he'd bought back in the '70s, and with some of that money he would be able to tide me over for a few more uncertain months of life in the city.

Always generous with me—at least when he had money himself—my father had a strange optimism about things financial. "Money," he maintained, "is something that comes and goes. Treat it that way, and it will show up when you need it." On the frequent occasions in my limping, liberal arts existence when my resources were low, my father would always tell me to relax. "Don't worry," he would say. "We'll free some cash up somewhere." For my father, it seemed, money was always on hand, even when you couldn't see it. Just stick a broom handle up into the money tree, poke around for a bit, and down it would come.

It was an idea I liked in theory but could not always accommodate myself to in practice. After all, it hadn't always worked that way in my life. Halfway through the extraordinarily expensive college I had chosen, for example, the money had run out, and it was only years later, thanks to my sister and brother-in-law, that I had ended up with a degree at all. As usual, the unknown—be it supernatural or just financial—held fear and uncertainty for me. It came down to the same old question it always did: How did my father *know* things would be okay?

It was perhaps a combination of my own fears about money and jealousy of my father's unfailing optimism that had led to the absurd situation I was now discussing on the phone. Right after my father had offered me further assistance thanks to his recent property sale, I started to take notice of my friend Elliott's remarkable good fortune in the stock market. Like me, Elliott was the product of an aggressively nonutilitarian liberal arts education. Classical music was his great passion, but in spite of this handicap he had somehow evolved, in the nine years since we had left college together, into someone actually capable of earning his own keep for long periods at a time. Recently, much of these earnings had been coming in thanks to a remarkable run of good luck on the stock market, which he had been dabbling in for years.

Ever more fond of my little bags of dope and ever more fearful of keeping myself supplied without taking one of those demeaning office jobs that I had had my fill of during my twenties, I hit upon an inspiration. Using a little of my father's money and Elliott's apparently magical stock insights, I would hop onto the big-money bandwagon myself. I would cultivate a little of that crazy optimism I was so used to seeing others practice and use it to harvest the secret abundance that rewarded those with positive attitudes.

My father, learning that I had among my friends a fledgling but already deeply accomplished stock impresario, had wired five thousand dollars Elliott's way and told me that he would hope for the best. If Elliott lost the money, so it went. If we made money, it was mine to keep. Elliott had been having such extraordinary success with his investments that it had come as quite a shock when, the very day after he received my father's five thousand and fed it into the market, two thousand five hundred of it had vanished irretrievably in a few short hours.

"Poof," Elliott had said over the phone that afternoon.

"What? What do you mean, poof?"

"I mean it's gone. The whole twenty-five I put in Intel stock. It was risky, but I had a real feeling about that stock, and usually when I have a feeling it works out right. I can't believe it. My luck has been so good up until now. You must be a jinx."

"A feeling?" I said incredulously, back for a moment among the crystal gazers and Tarot readers of my youth. "You threw away twenty-five hundred bucks on a *feeling?*"

"I told you when you got in, this stuff is imprecise. There are no guarantees. It's all about odds, and sometimes the odds let you down."

"Oh, God. What about the other twenty-five hundred?"

"That should be okay. It should be just fine. It could easily do so well that you'll still be in the black at the end of the whole thing. But we have to wait and see. Those options don't run out for another two weeks, and we might just be waiting up until the last day."

That had been over a week before. I had escaped New York, and the tangle of my romantic, chemical, and financial ineptitude, to wait out the second act of my stock debacle in the country. In addition to sporadic, unproductive, and unpleasant conversations with Rebecca, my primary phone conversations had been with Elliott. So far things had remained maddeningly vague, with the stock in question hovering a few points below where Elliott had bought in, presumably building up momentum for the burst he felt would inevitably come.

"Do you think you'll know any more later today?" I said now, staring at the ceiling and fingering my orange pill bottle as if it were an amulet.

"I doubt it. Call me tomorrow or the day after. Just keep your fingers crossed."

I had been extremely vague to my father about the five thousand, telling him nothing of the half that Elliott lost instantly. Fortunately, he was too preoccupied with other schemes and worries to ask me about it—not that he would have been upset if he had known. The news that his son, who up to this point had exhibited nothing but a lofty disdain for things financial, had tossed twenty-five hundred dollars into the void overnight, with perhaps another twenty-five to follow, would probably have engendered the same kind of tranquil, so-it-goes response that the destructive transgressions of my childhood had.

Even without the sting of parental reproach, however, I felt pretty bad. I had cost my father—not to mention my sister and brother-in-law—money for years, but never before had I actually thrown it out the window. Maybe I was no better than Radka, Zoltan, or any other of the legions of opportunists who had taken my father for sums large and small over the years. On top of that, there was all the credit card debt I had built up recently, drawing high-interest cash advances. All those newly minted twenty-dollar bills that I had summoned from Manhattan's ever-convenient cash machines, and all the little romantically named bags of powder I had transformed them into, danced around me now. From any angle, I was turning into one of those bad news types that I was always criticizing my father for consorting with, and I couldn't believe it was really happening. Or, more to the point, I couldn't figure out why something else—something better—had not happened instead. Elliott's luck had been phenomenally good for months on end—right up to the point where I signed on with him—and if it had just continued a little longer, I might have made enough money to relax, get over my little heroin and alcohol problem, and push a new writing project onto the tracks. It would all have been so convenient. But, to my amazement, it had not worked out that way. Now, the one financially related inspiration of my life had actually managed to send me further down into the ever-deepening swamp of weakness and worthlessness I was stuck in. As Elliott kept reminding me, I was "still down," and in every sense it looked like I might have lower to go yet.

"I'll talk to you tomorrow," I heard Elliott say again. *"Don't worry."*

"Okay. Right. I'll talk to you later."

I hung up, and realized that I had been in my room for over an hour and that it was once again creeping up on drink time. After all the commotion of the day, and all the bourbon I had managed to drink in the course of it, I wasn't sure if I was in such good shape for another drink hour. But with another pill or two the whole thing seemed like at least a possibility. My spirits, having been artificially buoyed all day, were aching to descend, but I was determined to fight that descent to the last. I opened the orange bottle, downed three pills, and chased them with another long pull from the sarcophagus bottle in the sock drawer. Then I went over to my nature library and took down *The World of the*

Prairie Dog—a good candidate for drink time browsing. In the kitchen, I found a beer in the refrigerator, and went outside. Out at the edge of the lawn, my mother was pushing a gasoline-powered hand mower back and forth, her small herd of dogs spread out behind her. Seventy-seven years old and there she was, mowing the lawn. I was thirty-three, and with each push of the mower I felt a little more useless.

I walked to the tree and sat down on the ground, leaning my back against the trunk and watching as my mother moved the mower back and forth, back and forth, getting all the little tricky areas where none of the fleet of sit-down mowers would reach. Looking down, I saw that beneath the grass growing about the roots of the tree some ants were at work, filing in and out of a little hole in the ground a foot or so away. Everybody but me, apparently, knew what they were doing and where they were going. Concentrating on one, then another of the creatures as they moved along their invisible paths, oblivious to the unemployed giant watching them from above, I found myself thinking of Quigley the calculator-eater.

Ants always reminded me of Quigley. He was, I had noticed, still sending my father packages after all these years. Poorly wrapped, with my father's name and address scrawled across them in large, ransom-note-style printing, these packages contained cassettes full of Quigley's utterances on topics ranging from government conspiracies and space aliens to problems of higher math and nuclear physics. For a long time now, Quigley had been reporting to my father on the state of the planet, and the messages he was bringing were bad. The toxins that humans had been dumping into the environment had reached the saturation point, Quigley maintained, and if old habits were not changed quickly and radically, the earth itself would not survive much longer.

One of Quigley's most consistent and reliable sources of information about the state of the planet was ants. They communicated with him telepathically, as did a number of other animals and insects. In addition to cultivating these sources, Quigley spent much time collecting dead animals and examining them for clues to their demise, that being one of the best ways to directly establish how advanced the state of the earth's toxicity was. Once, my father told me, a patrolman pulled Quigley over and, discovering six dead owls on his backseat, took him in for questioning with the suspicion that this bearded, wild-eyed individual was a Satanist of some sort. Once down at the station, Quigley managed to turn things in his favor when he noticed the bad reception on the station's TV. Quigley passed his hand over the set and, through some manipulation of electronic forces known only to himself, cleared up the picture. The amazed officers sent Quigley and his owls home.

I had met Quigley only once, long ago in the California desert, where he was living with his then wife and six children in an abandoned school bus. He had seemed benign enough, though there was something a little too Charles Mansonesque about his long hair and beard and his only-I-know-what's-really-going-on eyes. Plus, there were those six children, peering out of the bus at Peter, Betty, and me like feral kittens. If Quigley really had an inside track on what was going on in the universe, my mother had once remarked, he should have figured out where children come from and taken a few precautions against having so many— at least until he could afford better housing.

That meeting had taken place almost twenty years before, and except for occasional disappearances from the space-time continuum, Quigley had been a consistent presence in my father's life ever since. Over all this time, the cassettes had kept on coming: hour after hour of information, all of it animated by the same air of confident urgency. "Einstein was close, man, but here's where he went wrong. . . ." "Schrödinger *almost* had it. . . ." The tapes were full of such proclamations, always uttered in the same hushed, careful-someone's-listening tones.

Quigley was, as T.L. had once put it, "one frightened cat," but I had long suspected that this fear was not born out of any real possibility that the CIA was going to break down the door of his school bus so much as from the phenomenal amount of marijuana he smoked. It was T.L. who had originally told me about Quigley's enthusiasm for marijuana. He had witnessed it firsthand in the days he had spent with Quigley on a remote, tree-covered hillside in another part of West Virginia, several hours south of my father's present digs. This hillside boasted three skeletal wooden houses set high up on stilts in order to see over the trees surrounding them, and my father had purchased it during an episode of para-noia about the imminent collapse of the federal government. "The banks are going to go under, and when that happens everything will just turn to shit overnight. It's going to be every man for himself." My father's response to this presentiment was to buy the hillside property—which I dubbed Holocaust Hills—in the event that we would all need to pick up and flee the Barn quickly. T.L. was dispatched there to commence the homesteading process, and Quigley, then estranged from his wife and looking for a roof to shelter his conspiracy-tormented head, was sent there as well.

From his own stilt cabin, T.L. kept tabs on Quigley over in his, and this was how he had learned of the bushels of marijuana Quigley would smoke his way through as he labored at his math and physics. As T.L. was no slouch in the marijuana department himself, I could only assume that Quigley's intake played a part in fostering his paranoid sense of the universe.

I had never listened to enough of Quigley's ramblings to form an opinion on the maverick genius that my father was sure in-formed his prophecies and proclamations. But because of the large amounts of my father's cash that Quigley went through with all his marijuana and calculator consumption, my tendency was to write him off as just another drug-addled loser my father was either too gullible or too generous to abandon. Yet who was really to say, I thought ruefully now as I sat beneath the tree. My father always maintained that one should give everything a chance before dismissing it, and where did I—a drug-addled loser if ever there was one—get off pronouncing judgment on Quigley without giving his theories due consideration?

I kept staring down at the ants, who, like the Atlanteans of the primordium, somehow knew where to go and what to do when they got there, and wondered at how Quigley had managed to glean all those messages of planetary peril from creatures so small and remote from human concerns.

On the other side of the lawn, the power mower cut off and the tranquillity of the afternoon came flooding back in.

"Fuck," I heard my mother say as a breeze carried the mingled smells of cut grass and gasoline across the field. "Out of gas."

My mother pulled off her thick canvas gloves and walked inside, the dogs still trailing behind her. It was dinner time for "the boys" and drink time for her. Soon she would come down and join me beneath the tree, tired from her mowing and ready to enjoy the interval of relaxation and release from the burdens of the day that her handful of evening drinks brought her—drinks that she had earned, it seemed to me, in precisely the way I had not. I went back to staring at the ants.

Ten minutes later, my mother came out from the kitchen and made her way toward me as predicted, the dogs trailing after her.

"Hiya. How ya doin'?" she called ahead to me in an imitation Southern accent she sometimes used.

"Hi. Okay."

My mother sat down in the lawn chair, placed her drink on the little wooden picnic table beside it, and took out a cigarette.

"What are you looking at?"

"Nothing. Just some ants."

"Ants! Why don't I go get another chair for you."

"That's okay. I like watching them."

Ants were another creature my mother wasn't very fond of, but unlike her snake aversion, her feelings about them could be traced to a specific episode—one that occurred in this, rather than another, incarnation. While in Africa with her parents some time before meeting and taking off with my father, she and her mother had been spending the night in a friend's *banda*, a traditional African-style house with a gap between the walls and floor. Just before turning in, mother and daughter heard a strange sound coming from the far side of the primitive room. Down on the floor, marching in a crowded but straight line from one side of the *banda* to the other, were hundreds and hundreds of large, fierce-looking army ants. After staring aghast at them for a few moments, my mother's mother came up with a solution to the problem.

"Go step on them, dear," she said.

My mother dutifully went over to the spot where the line was at its thickest and began stepping. The ants, in turn, swarmed up her legs and covered her body in a series of bites that put her in a hospital for several days. This story, like so many others she had told me, seemed to me to illustrate the basic pattern of her parents' greeting a large and alien world with a willful and slightly malevolent naiveté, and my mother's paying the price for it.

"It's so *hot*," said my mother now, changing the subject. "I can't wait for summer to be over."

"I thought summer was your favorite season these days. You couldn't wait for it to arrive last winter."

"I couldn't?" My mother thought for a moment. "Well, you know me—fickle. Give me the fall, that's what I say today."

My mother's chair was turned slightly away from where I was sitting, and after a moment she turned her head around and stared at me the way she had the day before.

"Yesterday I thought you were getting a bit better, but now I'm not so sure. You're looking sick again. I think I'm going to call Dr. Quail after all."

"Don't get back on Dr. Quail!" I said a little irritably. "I'm fine. I'm just a little preoccupied."

"About what? It's not good to be so preoccupied all the time."

"I don't know. Life. Money. Rebecca. I'm still fighting a lot with her."

"Hasn't Peter given you some money? I thought he was going to put some in your account when his check from that property came in."

"That can't last forever," I said, suppressing a crazy desire to tell her about my stock debacle.

"Oh, if only I would win the lottery," my mother said. "Wouldn't that be fun?"

One leg crossed over the other, my mother sat with her drink and her slowly smoking cigarette and looked off beyond the ragged line of trees to where the sun was going down. Her invocation of the lottery reminded me of something I had noticed earlier on one of my passes through the kitchen.

"So, what's with that letter to Ed McMahon I saw on the kitchen table this morning? Are you still answering those stupid sweepstakes offers?"

"Oh, just every now and then. *Somebody* wins that money, and think how much fun it would be if I did. You could relax and do your writing; you wouldn't have to worry about anything ever again."

At some point in the '80s, during her time in the little house out behind the Barn, my mother had taken to buying lottery tickets and responding to the sweepstakes invitations that showed up in the mail now and then. Envelopes with Ed McMahon's plump, encouraging face started to appear with ever more frequency and were still coming in now, years later, out here in West Virginia. My mother, it occurred to me for the first time, suffered a little from the gambling bug herself.

And yet, as with drink, it was a compulsion she somehow managed to keep at a low volume. Over the years, she had probably frittered away several thousand dollars on lottery tickets and the endless magazine subscriptions that Ed and his associates were always pushing on her, but it had not really done anybody much harm. Like her drinks in the evening and her dogs and her "dumb" TV shows, these little indulgences were part of the bargain she had struck up with the world. If my mother might once have thought herself so special that Ed really would show up at her doorstep one day with a wheelbarrow of cash, I knew the pain and disappointment that life had brought her had long ago cured her of such illusions. Yet, for all that she had suffered, she still managed to keep a form of optimism about life intact. It was a weird and windblown optimism, neurotic and often nonsensical—or, as she said, "a little kooky"—but it was optimism nonetheless. And through those lotto tickets and subscriptions to magazines no one read, she had been feeding that optimism in small installments, like a daily sacrifice to a god who might or might not help in times of trouble but is worthy of daily tribute nonetheless.

I looked at my mother now, sitting with her drink and her cigarette, her back erect from all those years of enforced childhood discipline, and it seemed to me that she was waiting for something. For what? Ed McMahon? I didn't know, but I found myself swept with a feeling of admiration for her. In her quiet, "dumb" way, my mother had carved out a place for herself among the swirling wreckage of my father's world. Though wounded in important and lasting ways, she was, in the end, a survivor, and it was beginning to occur to me that I was not—or at least not for long. Sitting there with my back against the tree—relaxed and coherent thanks to the pills I had taken but due in exactly nine pills' time to fall back to pieces—I felt like one of my father's old lawn mowers or dishwashers. Adrift in a landscape of lost, broken machines, I was becoming little more than one of them myself.

I remembered a short walk I had taken after leaving Betty's apartment following our final talk together that August afternoon almost exactly ten years earlier. Sarah had found a parking spot by the time I got back down to the street, so while she was up with Betty I strolled along the crowded Georgetown sidewalks. So many people were swarming through the August air: people who each, to one degree or another, thought that they out of all the world were special and that certain things—the bad things—were not going to happen to them. Like my mother, Betty had not been so special that she could escape the wheel of blind mistakes and mundane disappointments, and in the end she had learned that. But what about me?

Suddenly I knew, with a weird and unsettling certainty that had a touch of calm at its center, where the second half of the money I had given to Elliott had gone, or would soon be going. Down into the void—the great, corrective vacuum that yawned beneath all who proclaimed themselves undeserving of bad things and deserving of good ones. I was no more exempt than anyone else.

My mother and I sat quietly for a while. Rudy, having temporarily misplaced all of his tennis balls, padded fretfully about, occasionally whimpering to himself. Soon it would be time to go up and help prepare dinner, and after that I would retire to my room, safe for another night. Tomorrow, perhaps, I would call Elliott again, and see if something had broken in my stock—something unforeseen and wildly fortunate—that would lift me up and out of all my problems. But even as I thought about how nice it would be if such a thing happened, I still knew that it wouldn't. The world, after all, didn't work that way. I didn't know much about the world, but I knew that.

The Last Days of Atlantis

"The black magician not only puts himself in touch with pernicious forces
that are the waste-matter of the Cosmos, but he also creates new ones
through his thought-forms, which eventually haunt him and tyrannize
over him. He pays for his criminal joy in oppressing and exploiting
his fellows by becoming the blind slave of tormentors more implacable
than himself—the demoniacal illusions, horrible phantoms and false gods
that he has made. Such was the nature of the black magic which
developed during the decline of Atlantis to an extent greater than
has ever since been reached. There were monstrous cults; temples
dedicated to gigantic serpents, or live pterodactyls, who devoured
human victims; while the men who had attained power were worshipped
by troops of slaves and women."
—Edouard Schuré

I looked at my watch. Nine A.M. First in fragments and then a
steady flow, the details of the night before came back to me. Dinner had been pleasantly routine. More complaints from my father
about the food to be had at the local markets, and a somewhat
confused interchange between my mother and father about leaving
the body. For years I had heard about my mother's ability to
leave her body and float above it. The naturalness with which she
described the activity had probably done more to convince me of
its reality than my father's confident theorizing, and it always
struck me as ironic that she, and not he, was the one who had
been born with the knack. My father, meanwhile, had been read-

ing about the ability of certain clairvoyants at the turn of the
century—the theosophist Charles Leadbeater most importantly—
to get outside their bodies and describe the inner structure of
various elements. "Do you know," my father had turned to me
and asked at a certain point, "what Leadbeater found at the heart
of the atom?"

"Yeah," I had answered with exaggerated boredom. "A tiny
little grain of consciousness."

"How did you know that?"

"You've told me before."

"Well, don't you think it's staggering?"

"Actually, no. I think it's kind of simplistic. These clairvoyant
physicists of yours always seem to be quantifying consciousness
in their subatomic investigations, as if it were some kind of substance you could keep your eye on and measure, like ball bearings
or chopped liver."

"They don't simplify it at all. Quite the contrary. You just think
so because you haven't read the material yourself."

"It's true, I haven't. Somehow I just can't bring myself to read
Leadbeater. I think what holds me back more than anything else
is that he was such a pederast. From what I've read about him,
he seems to have gotten into quite a bit of mischief in those boys'
groups he was always organizing."

"There's no doubt he was a fellow with strange tastes, but
he was vilified as well. You shouldn't necessarily believe all that
bad press."

"I know I'm very stupid," my mother had thrown in around
this point, "but I don't see what chopped liver has to do with
consciousness."

The dinner rambled on for some time in this vein, and while
no satisfactory conclusions were reached, I felt sharper, more in
command of my thoughts, than I had for some time, and talking
felt good. Once again I had done the dishes, then retired to my
room for a few late evening pops of bourbon, followed by chemi-

cal cold storage courtesy of my orange bottle. Looking down at
the floor now, I saw that *Cosmic Memory* was lying open next to
a pile of scraps and clippings from the Atlantis box. I had a hazy
recollection of looking through its pages while waiting for the pill
curtain to descend and take me away from the burdens of ordinary
consciousness, but the content of what I must have read escaped
me.

With the previous night successfully accounted for, I turned
my thoughts to the day ahead. Sitting up, I assessed my physical
condition first. My head and my lungs hurt, my stomach felt like
a burlap sack full of instant oats that someone had left out in the
rain, and the disorder of the room around me seemed only a rung
or two below that which reigned out in the storage barn. I lay
back on the bed and contemplated the spilled contents of the Atlantis box on the floor. Across the room, looming above the sea
of Atlantean scraps, the bounty of my childhood of nature book
collecting stood row upon row on a set of hastily hammered-
together shelves. *Of Whales and Men*; *The Social Insects*; *Animal Wonder World*; *Chipmunk Portrait*; *The Natural History of Seals and Sea
Lions*; *My Beaver Colony*; *The Serengeti Lion*; *The Sex Lives of Animals
Without Backbones*. Each worn title stared down at me accusingly.
Was this, they seemed to ask, what it all had come to? Returning
home to this room was always at once comforting and discon-
certing—revisiting a childhood that seemed waiting to either embrace or devour me. Curiously enough, the room was laid out
exactly as my room in the Barn had been, and sometimes, for a
moment just after waking up, I would get the sensation that I was
back there, with no distance between the child I had been and the
adult I now presumably was.

Lying there in bed, sweating already from the humidity, it
seemed to me that this would have to be the day of my family
vacation when I did something definitive—when I took the action
that would dislodge me from the clutches of stasis and power-
lessness once and for all. The main reason for choosing today for

this definitive action, whatever it was going to be, was the ugly fact that the orange bottle discovered two days before contained only six more pills. Without question, they would be gone by sometime tomorrow, if not before, and I knew that with their end I would swiftly cease being the relatively busy creature I had been over the last two days, venturing out around the property, carrying the occasional box, wrestling the occasional snake, and actually coming up with some conversation at mealtimes. Thanks to the preposterously trivial fact that I had used up this stumbled-upon bottle, my entire approach to life would suffer a crippling blow. It would be back to bed all day long, waiting to work up the energy for a trip down to the 7-Eleven, and no energy for any real thought or action, be it large or small, inspired or foolish.

Perhaps because I had for so long been coached in accepting the primacy of things supernatural over things material, it was never easy for me to accept that the workings of my mind could really be dependent upon something as mundane as the supply of chemicals I fed it. Of all the physical dimension's tyrannies over the spirit, this was perhaps the most nonsensical and cruel. But I wasn't out of pills just yet, and with a burst of the intermittent optimism that is the trademark of the pill addict, I now decided that in the hours of reprieve left to me, I would take steps to ensure that when I did run out I would not feel as bad as I feared. The crazy belief that I could will myself out of the condition of addiction while under the influence of the very stuff I was addicted to was something I had fallen prey to before. Deep down I knew full well it wouldn't work. But I decided it couldn't hurt to try.

Fully clothed as usual, I sat up and put my feet on the floor. The pounding in my head rose a level or two, and without thinking I grabbed the bottle and downed three more pills. God, only three left now. The ceiling was coming down rapidly, and the prospect of solving all my problems in one day already seemed less realistic than it had a moment before. Still, I should act while action was possible.

I tottered into the bathroom, knocking over a carton of Epsom salts that Lena had brought the previous week to help me "remove the toxins" from my body. Because Lena was someone I felt very comfortable talking with, she knew a good deal more about my present dilemma than either of my parents did. In her well-meaning way, she had been very persistent about the curative properties of these salts, but at the moment the idea of getting in a hot bath full of salty water made me feel a little faint. I had a suspicion that, immersed in a tub full of them, I might simply dissolve away into nothing, or perhaps explode. No. For the moment I would take the path of more, not fewer, toxins. Perhaps later, when the pills ran out, I would lock myself in the bathroom, sit in the tub with that carton of salts, and not emerge until I was radically and triumphantly transformed.

In the bathroom, I was pleased to discover an unopened beer, brought in from the kitchen at some point during the previous night and forgotten about. I opened it and brought it into the shower with me, and felt so much better once I had downed it that I even had the energy to shave. By the time I was back in my room some twenty minutes later, the pills were taking effect. I was ready to seize the day!

But how to seize it? Should I concentrate on the Atlantean material? There was something in that box of scraps and snapshots and journal scribblings that appealed to me. Not, perhaps, what appealed to my father, but something worthwhile nonetheless. Though I had never been able to conjure up much more love for the lost continent than I had back in the Bimini days, there was a sense of melancholy and lost grandeur to the Atlantis myth that appealed to my essentially romantic temperament. It wasn't Plato's myth, with all its boring details of waterways and jurisprudence, that spoke to me, nor was it the occult Atlantis, with all its preposterous ideas about seven-foot-tall warriors with metallic black skin and laser-belching death crystals. It was something else—something more mysterious and intimate. Perhaps if I could isolate and pursue this elusive aspect of the Atlantean story that did attract me, there would be something for me to write about: something that would please both my father, with all his irritatingly concrete talk of glacial floodings and pole shifts, and me, with my predilection for the mythological and the romantic. Then I would set myself to writing, and all the problems I had to contend with at the moment would magically vanish, one after another.

I wandered out into the kitchen, where my mother was making her coffee.

"You're up early," she said. I couldn't tell whether the casualness in her tone was friendly or suspicious.

"It's the weather, I guess. Hot already!"

"The dogs hate it. I think I'm going to take them to town to have them clipped. Seeing as you're feeling better, can you do me a favor?"

"Sure," I said, delighted that my new "feeling-better" image was apparently still going strong.

"Go down into the laundry room and bring out the big laundry basket that's on the floor. I'd get it myself, but I think it's more snakey down there in the mornings than it is in the afternoon."

I stepped out of the kitchen area through an alcove and down into a small, cement-floored room where my father kept a working washer and dryer. Low, damp, and cluttered, the room was, in fact, particularly attractive to snakes, and I took care where I stepped myself, not being in the mood for another encounter so soon after yesterday's adventures. On one of the walls hung a primitive-looking oil painting that depicted a woman and a young boy, each with an arm around the other and with a hand on the other's genitals. As my father had explained it, the artist was attempting to address certain key elements of the Oedipal drama in a manner that bypassed the academic explanations of the psychologists. Though the artist, now deceased, had been a good friend of both my mother and my father, my mother had never seen the brilliance of this painting herself, and it was perhaps her dislike of it that had made my father consign it to the laundry room.

Just beneath the mother-and-son painting, partially obscured by a short white bureau with one drawer missing, was a big plastic grocery bag. Peeking inside, I saw a six-pack of very cheap Mexican beer that my father had purchased over a year before on one of my visits and which I had urged him to return. I was extremely open-minded about the alcoholic beverages I was willing to put down my throat, but this particular beer tasted so poor that it offended even me. Obviously, my father had neglected to return the stuff, and it had been sitting there for all these months. There I had been, so desperately thirsty a few days before, while the wished-for reserve had been there all along.

I brought the laundry basket up and placed it on a bench by the kitchen table.

"There you go. No snakes down there this morning. I think I'll do a little laundry myself, seeing as I'm up."

"Good idea. I'm not going to do mine till a little later."

My mother went back to her room and I went back to mine to collect some laundry from the floor, being careful not to stuff any stray Atlantean clippings in the pillowcase I was using for a laundry bag. Humming cheerfully, I headed back to the laundry room, stuffed my clothes in the washer, turned it on, packed the bag with the beer inside the now-empty pillowcase, and returned to my room. Perfect! There was still a good half of the big, sarcophagus bourbon bottle for the afternoon, and now, with the discovery of the Mexican beer, I had a little something to take the edge off the midday hours. If only every day fell into place this easily, what wonders would I not perform.

I sat on my bed and looked down at the Atlantean material spread across the carpet, my mind occupied with the great defining action that I was to take. What was it to be? Perhaps a really thorough reading of Steiner's *Cosmic Memory*—such as I had not yet managed despite all the time it had spent covering my face. As Steiner was to my mind far and away the most fascinating intellect among the occultists, and as he was also one of those happy authors both my father and I admired, maybe I would find something in his thoughts on the Atlanteans that would give me the spark I needed to get my Atlantis project going in earnest. The way I saw it, Rudolf Steiner was where it all either came together or fell apart as far as things New Age were concerned. There was so much of interest in his writings and lectures, so much that was unarguably brilliant and revolutionary, and so much that was deeply bizarre and difficult to believe, that it had been so far impossible for me to come to any comfortable conclusions about him. Like my father in his own way, Steiner represented to me both that which was deeply commendable and that which was wildly irritating about the New Age, along with the hopelessness of ever disentangling the two.

Steiner's Atlantean material, supposedly gleaned from the Akashic record, was perhaps the greatest stumbling block for someone interested in accepting and pursuing what he had to say on other matters. It was the weird tale that was so weird it rendered all the rest of what he had to say suspect. How was one to take it seriously?

I picked up *Cosmic Memory* and flipped about randomly.

Think of a kernel of seed-grain. In this an energy lies dormant. This energy causes the stalk to sprout from the kernel. Nature can awaken this energy which reposes in the seed. Modern man cannot do it at will. He must bury the seed in the ground and leave the awakening to the forces of nature. The Atlantean could do something else. He knew how one can change the energy of a pile of grain into technical power, just as modern man can change the heat energy of a pile of coal into such power.

The passage was, as usual, at once intriguing and frustrating. I thought of Charlie Citrine, the narrator of Saul Bellow's novel *Humboldt's Gift*, and the struggles he endured trying to figure out whether Steiner, with his strange tales gleaned from the infinite stacks of the Akashic library, was a true revolutionary or just a remarkably talented quack. In the course of that book, accepting or rejecting Steiner had grown into a fundamental problem for Citrine—an issue relating to his essential identity and how he approached the world. Bellow himself, I suspected, took Steiner very seriously indeed, but there was no telling how much of what he had expressed in his novel was his opinion.

As for me, I was not a character in a novel but a living, flesh-and-blood person—whose flesh and blood was at the moment in a well-advanced state of toxification. What I thought about all these things—Atlantis, Steiner, my father, and the whole rich, bizarre bouillabaisse of influences that made up my life—was tied up with the toxic state of my body and soul. But where to go with this fact, I couldn't say. If I had known, back in my days of floating over the great white Road, that I would one day actually consider writing something about Atlantis myself, I'm sure I would have shuddered with distaste and disbelief. Still, here I was, being pushed closer and closer toward my own confrontation with the lost continent.

And confront it I would. I would haul myself out of the quagmire of chemical debilitation I had landed in through the sheer force of intellectual enthusiasm. I would get excited about a subject—the way I had in the old days—and the subject I would get excited about was Atlantis. Pills or no pills, the energy generated by that excitement would hold me together, just as it had in times past.

Sitting there on my bed with Steiner's Atlantean musings in my lap and the pills dissolving into my bloodstream, it felt like I had accomplished my mission already. Of course, there was no sense fooling myself. I knew full well that the feeling of victory coursing through me had to do with the fact that the pills I had taken an hour before were approaching maximum effect. But something of this feeling would have to remain after that effect had gone—it couldn't *all* just fade away. . . .

For the moment, what I needed was a break—something to separate me from all the concerns that had been swirling through my head. I needed to get away—away from the mass of twisted yellow clippings and glossy photos of the great white Road, away from the natural history books staring down at me—away from it all. My mind needed to be able to travel for a while, healthy and relaxed and free, so that I could commence with my Atlantean project with a clear head. Tomorrow. Today, I now decided, I would relax.

Fully in the grip of this inspiration, I snatched up the six-pack of Mexican beer and walked over to one of the shelves where my books on subjects other than the natural world were lined up. Immediately, a title shouted out to me. *Selected Poems of Rainer Maria Rilke*, translated and introduced by Robert Bly. This had been a favorite of mine in college, and though I hadn't looked at it for a long time, it might be just the thing to take me where I wanted to go today. I stuck the book, the beer, and Steiner's *Cosmic Memory* (just in case I decided to get going on Atlantis today after all), in a canvas tote bag that I had brought down from New York. I walked out through the kitchen area to avoid the still-broken door, calling over toward my mother's room as I did so. There was no answer. Oh, well. I wandered into the front garden and snatched up one of my father's troop of folding garden chairs, then went around to the back of the house.

I set off down the path my father and I had taken two evenings before, thinking that I might follow it to a small, secluded clearing that lay at its very end and spend a few hours by myself there with my newly discovered beer and Rilke.

As beautiful as the landscape on the hill could be at certain hours of the day, other hours could rob it of its charm completely, rendering what before had been a green and golden countryside into a gray, spongy wasteland of suppurating vegetation and dead air. As I made my way down the path, I could tell that this was going to be one of those choked and cheerless days. The vegetation on either side of me already had a cluttered and vaguely malevolent feel to it, and it was probably only going to get worse as the morning wore on.

It was no great surprise when, only twenty yards or so down the twisting path, another of the hill's rat snakes lay stretched out across it. Amazingly, it looked a little bigger than the one my father and I had carted off yesterday. I squatted down and took a close look at it, and with its small black eyes it looked back at me. I picked up a stick and slid it under the snake near its midpoint. It was fascinating how relaxed these creatures were in the presence of humans—provided those humans didn't try to pull them out of holes or grab them around the neck. Hoisted in the air, the snake contracted a little and turned its small head more pointedly in my direction, its tongue flashing in the air for a fraction of a second and then retracting. "And . . . ?" its expression seemed to say. I moved the stick over into the long weeds at the side of the trail and slid the snake off onto the ground. With a measured, inevitable movement, it flowed off into the underbrush, and I continued down the path.

No further members of the local serpent community blocked my way for the remainder of my walk, which followed the twisting route blazed by my father's mower deeper and deeper into the weedy mass that seemed to stretch forever behind the house. I stopped one more time and picked up a golden yellow tennis ball that Rudy must have left behind on one of the infrequent occasions when my mother had come down the path. I was still wearing my shorts with the big pockets, and the ball fit in them as easily as the bourbon bottle had the day before. Perhaps I should have taken a little bourbon with me as well? No, that could be dangerous. After all, there was a full day ahead of me, and with beer, I always knew where I stood.

Slowly and mercilessly, the day was heating up around me, and the chirring Martian sound of locusts increased along with it. The path wound on and on, and as I followed along it I felt the effect of the breakfast pills was leveling out. The noise of the locusts was still somewhat calming and affirmative, the vegetation on either side of me still more lush and comforting than oppressive, but I could feel the euphoria slackening off and knew that as it did the landscape would grow increasingly poisonous. I had left the final three pills, along with the bourbon, back in my room on the chance that I would get too cheerful out in the bush and decide to take them as well, so I had only the Mexican beer to keep my spirits up. With luck, the residue of the pills would hang on long enough for that to suffice.

Slogging dreamily along, I passed the spot where, two days before, my father and I had veered off through the woods to the apple orchard. Just as I was starting to wonder if the trail blazed by my father through the endless, baking mass of vegetation was ever going to come to a stop, I arrived at the clearing. At its center was a tall, hearty, dignified tree that looked like it didn't really belong there, in deference to which the mass of cluttered vegetation backed away a bit on all sides.

I unfolded my lawn chair, placing it on the grass in as level a manner as I could, and sat down. I pulled one of the beers out, and with a key I had thought to bring along, wrenched the cap off. The short walk seemed to have heated the stuff up a bit, and as I pocketed the cap I wondered what this might do to the beer's already unpleasant smell and aftertaste. The first sip gave me my answer. Barely drinkable cold, the stuff now bordered on nauseating. Yet, with the pills wearing down and my hangover threatening to return, it was no time to be fussy. Steeling myself, I downed the contents of the bottle and dropped it onto the grass.

With that done, I settled down to my reading. Scarcely had I opened the book, however, than the thought came to me that I'd better open another bottle and work on it as I read. After all, there was no sense in letting the remaining supply get any hotter than necessary. Amazingly, the second bottle tasted even worse than the first, and on finishing it I realized that I had no rational choice but to get all six down as swiftly as possible or abandon the project of drinking them altogether.

In no time I had four of them successfully under my belt, and my bad feelings were once again on the retreat. With my sense of feistiness and assurance returning, I opened my Rilke at random and began to read.

> It's possible I am pushing through solid rock
> in flintlike layers, as the ore lies, alone;
> I am such a long way in I see no way through,
> and no space: everything is close to my face,
> and everything close to my face is stone.

Meditating on the apt grimness of this passage, and wondering how close Bly's notoriously relaxed translation method had come to capturing the original German, I opened bottle number five and gagged it down. I turned to a different page and read some more.

> Slowly the west reaches for clothes of new colors
> which it passes to a row of ancient trees.
> You look, and soon these two worlds both leave you,
> one part climbs toward heaven, one sinks to earth,
>
> leaving you, not really belonging to either,
> not so hopelessly dark as that house that is silent,
> not so unswervingly given to the eternal as that thing
> that turns to a star each night and climbs—

leaving you (it is impossible to untangle the threads)
your own life, timid and standing high and growing,
so that, sometimes blocked in, sometimes reaching out,
one moment your life is a stone in you, and the next, a star.

Whether it was the fault of Rilke, Bly, the looming wall of weeds and tattered trees about me, the shrill mechanical chirr of the locusts, the beer, the fading pills, Atlantis, or some combination of all these factors, I suddenly felt that I was going slightly insane. Reaching for the last of the beers, I popped the cap and sent the liquid down to my now uncomfortably bloated stomach to do what it would. Then I opened the Rilke again, this time to "Archaic Torso of Apollo," which had always been my favorite poem in the book. Moving quickly over the first few stanzas, I zeroed in on the famous last lines.

. . . there is no place at all
that isn't looking at you. You must change your life.

I lifted my head to look around at the wall of weeds and the trees rising up behind them, and shuddered slightly as an old and very familiar sensation rose up inside me. It was a sensation that lay at the exact midpoint between joy and fear, and I had experienced it in countless odd moments over the years, from my bed in the Barn at night to the blue waters of Bimini and all sorts of other places besides. It was the sensation of being watched.

The more I looked out into the mass of green in front of me the stronger the feeling got, and after a moment I dropped my eyes back down to my book. But it was impossible to read now. My concentration was gone, and I realized that if I was going to stay there any longer I would have to take action to clear my head and lose the uncomfortable sensation that something out there— be it a host of nature spirits or Bigfoot or the sinister Larry himself—was monitoring me. Noticing the empties that lay scattered around the lawn chair, I felt a sudden, urgent desire to get rid of them. One after another, I picked them up and lobbed them into the surrounding vegetation like a commando tossing out random grenades.

If the surrounding greenery was offended by this action, it gave no sign. The bushes and the trees and the grass all remained as they had been, and I heard no thudding footsteps as the Invisible Presence, aware that I was onto it, retreated into the bush. A slight breeze—just slight enough to create the desire for a stronger one— moved the leaves of the trees and bushes, then died down again.

The obstinate being-watched sensation reminded me of an experience I had had off and on over the years. I didn't know why I hadn't thought of it at the time, but it occurred to me now that it would have been very helpful to Michael in his attempts to figure out the significance of the mysterious Larry entity two days previously.

Sometimes, towards the end of an evening's drinking with my old girlfriend Sarah, I would suddenly look up, scan the room, and pointedly say to her, "Where'd he go?"

"Where did who go?" Sarah would inevitably answer.

"Oh, come on. You know who I'm talking about. Where is he?"

"Ptolemy, there's no one else here. It's just you and me. We haven't talked to anyone else all evening."

"Look, I know he's here, so just come out with it and tell me where he went."

"Where *who* went?"

"The other guy!"

Over time, "the Other Guy" became a familiar figure in Sarah's and my relationship and a gauge of sorts of how much I had had to drink. Basically, if the Other Guy showed up, I knew I had drunk a great deal. His appearances also seemed to be based on my anxiety level. The more worried or frightened I was, the more likely it was that the Other Guy would make an appearance if I drank enough.

Some years after Betty died, I began to have a recurring nightmare in which I would see her floating before my eyes, reaching out to me for the compassion and support that I had so steadfastly refused to give her in the terrible last months of her life. Eventually, she and the Other Guy blended in my imagination. They became, together, the chief representatives of the shadow side of my life—the side that watched and stood in judgment of me, that spoke to me in moments of sleep or extreme inebriation but whose words I could never remember when I came to my senses.

Sweating away on my lawn chair, I continued to stare out into that chaos of green. To my surprise, I found that I was unthinkingly courting the being-watched feeling now. If ever there was a good time for Larry, or Bigfoot, or the Other Guy, or whoever, to just come out and show himself, surely this was it. Had he been waiting, all these years, for me to reach the end of my tether? If so, the wait was over. I was no longer the overanxious, overimaginative young man with a penchant for mild spells of alcohol-induced dementia that I had been throughout my twenties. It was a different game now—I had graduated to a new level—and it seemed that the least he could do was acknowledge this achievement by stepping out into the clearing in full daylight so that I could at last see who he really was.

From the woods all around me the sound of the locusts continued, building in intensity, then breaking off suddenly, only to start all over again after a moment. Otherwise, everything was quiet. My eyes still fixed on the wall of green, I tried to picture what the Other Guy would look like were he to satisfy my curiosity and actually show himself. I was never able to describe the Other Guy to Sarah, and I had no more success at imagining him now than I ever had.

He was everybody and he was nobody. He was the mummy on the cover of that comic book I bought when I was eight. He was one of the zombies scratching and clawing at the door in *Night of the Living Dead*. He was that sinister, balding figure named

Larry that Michael had so skillfully identified moving around the perimeter of my psychic space. He was the shark in *Jaws*, and he was the cancer that killed Betty. He was the alcohol in my stomach right now, and the pills too. He was everything that threatened and promised to change my world once and for all: to blow away the fabric of lies and cheap illusions and reveal things for what they were, for good or ill, for better or worse. He was what I loved, and what I feared, more than anything else in the world, and he had been born specifically from the life that I had lived so far; a life where the world was always just about to become the true, vivid, and rock-solid place it was supposed to be, and to cease being the forest of confusions, falsities, and failings that it actually was. The Other Guy. The figure from the hidden side of things, here at last.

I had not gotten up to urinate for about ten minutes, and realizing that I needed to badly, I raised myself from the lawn chair and stepped over to the periphery of the clearing where the long grass started to grow up. As I stood there, staring absently off into the woods as the Mexican beer drained out of my body, a white shaft of fear shot through me. Several yards away, a man was standing. Tall, pale, slightly hunched over, he resolved back into the stump of a tree, broken off at about six feet, just as my eyes and brain were assuring me that he really and truly was a man, watching me from his place amid the trees.

The trick of vision had lasted for only a second, but it was all that was necessary to wipe the slate of my mind of all thought and all composure. My heart going fast and heavy in my chest and a remaining bit of urine running down my leg, I walked stiffly and briskly back to my folding chair. I threw Rilke in the canvas bag, left the lawn chair where it was, and set off swiftly down the path, my eyes fixed on the grass straight in front of me.

Before too long the windows of the Milk House loomed up once again out of the foliage, and with them the fear that had been following close behind all the way from the clearing fell away. Taking a deep, relieved breath, I walked past the little pool, stepped purposefully up to the rear door, and pulled on the knob. The whole thing gave way with remarkable ease, falling into my arms like a fainting giant. Now both hinges were completely off, and my father would have double the work reinstalling it. Perhaps he was off at the store buying the screws to do so right now. I hoped he was buying a lot of them. In any case, I would worry about that, about everything, later. For suddenly, with the fear gone, exhaustion was flooding in to take its place, and I felt very much in need of a nap.

Atlantis Sinks

"Such was the dream-paradise of the primitive man of Atlantis. At
night he drank deep of the waters of Lethe, forgetting the days of
sweat and blood; but throughout the day he remembered fragments of
his splendid visions, and still pursued them in the chase. These
visions were to him as a sun bringing rays of light into the confusion of
his tenebrous forests. After death he recommenced his dream on a vaster
scale, from one incarnation to another; and when after many centuries
he was reborn in a cradle of creepers under the leafy boughs of his scented,
suffocating forests, there remained with him vague memories of his
cosmic voyage, which haunted him like an intoxicating dream.
"So, in these primitive ages, night and day, sleep and waking, vision
and actuality, life and death, the here and the beyond, were all
mingled for man into one vast dream, like a moving panorama of
transparent tissue which seemed to stretch to infinity. Neither sun
nor stars could penetrate the cloudy atmosphere, but man, guarded by
invisible powers, sensed the Gods everywhere."
—Edouard Schuré

SOMETHING woke me up. I raised my head and looked out
my bedroom windows. For a moment I was afraid it was dark—
that along with the fact that the pills were almost gone I would
have to face the embarrassment of having slept through dinner.
But no—it was still light outside, and judging from the warm look
of the vegetation around my window, there was at least a good
hour or two left in the day. The air looked vivid, not white and

choked as it had been earlier. Another wind must have come through and blown away the hot white haze of midday, rescuing the afternoon. I seemed to be sleeping through so many winds these days.

The beer from my adventure out in the woods had had time to seep into my entire body and soul while I slept, and as I staggered into the bathroom to rid myself of some more of it I felt climactically and definitively poisoned. I came out and sat back down on the bed and, once again, I uncapped the orange bottle and threw the last three pills down my throat. Then I lay back and stared up at the planks in the ceiling, with their familiar knots and water stains, gathering energy. To my surprise, the idea that I had been toying with since arriving here in West Virginia, and that had come into such sharp focus during my morning pill giddiness, was still there.

Atlantis. Maybe there really was something to the lost continent that I had missed so far—something that could feed and excite me in the way it had so successfully fueled my father over the years. Beyond all the foolishness, and all the questions about what body of land had been flooded in what eon and what psychic was right, there was something about the world of the Atlanteans and the lesson that had come from the decline and death of their continent that was real, and alive, and useful still, no matter how real or unreal the Atlanteans themselves had been. I didn't understand any more than this at the moment, but I knew that if I tried hard and thought about it enough I would. It had to be so.

With a determined heave, I set myself on my feet again and got into the shower, staying on my feet with some difficulty for the time it took to scrub the lingering essence of sour Mexican beer from myself. Emerging from the shower, I noticed that my mother had finished the wash I had started earlier, leaving my clothes folded in a neat stack by the cables of my old computer. I dressed and headed out toward the front of the Milk House. Stepping onto the porch, I was relieved to see that the haze and oppression of midday had indeed gone. White, swift clouds moved across the sky, riding the remains of the wind that must have swept through, and the sun was once again turning everything to gold. Beneath the big tree at the side of the field, my mother sat in her little chair, the dogs spread out around her. I looked at my watch. It was six-thirty. Drink time.

I went over to the refrigerator and rooted around in it for one of my father's higher quality beers to counteract the effects of the nauseating stuff I had drunk in the woods. I found one, opened it, took a swallow and felt, somewhere in the liquor-swollen cells of my body, how good it would have tasted if I had been a normal human being having my first drink at the end of the day. It was time to go out and join my mother under the tree, but within myself I could feel an absence as I had so many times in the days before—as if the "real me" was once again on holiday and would not be coming back for quite some time, if ever. I put the beer down and headed back to my room and the sock drawer. The big bottle lying inside still had almost half its contents left, and I took a long drink, followed by another and another. I concentrated and tried to feel, deep down inside myself, if anything was stirring— if, thanks to this final deposit of pills and bourbon, the person I knew and wanted myself to be might be revived at least one more time.

Yes. Down there somewhere, something was indeed stirring. I left my room, passed through the kitchen to get the bottle of beer I had left there, and went out the door. By the time I was halfway across the lawn toward the tree where my mother and her dogs were sitting, I was fully myself again. For the thousandth time, I wondered at how it was possible to be so distanced from myself at one moment and so wonderfully centered the next, all thanks to a bottle of booze in a sock drawer and a bottle of pills found by chance under a burgundy BarcaLounger. From these random items, a successful rescue from the world of shit had once again been effected. How could such a thing be? And what on earth

was I to do now that the time of rescue had passed and the world of shit was going to be flooding back in at full strength?

It was a question, I realized, not altogether unrelated to the story of Atlantis. The Atlanteans, as my father was fond of saying, had "blown it." Manipulating the energies of their world for their greater gain and glory, they had created such an imbalance in those energies that ultimately the very ground had fallen away beneath them. The skies had opened up and the ocean's waters had boiled over, and when it all was finished, those who were still alive found themselves in a land they didn't even recognize. At loose ends in this new, fragmented world, where the gods no longer appeared or spoke to them and the air itself felt thinner and weaker than it had before, the Atlanteans had a choice. They could turn away in fear and refusal, envying those who had perished in the catastrophe and thus been spared the sight of this cold new world altogether. Or, gathering all their courage, they could step out into it, carrying the memory of that other, kinder existence they had left behind as both a cherished memory and a promise of things to come.

The longer the Atlanteans spent out in the air of the new world, the more difficult it was to remember the old way of living. Everything now was more demanding, more confusing—everything was a job instead of effortless play. Who could be at home in such a world? After a while, the surviving Atlanteans began to realize that this work of feeling at home was the most necessary of all the tasks now demanded of them. For the wisest of the Atlanteans—those who still retained some of their old clairvoyant powers—sometimes sensed, in the sound of the wind or the rushing of the water, the voices of the old gods who had once cared for them. And what those gods told them, in voices so dim and soft they could barely be heard, was that the time of their presence in human affairs was over for a reason. "Do the work yourselves now," the gods said over the terrible distance that now separated them. "Our work for you is done."

At the other end of the field, Rudy was searching for his ball along the thick periphery of weeds. The sun's rays, spread out low across the countryside, struck the Milk House and made its strange pink paint glow. It was the hour of the day when everything stopped—when the air itself turned gold and all things seemed suspended in it, as they are in the halls of the Akashic record, where all moments, good and bad, are stored just as they happened, forever. All three pills were at work now inside me, flooding my bloodstream, raising the better part of me up, separating me from the world of shit so that once again I could look down upon that world and all the poor, petty, opaque garbage shuttling about in it and find it forgivable, and even good.

I had brought with me the golden tennis ball I had found earlier, and I waved it in the air, calling to Rudy as I did so.

My mother turned from her position facing the sun.

"Oh, hi there. He's been looking *all over* for a ball. He's lost every last one."

"I found this one on the trail behind the house. I was out there reading earlier."

"Is *that* where you were. Peter had some lunch for you but couldn't find you anywhere. Then I looked in your room later and you were asleep. You've sure got a strange schedule these days, mister."

"I'm going to change it," I said, not worried by the tone of suspicion in my mother's voice. My father was right. Michael the aura reader was right. And the child that I once had been was right as well—at least to a degree. People just didn't understand what kind of world it was. They didn't know that there was another place—another world, behind this one—and that this secret world was watching all the time, waiting to see if we could figure out what to do among ourselves, stuck down here in the shit. And maybe if you could really manage to believe in that other world, to keep it in mind even when all the evidence for it was gone and you felt like just another drifting piece of flotsam in a sea of pointlessness and clutter and empty fear—maybe things got better after a while. Maybe, eventually, a person could really live down here without it hurting so much.

Rudy was at my feet now, running around in circles and looking up, his eyes trained on the ball. I wound up and sent it high into the afternoon air, and it came down out in the weeds and tall trees beyond the periphery.

"Oh, Ptolly! Now he's going to go crazy trying to find it again."

"That's okay, the work is good for him. Things should never be too easy, you know."

I sat down under the tree at the spot I had been the previous afternoon and looked down to see if Quigley's ants were still there, hurrying about on their errands. There they were, all urgency and purpose, just as before.

"Thanks for doing my laundry," I said. "You don't have to do that for me you know, just because I'm visiting."

"I like doing it! You don't want to take an old woman's remaining pleasures away from her, do you?"

"Nope. I wouldn't want to do that."

The pills were making me feel so good, sitting beneath the tree with the ants and the dogs and my mother and the sun coming down on us all, that it felt like I might have broken into Akasha itself and that this particular, golden moment we were in now would never end—that we would not all have to get up and move out of it but could stay within it, just as it was, forever.

Of course, that was not to be the case. Later that night, when the pills inside me wore off and there were at last no more to take, I would drink the rest of the bourbon in my sock drawer and pass out on my bed. Later still, in the small hours of the morning, I would wake up, my head pounding as it had never pounded before and my body trembling in a new and catastrophic way, and I would stagger upstairs, past the open suitcases and the big burgundy BarcaLounger where I had found my cache of pills, and wake my father. He would put on his robe and get a glass of water and some aspirin, and as I sat on his bed shaking he would ask what he should do. And I would realize, when he asked me this, through all the pain and sickness and humiliation I felt, that for perhaps the first time in our long and eventful relationship I was presenting him with a problem he had no answer for. And, realizing this, I would feel a little better. After a while the pounding in my head would diminish and I would go back down to bed, and when I woke up the next day I would call New York and Rebecca, in a car borrowed from my sister and brother-in-law, would come down and take me to a hospital far away from the hill, with its golden, heavenly afternoons and its black and horrible midnights. And when I next returned to it I would be different than I was now—different in ways that I had not imagined possible, despite all the imagining that I had done for so long.

But that was all far away—hours and hours away. For the moment, there was only the beautiful feeling in my stomach, the feeling of the pills and the bourbon making me whole and happy, as the Atlanteans had been whole and happy long ago, when the gods of the invisible world had taught them all they needed to know and done for them all that needed to be done.

"It's a nice afternoon," I said to my mother, from that old familiar place.

"Yes," she said. "Just beautiful."

About the Author

Ptolemy Tompkins was born in Washington, D.C., and was educated at Sarah Lawrence College. He is the author of several works of nonfiction, including *This Tree Grows out of Hell*, a study of Mesoamerican myth and ritual. He lives in New York City with his wife and stepdaughter.